KENT ARCHAEOLOGICAL SOCIETY

KENT RECORDS

VOLUME XXV

1988

KENT RECORDS

General Editor: A.P. Detsicas, B.A., M.A., D.Litt., F.S.A.

SEVENOAKS WILLS AND INVENTORIES IN THE REIGN OF CHARLES II

Edited by

H.C.F. LANSBERRY, M.A., Ph.D.

Published by the Kent Archaeological Society
The Museum
St. Faith's Street, Maidstone
Kent

1988

Front Cover: Rembrandt: *Saskia im Bett mit einer Amme.* (Reproduced by kind permission of the Staatliche Graphische Sammlung, Münich.)

Published for the Society by
Alan Sutton Publishing, Gloucester
Printed in Great Britain
by J. W. Arrowsmith Ltd

ISBN 0 906746 13 2

CONTENTS

ILLUSTRATIONS

Goods and chattels of the seventeenth century in Maidstone Museum. (By kind permission of the Curator, Maidstone Museum).

PREFACE

Preparatory work for this volume was begun in Sevenoaks in a research class in local history for the University of Kent at Canterbury. I would wish to thank the members of the class who, over several years of painstaking transcription, maintained their initial enthusiasm and interest about the lives and possessions of their predecessors, the inhabitants of Sevenoaks of three centuries ago. Whatever merit the introduction may have is due largely to the helpful criticisms of Dr Joan Thirsk, to whom I am most grateful. Also, I should like to thank Dr Alec Detsicas, the General Editor of this series, for his practical help in the editing of this volume.

Each document has been transcribed in full except for the probate clause. The spelling, punctuation and capitalisation have been left as they were found in the original document. Abbreviations have been expanded except for the more obvious. The wills, and the wills with their accompanying inventories and the inventories without wills, are listed in the chronological order in which they were made. Seven pieces of information head each document: (i) the sequential number; (ii) the name of the testator or the inventoreed; (iii) their social or occupational ascription; (iv) the date of burial, if known; (v) the date of the will or inventory; (vi) the date of probate; and (vii) the PRO or KAO reference number.*

* The parish of Sevenoaks was in the Peculiar of Shoreham in the Deaneries of Shoreham and Croydon. Lambeth Palace Library now holds the complete set of original registers, act books and probate papers for the deaneries, but a micro-film of all the material transferred in 1983 to Lambeth from Maidstone is available in the Kent County Archives Office (ref. PRS). To this extent the information relating to the probate records of the two deaneries contained in the *Guide to the Kent County Archives Office* (1958), 122–3, and the *First Supplement 1957–1968* (1971), 92, needs to be amended.

ABBREVIATIONS

Arch. Cant.	*Archaeologia Cantiana*
BL	British Library
CALC	Cathedral Archives Library, Canterbury
I	Inventory
KAO	Kent Archives Office
NW	Nuncupative will
PRO	Public Records Office
Prob.	PRO reference
Prov.	Date of probate
PRS	KAO reference
SL	Sevenoaks Public Library
W	Will

SEVENOAKS WILLS AND INVENTORIES IN THE REIGN OF CHARLES II

INTRODUCTION

Can we infer much about the way people lived from the records of their estates and their dispositions at their deaths? It would be comforting to believe that we can, for Kent is peculiarly rich in the quantity of its probate records which survive, far exceeding that of any other county in England. Most historians would agree that wills and inventories provide an incomparable source of information about the personal possessions of a wide spectrum of the population. They indicate in great detail something of the intricacies of personal relationships and obligations and also of the way in which husbands provided for their wives and children. Professor Stone has observed the development in the late seventeenth century of a more equal partnership between the spouses in middle and upper class families.[1] We may conclude, after analysing the priorities, which occupied the testator's mind, that mutual love and concern for children's welfare had some basis in family life further down the social scale.

The thousands of pieces of information which follow allow us to build up a fairly comprehensive account of living conditions in Sevenoaks between 1660 and 1685. If at times the emerging picture appears a little thread-bare and worn one might reflect that, for the first part of the reign, it is the image of an older generation whose material possessions reflect more nearly the conditions existing under Cromwell rather than those that we might imagine under Charles II. However, one death might have changed this picture. The goods of Thomas Greene, mercer, who died in the first year of the reign of William and Mary, required an inventory over six feet long. Scores of items, a variety of foreign cloths, currants from the Levant and spices from the East would have given some weight to Sir Edward Dering's complaint that the reason for the decay of rents in Kent was 'the neglect of our native commodities and fondness for foreign.'[2]

[1] L. Stone, *The Family, Sex and Marriage in England, 1500–1800*, (Pelican ed., 1979), 149.

[2] (Eds.) J. Thirsk and J.C. Cooper, *Seventeenth Century Economic Documents* (1972), 85.

Undoubtedly these goods were being bought by the people of Sevenoaks in Charles II's reign. One ought perhaps at this point to sound a cautionary note. The goods recorded in the inventories are the very minimum that the deceased possessed. Then, as now, we can be sure that certain choice articles, desirable consumer goods such as curtains, clocks and mirrors, had been prudently removed before the inventory appraisers arrived.

Even so, by the time we have finished reading these last words from Sevenoaks, we may feel that they describe scenes from life rather than death in a small but thriving Kent market town. We shall know that the bedsteads, with their furnishings, are going to be the most expensive pieces of furniture in the house; that the great chests will be carefully packed with labour-intensive linen which will be more highly valued than the furniture. We shall recognize the socially aspiring from their Turkey-work chairs; that green appeared to be the 'in' colour; that everyone had the jointed tables and stools which now form such alluring and expensive items in antique auctioneers' catalogues. We shall note where they cooked and what they cooked on, and that pewter-ware was almost universally used for eating and drinking. But where, apart from Thomasin Weston's spirits shop, are the drinking glasses with the inverted baluster stems and folded feet, which we know must have existed? The glass cases or cages are there, but the glasses were just too desirable to be left around it seems.

Perhaps it may be worth noting here that by the second half of the seventeenth century wills contained less detailed information about the personal goods of the deceased than they had done at the beginning of the century. Dr Jules De Launay's, *Cranbrook Wills, 1396–1640*, shows that clothing is described more carefully than in any of the later Sevenoaks wills or inventories. Edmund Iddenden, broadweaver, in 1600 left his best suit of apparel, viz. a cloak, doublet, Venetian hat, cambric ruff-band, a pair of worsted stockings and his best shoes to a brother, George, and to another brother (in-law) John Longe, 'my doublet, cut upon green, my venetians with three velvet laces and a cambric ruff for a band that is not yet made.'[3] One would seek in vain for that sort of detail among the Sevenoaks wills and inventories, where the clothing was usually lumped together as 'both linen and woollen' and accorded a suspiciously standard valuation. Nor is the detail simply indicative of the professional concern of a Kentish weaver. George Miller, a Hertfordshire yeoman, in 1609 after disposing other items of his clothing left 'unto Thomas wynn gent the Night gowne which was sometymes my Master

[3] J. De Launay, *Cranbrook Wills 1396–1640* (1984), 229.

Sir Charles Morison, prayeng him to weare it for his sake'.[4] We may, indeed we must, categorise these people for the purposes of analysis, but statements like that point to the at times almost unbridgeable gap, which separates the present-day reader from the social structure and the social pre-suppositions of later Stuart times.

In most cases the occupation or the social nomenclature of the testators and of those who died intestate is noted, either by themselves or by their appraisers. They may be grouped as follows:

		% of the whole
Agriculture, i.e., yeomen, husbandmen and a gardener	25	22
Widows, spinsters, widower	22	19
Craftsmen	20	17
Innkeepers, victuallers	11	9
Gentlemen	10	8
Tradesmen, shop-keepers	9	7
Professions, i.e. vicars and a schoolmaster	3	2
Labourers	3	2
Seamen	1	1
Not known	9	7
Total	113	

If one adds two widows and two cordwainers who were also farmers, the percentage of those who were engaged in agriculture increases to just over 25 per cent. Two widows were also shopkeepers and another sold home-made gin.

The large percentage engaged in agriculture reminds us that the parish of Sevenoaks included not only the town but also Sevenoaks Weald and Riverhead. About 75 per cent of the population of the parish lived in the town, 26 per cent in the Weald and 16 per cent in Riverhead. This may also account for the high proportion of gentlemen, about as many as tradesmen and shop-keepers. Much depends upon the definition of a gentleman, and this is discussed

[4] (Ed.) L.M. Munby, *Life and Death in Kings Langley: Wills and Inventories 1498–1659* (1981), 55. In (Eds.) B. Trinder and J. Cox, *Yeomen and Colliers in Telford: Probate Inventories for Dawley, Wellington and Wrockwardine, 1660–1750* (1980) and (Ed.) J. S. Moore, *The Goods and Chattels of our Forefathers: Frampton Cotterell and District Probate Inventories 1539–1804* (1976), wearing apparel tends to be grouped together.

later. Nearly one-fifth of the total are women. Naturally this is a socially amorphous grouping and they include Dame Margaret Boswell at one end of the spectrum and Elizabeth Clifford, with only basic household articles to bequeath, at the other. The great majority were widows, and Kentish widows at that. As such they enjoyed greater advantages than their sisters in most other areas of England. At least two of the widows were shop-keepers. One might best be described as an ironmonger, the other's shop goods were not specified but amounted to £30. Thomasin Weston sold stilled waters and syrups. The male shop-keepers and tradesmen comprised three butchers, a haberdasher, mealman, cheesemonger, tobacconist and two mercers. Mercers did not only deal in fabrics. Thomas Wickenden's inventory notes drugs and grocery wares while Thomas Weston appears to have been little more than another tobacconist. The craftsmen, the next largest category after the widows, worked with wool, leather and wood. Apart from the finishing side of the industry, it would seem that the wool-workers had seen better days. The leather workers, somewhat grandly describing themselves as cordwainers, were notably better off. The remaining significant grouping is the innkeepers and victuallers. We know of the importance of inns in the economy of market towns, and Sevenoaks was no exception.[5] They ranged in size and facilities from the grandest, like The Crown, to the more humble fare provided by Gilbert Kipps, but we can be sure that the carriage trade to the wells beyond Tonbridge favoured Sevenoaks' inns. Three members of the professions, three labourers and a seaman complete the collection of known groupings. What kind of sample of Sevenoaks' inhabitants does this provide?

To some extent the value of probate records for the social historian depends upon the numbers which survive. For Sevenoaks in the period 1660 to 1685 I have found 85 wills and 68 inventories. No doubt there are more. 41 of the inventories were attached originally to the wills, of the remaining 27 some were returned to the courts in response to letters of administration which were granted to the next of kin when a person died intestate. So we have information about the estates of 113 people who died in Sevenoaks between 1660 and 1685. Is this a useful proportion?

In 1695, Gregory King calculated that there were 1572 persons in the parish of Sevenoaks.[6] King obtained this figure by taking the total

[5] A.E. Everitt, 'The marketing of agricultural produce,' in (Ed.) J. Thirsk, *The Agrarian History of England and Wales 1500–1640* (1967).

[6] PRO., T64/302 ff. 14–17. Quoted by C.W. Chalklin, *Seventeenth Century Kent* (1965), 36.

number of households returned for tax purposes and multiplying that figure by 4, which was his estimate of the average number of persons in a household. Modern demographers would consider this multiplier slightly too low and use 4.5.[7] By making a similar computation to that of King and using the Hearth Tax returns of 1664[8] the totals for the parish of Sevenoaks are as follows:

Sevenoaks Town	186 households
Sevenoaks Weald	85 households
Riverhead	55 households

The total of 326 households when multiplied by 4 gives 1304 inhabitants, and by 4.5 gives 1467. A cross-check using the rule of thumb method of taking the average number of baptisms for a decade and multiplying that average by 30 gives roughly the same totals. There is a gap in the parish registers from January 1665 to January 1671, but for the periods 1661 to 1664, 1671 to 1675 and 1681 to 1685 the average baptisms are 50, 49 and 52, respectively. Multiplying by 30 one arrives at: 1661 to 1664, 1500 persons; 1671 to 1675, 1470 persons; and 1681 to 1685, 1560 persons.

Between the years 1665 and 1668 and the years 1677 and 1680 disease appears to have caused a higher than normal mortality. In 1665, the disease was probably the plague and, in 1677, it may have been influenza or smallpox.[9] There are no burial figures for the years 1665 to 1668 but there are 50 per cent more wills and administrations for these years than for any other four-year period between 1660 and 1685. Also, it may be significant that the rental for the manor of Sevenoaks was remade in 1665, for it has been suggested that 'the drawing up of rentals might serve as a demographer's guide to exceptional mortality.'[10]

Usually, it was the head of the household and some widows, who may or may not have been heads of households, who made a will. If we subtract from our total of 326 households those who were too poor to leave anything worth bequeathing, probably 40 per cent of the parish, [11] we are left with about 200 households from which one might have expected some form of will. The 113 wills and administra-

[7] (Ed.) E.A. Wrigley, *An Introduction to English Historical Demography* (1966), 177–8.

[8] KAO., Q/RTL. Reproduced as Appendix A.

[9] Chalklin, *op. cit.*, 38–41.

[10] C. Howell, 'Peasant Inheritance Customs in the Midlands, 1280–1700,' in (Eds.) J. Goody, J. Thirsk, E.P. Thompson, *Family and Inheritance* (1976), 122.

[11] See page xxxiv.

tions may represent a cross-section of about half of the non-pauper households in the parish in the reign of Charles II.

Only 13 of the 86 testators, when they drew up the preamble to their wills, claimed that they were in good health; 32 admitted that they were sick; 16 said that they were aged and weak; 14 gave no indication of their state of health and the remaining 10 were nuncupative wills, i.e., brief death-bed statements made before witnesses which were acceptable for the purpose of probate. Nearly 70 per cent of the testators postponed making a will until they thought that they were going to die. Of 39 whose burial dates can be verified, 25 per cent were buried within one week and 50 per cent within one month of making their wills. Perhaps, as has been suggested, 'some thought it unlucky to make an early will because many people died after doing so.'[12]

Tradesmen in the market town

The market area and the shops which grew up around it were of fundamental importance to Sevenoaks. According to H.W. Knocker, Sevenoaks was unusual in that its development followed an inverted sequence. First came a toll-free market of such antiquity that its origins cannot be traced, then the church was built, finally the manor was created in the middle of the sixteenth century out of a part of the Honor of Otford.[13] The siting of Sevenoaks at the junction of the road from Dartford with the London to Rye road, was superior to that of its rival markets of Kemsing, Shoreham, Seal and Otford, and it enabled Sevenoaks to survive the economic vicissitudes of the fourteenth and fifteenth centuries.[14] Also, the preference of the archbishops of Canterbury for Knole rather than Otford and their interest in the economic activity of the town helped to stimulate trade in the late fifteenth century. This was particularly true of Archbishop Morton who possessed thirteen shops in Sevenoaks market place.[15]

Nineteen shops are noted in the manor rental of 1665. It is probable that several more shops are listed as tenements. For instance, it seems likely that two of John Blome's tenements near to the market cross were shops or had been shops. The tenants were

[12] K. Thomas, *Religion and the Decline of Magic* (1971), 746

[13] H.W. Knocker, 'Sevenoaks; the Manor, Church and Market', *Arch. Cant.*, xxxviii (1926), 51–67.

[14] A.E. Everitt, *op. cit.*, 465

[15] F.R.H. Du Boulay, 'The Assembling of an Estate: Knole in Sevenoaks 1275–1525', *Arch. Cant.*, lxxxix (1974), 9–10.

Isaac Day, mercer, and Gilbert Kipps, innholder, in whose inventory was a room called 'the old shop' (93). Some shops might be accurately termed workshops. David Jeffery, clothworker, had shears, shearboards, weights and brushes in his shop at Greatness Mill, but there were scales and beams in the kitchen and he may have traded from the Mill (34). Seven of the shops were occupied by butchers, one of which was noted as 'new built' in 1665. There was also a chandler's, a tailor's and a leather shop.[16] From the inventories it would appear that the most common layout was that the shop chamber took the place of the parlour in the typical timber-framed Wealden hall-house.[17] By the latter part of the seventeenth century there were usually chambers above the shop and hall, although some of the butchers' shops did not have a room over the shop as they required the extra height for ventilation.

In most of the tradesmen's inventories the saleable items are not listed separately. There were £30 of drugs, grocery wares and utensils at the mercer's, £6 of butter and cheese at the cheesemonger's and £5 worth of leather and shoes at the cordwainer's. 475 pounds of tobacco and two gross of pipes made up the stock of another mercer, Thomas Weston (61). The most detailed account is of George Johnson's shop (60). Although the total value of the inventory was only £31, three appraisers conscientiously listed every item even down to a tin candlestick, valued at sixpence, in the hall. Stockings, shirts, frocks, waistcoats and dimity drawers are carefully priced. With only one shilling remaining in his purse business does not appear to have been very brisk in July 1668. Possibly there was little demand for woollen stockings, kersey hose and flannel waistcoats in midsummer: more probably his widow had removed the surplus cash before the appraisers arrived.

Inventories often show the debts owing to the deceased as sperate – hopeful and desperate – hopeless. The sperate or good debts are usually included in the total value of the deceased goods, the bad debts are excluded. But, as Professor Everitt has pointed out, at this time 'The whole structure of private marketing rested on a basis of credit'[18] and in the following table good and bad debts have been added into the total to show the percentage of credit extracted from the various groups.

[16] KAO. U.1000/7 T.60. Title deed to a shop in the Leather Market.

[17] See illustration in (Ed.) E. Melling, *Kentish Sources*, vol. 5 *Some Kentish Houses* (1965), 4.

[18] Everitt, *op. cit.*, 557 and fn. 3.

	Total value	*Debts*	%
Craftsmen	£ 603	£212	35
Victuallers	£ 964	£155	16
Tradesmen	£ 584	£ 77	13
Yeomen	£1985	£ 72	4

The butcher, Thomas Taylor's inventory is notable because it contains a list of the debtors to the deceased (27). Almost £50 was owed by one man, Sir Bernard Hyde of Sundridge. £8 was owed by the parishioners of Sevenoaks. One of the desperate debts, Thomas Wickenden, mercer, had died one month previously. Some of the debt of £150 owing to Spilstead, the weaver, may have been his charges for weaving yarn into cloth for local inhabitants, for one item in Robert Everest's inventory is for 'certain flax, hemp, tow and yarn at the weavers' (147).

Shortage of coin may have forced tradesmen to give credit, at least for small sums. During the Commonwealth period, no copper coinage was officially issued, consequently copper tokens representing small denominations of a farthing and a halfpenny were issued by tradesmen. These tokens first appeared about 1649 and were in use until at least 1672 when a royal proclamation announcing a new copper coinage ordered the withdrawal of the tokens.[19] Wickenden was one of about a dozen Sevenoaks tradesmen who issued tokens during the 1650s and 1660s.[20]

If one looks at the evidence of probate records one gets the impression that no great fortunes were to be made from trade in Sevenoaks in Charles II's reign. One is struck by the paucity of shop-keepers' wills and inventories. There were people like the Blomes and the Thorntons who recognized the potential of Sevenoaks position, particularly as the wells beyond Tonbridge and the building or reconstruction of bridges encouraged the carriage trade. But their financial inducement appears to have been rent. Before 1685, the only evidence that Sevenoaks folk knew that there were worlds elsewhere were tobacco and wine. The shops appear modest, some even primitive, and with repeated references to old furniture and worn fittings, a little rundown and threadbare.

[19] E.W. Tilley, 'The seventeenth Century Token Issuers of Gravesend and Milton', *Arch. Cant.*, lxxxv (1970), 149.

[20] G. Ward, *Sevenoaks Essays*, (1931), 131–5.

Craftsmen

Twenty craftsmen left wills or inventories and they may be grouped under the cloth, leather and wood trades. Ten, including five tailors worked in cloth, six in leather and four in wood. The most prosperous trades appear to have been the cordwainers and the cloth finishers. The cordwainer, Richard Cakott's inventory totalled £134, but he also left the leases of three farms to his two sons (81). John Hayns, cordwainer, left the lease of his farm to his son, who when he died left his land and estate to his brother (47. 143). The inventory of another cordwainer, William Floate, totalled only £6, but he left two houses to his nephew and his niece.

The religious non-conformists, David and John Jeffery,[21] described themselves as clothworkers and seem to have been cloth finishers, for they owned the mills at Greatness, one of which was a fulling mill. When David died in 1666 the tools of his trade were valued at only £5 15*s*. in an inventory which totalled £174. But his farming stock and ground amounted to over £80 and included 4.5 acres of hop grounds and 5 acres of grass on which were his tainters (33). Carpenters in an area of timber-framed buildings were the equivalent to builders. Tristram Mantle left two houses in Sevenoaks to his son, and John Soane left the 'old messuage', which had been divided into two tenements, to his brother (142.14).

Weavers and tailors may have been less fortunate. Although William Spilstead's inventory totalled £196 that included £150 of debts; £140 were hopefully ascribed as good debts (147). Samuel Harmon and John Rowett left their looms to their sons (49.7). Spilstead's two looms were valued at £5. The tailor, William Everest, left what appeared to be a competence with a share of a hop ground to his widow and son, but the burden of numerous legacies may have accounted for the apparently reduced state of his son, William (55. 56: 131. 132). Diversification into farming or hop-growing must have had its attractions to those craftsmen who could obtain a lease of land.

Innkeepers and victuallers

By the second half of the seventeenth century, Sevenoaks had something in common with Tonbridge, the next market town on the

[21] B.L., Egerton 2985, Heath and Verney Papers, vol viii, f. 249. The widows of David and John Jefferys presented as recusants to the magistrates meeting at Riverhead 5 Jan. 1681/2.

same road to the coast.[22] Although there were still families engaged in the clothing trade, it was in decline. Providing for travellers on 'the well frequented road conveying you to the readiest passage to Diep . . . whence you have the shortest land passage thence to Paris'[23] was a more extensive and valuable business in Sevenoaks and it was an expanding one. The number of innkeepers and victuallers recognizances returned to Quarter Sessions increased from a dozen in 1665 to over twenty in 1678.[24] Twelve, possibly thirteen, inns are shown on Sir John Dunlop's map of Sevenoaks in 1687,[25] and there were at least four more inns at Riverhead, including The Porcupine, shown on Ogilby's road map of 1675. Some inns changed their names several times in the second half of the seventeenth century: thus the White Lyon of 1650 became the Kingshead of 1675 and the Black Swan of 1694. The Pydbull, The Bell, The Blackboy, The Porcupine, The Hand and Pen, The Catts and The Kingshead are all mentioned in the manor rental of 1665.[26]

By far the greatest inn in Sevenoaks was The Crown. The inventory of Francis Best, the proprietor, who died in 1669 indicates that the building was large and of an unusual configuration (69). The first chamber noted was called 'the Forten' and it was large and lavishly furnished. As well as a bedstead with all its furniture and a trundle bed there were one long table, two short tables, a court cupboard, eight leather chairs, three green stools, a dozen cushions and, touches of luxury for Sevenoaks, four carpets, two window curtains, a looking glass and brass-trimmed fire dogs. Other accommodation included a gatehouse with two chambers and two garretts over it, a little hall chamber, The Star, The Crown and The Green chambers. All these rooms were furnished with beds and, if one allows only two persons per bed and one per trundle bed, then The Crown could accommodate about forty people, including servants. There was a barber's shop and the kitchen was equipped with two and a half hundredweights of pewter dishes, ninety-four pounds of flagons and wine pots and five spits. In the brew house was the most valuable item of the inn, the brewing equipment. In the cellar were £10 worth of beer and wine. Best beer and ale were ten shillings a barrel and small beer and ale were six shillings a barrel in 1675.[27] Best appears to have grown some hops for his own use: the poles in the hopgarden were valued at £13 10*s*. 0*d*. 5000 old hop poles were valued at £10 in

[22] C.W. Chalklin, 'A seventeenth Century Market Town: Tonbridge', *Arch. Cant.*, lxxvi (1961), 152–62.
[23] John Ogilby, *Brittania* (1675), 61.
[24] KAO., Q/RLV 1/13–1/25.
[25] J. Dunlop, *The Pleasant Town of Sevenoaks* (1964), 121.
[26] See appendix B.
[27] BL., Egerton, *op. cit.*, f. 146.

1665 and two acres of hop poles were valued at £6 in 1679 (31. 127), so he may have had four to five acres of hops. In the yard were 1000 faggots for the ovens, six cords of wood for the fires and in the barn oats and beans for horsemeat. The whole inventory presents a picture of a thriving establishment offering the most comfortable accommodation and the best fare in Sevenoaks. The inventory totalled £510, but £200 of this is described as 'money in the deceased's purse and owing upon bills, bonds, book debts and otherwise.'

Two other innkeepers had inventories which totalled £133 and £147. The latter applied to John Thornton who, in 1665, had been the tenant of The Pydbull. By his will (53) he also left six tenements to three daughters and an unspecified number of tenements to his son John. He had another house in Tonbridge and he left an annuity of £8 a year to his mother. Gilbert Kipps and Edward Baker seem to have kept more modest establishments.

Thirteen brewhouses are noted in the inventories. The equipment in them varied but a furnace, needed to heat water and malt to convert it into wort, was essential. The wort was then boiled with hops, strained and cooled. If large quantities were being brewed a hop back or cool back was employed. Good equipment was expensive. At The Crown Francis Best had 'One meash fatt (vat) and one under pate (plate) and one tun with two Collers (coolers) two shoots (funnels) one pump with two small beareing tubs and one lardge Furnace' which was valued at over £25. Edward Baker's equipment amounted to £14 of his £35 inventory. But for most people who brewed for their own households a furnace, mash tun and keelers – shallow bowls or tubs for cooling liquids – had to suffice. Usually, the brewing was done with the furnace and copper in the kitchen. Only twelve cellars are recorded, most of them belonging to the innkeepers. For the majority of householders beer was kept in the beer or drink buttery, or in one case, in the drinkhouse.

The recognizance for good behaviour which Best gave, and to which all innkeepers were required to subscribe, is reproduced as Appendix C. If fully observed it would have soberly modified the picture we may cherish of Restoration conviviality and tavern society. Fortunately, such latter-day Puritanical echoes did not inhibit Charles, the sixth Earl of Dorset of neighbouring Knole who, according to Pepys, was arraigned before Chief Justice Foster for having in the company of Sir Charles Sedley, another noted rake, committed various acts of gross indecency in a public place to wit the balcony of an inn or brothel.[28]

[28] (Eds.) R. Latham and W. Matthews, *The Diary of Samuel Pepys* (1971), vol. iv. 1663, 209–210.

Agriculture

There are wills or inventories of 25 yeomen or husbandmen and a gardener who died between 1660 and 1685. Five others, two widows probably of yeomen, two cordwainers and a butcher, did some farming, also. Twelve yeomen, four husbandmen, two widows, two cordwainers, the butcher and the gardener have left inventories, which give some indication of the sort of farming that they pursued. Thomas Fuller was described as a husbandman, but left no stock, crops, working tools or furniture of any kind. At his death he was owed £5 for wages. The list of his personal clothing is the longest and most detailed in any Sevenoaks inventory. Thomas Beecher was described as a yeoman yet he had no stock or crops and only the simplest tools such as spades and sickles. In his will he does not refer to a farm or the lease of a farm. £60 of his personal estate of £70 was in cash. No doubt in Kent, as in Cambridgeshire, some yeomen sold their farm stock and leases, laid out the money on loans or mortgages and retired.[29]

The land in the parish varied from the lighter and in some cases sandy soils on the ridge on which Sevenoaks was sited to the heavier clays of the weald. All the farms, with the possible exception of Richard Cakott's, appear to have had some arable land, and, with corn prices falling fairly steadily after 1660, it is not surprising that the emphasis was upon pasture farming.[30] Parnell Hunt's farm at Blackhall was on the yellow and red sand of the chartland.[31] In August 1666, her barns contained the unthreashed harvest of 213 cops of oats, 55 cops of wheat, 36 cops of oats and teares, 3 loads of peas and there were also 7 loads of hay. Cops or coups were heaps of grain in straw. The value of these crops was estimated at £63, the livestock at £114 and the farming tackle at £6 (36). Of her liquid farming capital, excluding the value of any leases of land, 34 per cent was in the crops and 62 per cent was in the livestock. John Everest, whose land was in the Weald around Else's Farm, also had a harvest inventory. In his barn were 50 cops of oats, 33 cops of wheat, 10 loads

[29] M. Spufford, 'Peasant Inheritance Customs and Land Distribution in Cambridgeshire from the 16th to the 18th Centuries', in (Eds.) J. Goody, J. Thirsk, E.P. Thompson, *op. cit.*, 163.

[30] Cf. J.H. Bettey and D.S. Wilde, 'The Probate Inventories of Dorset Farmers 1573–1670', *The Local Historian*, vol. 12, no. 5 (1977), 230. And for Gloucestershire, J.S. Moore, *op. cit.*, 29. Also, J. Thirsk, 'Seventeenth Century Agriculture and Social Change', in J. Thirsk, (Ed.) *Land, Church and People* (1970), 148–77.

[31] H.G. Dines, Buchan, Holmes and Bristow, *The Geology of the Country around Sevenoaks and Tonbridge* (1969), 72. 83.

of hay and there was 10 shillings' worth of barley still on the ground (88). Adding the 4 quarters of wheat and 5 quarters of oats in his garret, his crops were estimated at £28, his livestock at £81 and his farming tackle at £5, i.e., about 24 per cent of his farming capital was in crops and about 72 per cent was in livestock.

Hops were grown around Sevenoaks in some quantity. Their value as a crop was reflected in the actions, which rectors and vicars brought against hop growers reluctant to pay their tithes.[32] An indenture of 1677 refers to a hop garden and hop field of 8 acres bounding upon The Vine.[33] The largest area noted in the wills and inventories was of 4.5 acres held by David Jeffery, a clothworker. Fifteen inventories show evidence of hop growing, but only five of these belonged to yeomen. Three innkeepers, Edward Baker, Francis Best and Richard Everidge grew hops, presumably for their own brewing. The other growers, including the vicar, no doubt supplied their own requirements and other home brewers. Some beer may have been brewed on a commercial scale for John Wood of Sevenoaks, 'Beerebruer' bought two houses near to the vicarage in 1645.[34]

Oxen were most favoured for working the land, particularly the heavy clay of the Weald. There were seven teams of four and one team of six oxen. All the farmers who had oxen had three or four young steers for replacements. The oxen were the most expensive farm animals, their price varying from £4 10*s*. to £4 15*s*. Horses and mares were usually priced at £3 or less. Cattle which were being fattened up for the table fetched half as much again as the normal run-of-the-farm animal. Thomas Taylor, the butcher, had three 'fatling steers' which were valued at £20, as much as his four oxen and three ordinary steers (27). His sheep were valued at 9*s*. 3*d*. whereas the farm price was around 6*s*. 8*d*. Similarly, the sheep penned in the yard of The Crown were priced at 10*s*. and the fat hogs at £1 5*s*. It seems likely that the most common meat for sale in the numerous butchers' shops in Sevenoaks was mutton and pork, although George and Richard Wood, two farmers who had no ox teams, kept bullocks (135). Tables of the prices of grain and livestock are included in Appendix D.

[32] H.C.F. Lansberry, 'Improper Impropriators and "Autiel Petit Choses"', in (Eds.) A. Detsicas and N. Yates, *Studies of Modern Kentish History* (1983), 104–107.

[33] SL., Gordan Ward Notebooks, S XIII, indenture 13 April 28 Chas. II.

[34] KAO., U.1000/5 T41.

Gentlemen

What credence can we give to the gentleman, often self-styled? The Heralds' Visitation in Kent in the 1660s rejected fifty-one claims to coat armour.[35] Probably only a minority of Sevenoaks' gentlemen would have claimed that sort of gentility. Birth, education, the ability to live without undertaking paid employment, to be able to 'go' like a gentleman, in fact, all the criteria which might have been used before the Civil War and Interregnum, no longer applied to most of the claimants. One might suggest perhaps that the format of the will engendered the title in some cases. Those who had insufficient land to be dubbed an esquire opted for the suffix of 'gent' as representing a half way stage between 'esq' and the prefix of master. But, as the will might not show the real estate of the deceased, attempting to interpret the standing of a gentleman from probate records is more speculative than that for any other group.

Can one accept the designation of the testator's contemporaries? Thomas Buckminster (104) was called a gentleman by his appraisers even though the total value of his inventory was less than £15. In his will (103) he called himself a tanner and the only property mentioned was a mortgaged house in Hen Lane, Sleeford, Lincolnshire. Edward Courthop also was described as a gentleman by his appraisers, both of them mercers (29). The cases of silver, steel and tortoise-shell instruments of chirurgery, the galley pots and the bottles of stilled waters and drugs suggest that he was a surgeon-apothecary. But his house was large containing twelve rooms, including a shop, and it had four hearths. It was furnished better than most. In the parlour were six Turkey-work chairs and four leather chairs. There were hangings on the walls, three carpets and a window curtain and, although his napkins were 'worne very thyn', they were of damask. Signs of better days? Like the apothecary's scales, the evaluation of a gentleman seemed to depend upon delicately balancing variables. Some, like the Blomes, were on their way up, others like this branch of the Courthops may have been on their way down. A John Courthop of Brenchley, Kent, who had been a gentleman pensioner of Charles I, was imprisoned, prevented from returning to the late king and soon after died, his wages then being £800 in arrears.[36]

Edward Cosier was described as a gentleman by his appraisers and by himself in his will (42. 43). Yet, the total value of his goods was only £13. Once again there were signs of grander times. He left a

[35] L. Stone, *The Crisis of the Aristocracy 1558–1641* (1967), 39.
[36] *Calendar of State Papers Domestic, 1660–61*, 31.

silver cup, two pictures and several 'escutchions'. Although only two rooms were noted, his bed chamber and dining room, that was the only dining room recorded in Sevenoaks. To the poor he gave ten shillings; to his friends, his clothes, which included a 'darke grey coate with gold buttons', but to his loving friend, the *éminence grise* of Sevenoaks, Mr John Blome, he gave the remainder of his estate both real and personal. And that may have been considerable for, according to the manor rental, it included a butcher's shop and a tenement and land whose rent of 1*s*. 8*d*. might be compared to that of Francis Farnaby, who paid only 1*s*. 4*d*. for his house and garden of Great Kippington. At one time the estate of Kippington had extended to over 200 acres and had been owned in the late sixteenth century by a succession of cloth workers, the last being Richard Cooper, a dyer, whose son, John, sold the estate to Thomas Farnaby in 1630 for £2200.[37]

John Couper's will and inventory of 1665 present a contradictory picture, also (21. 22). His personal estate amounted to £6 of which £2 was for some old hop poles. After leaving forty shillings each to his two daughters, all the rest of his house, leases, tenements and goods he left to his youngest son. In 1649, John Cowper of Sevenoaks, gentleman, had sold 'an old, old house', large enough to be split up into three tenements, and other property in Brands Lane, to tradespeople.[38] By 1664, only one member of the family was recorded in the Hearth Tax return, a Mr John Cooper who lived in a house with twelve hearths, almost as many as the Lambards of Sevenoaks Park.

All the remaining gentlemen were property owners. Charles Beswick bequeathed a messuage in London near to Temple Bar (150). Edward Besbeech owned a house and lands in Staplehurst and a capital messuage, orchards, meadows and woods in Sevenoaks (13). Part of this may have been made up of the meadow called Blackmead, which had been bought by a Mr Besbeche from the recusant George Lone in 1652.[39] Robert and John Smith had lands in Sundridge and Chevening. Walter Smith, who appears to have died suddenly during the time of the plague, had received lands from his father-in-law, Robert Smith (23. 116. 46). William Wall, who held lands in Sevenoaks, Chevening and Yalding, a share of the manor of Otford and the Forest of Whitcliffe and the advowson of the parsonage of Farnborough and Chelsfield, was termed a gentleman by his appraisers but, modestly, not by himself (143. 144).

[37] SL., Farnaby-Austin MS., indenture 1 Nov. 1630.
[38] G. Ward, *op. cit.*, 196.
[39] KAO., Lambard MS., U 1000/2 T1. 9 Nov. 1652.

Professions

Of this small group comprised of John Hooper, schoolmaster, and the Richard Bosses, father and son, vicars of Sevenoaks, the will and inventory of the schoolmaster presents the most intriguing picture (2. 3). If one includes the service quarters, there were 19 rooms or chambers in Hooper's house and two cellars. Some of the students must have slept upon the 23 bedsteads and trundle beds within the house. A further 9 bedsteads with mats and cords but without beds or linen were stored 'over the Schoole'. No mention is made of any furniture in the school, and only one desk, one 'study late set up of fir boards' and one hanging table in the little study were listed in the house. In his will Hooper reserved his library for his sons, and his appraisers, who included Thomas Lambard, esquire, did not refer to it. Hooper admitted that there 'may be several small sums owing to me for the boarding and teaching of scholars' and he urged his wife to take some pains to assist his executor gathering in these arrears. By the time that the inventory was taken, they had not been very successful for his appraisers included £440 of desperate debts in his personal estate of £747. Hooper also forbade his wife to give away more than 20 marks (£13) at any time during her life or at her death, a somewhat uncharitable valediction in view of his own inability to balance his books.

Richard Bosse, the elder, by his will (19) also left his library and his sermon notes to his son Richard, who in turn (117) left the library, valued at £73 in 1677, to his two sons, if they qualified for the ministry. Apart from £300, which he had loaned out on security, the library was by far the most valuable item in his inventory. The younger Bosse who, shortly before he died had been appointed domestic chaplain to the Earl of Dorset, liked his creature comforts. He slept upon one of the two down beds in Sevenoaks and bestrode the most valuable horse in the parish. The produce of four thousand hop poles kept the brewhouse well supplied. His death on 1st of February 1677 was lamented by the whole parish.[40] The only other man in Sevenoaks with a notable library was Edward Courthop, gentleman, whose library of 160 books valued acording to size totalled £11 17*s.* 6*d.* If Bosse's library was valued on the same principle, it might have amounted to about 1000 volumes. Books are noted in another eight inventories. Eight Bibles were owned by five inhabitants, two of them by Robert Skinner, as befitted the wearer of an old buffcoat.

[40] SL., Gordon Ward Notebooks, SVII. 32.

Widows

Customarily, widows have been the most carefully protected members of the family and with good reason. If the husband died young, his widow might have the responsibility of bringing up his children. Usually, the wife's presence would have ensured that thoughts about her future would be uppermost in the sick man's mind. The following scene, enacted at the death bed of a Mr Franklyn of Wye in Kent, could have been matched many times at Sevenoaks:

'Upon a day happening some six or seven days before the death of the testator, Mr. Franklyn, he this deponent, being his servant was sent for to come unto him, went and found him the said Mr. Franklyn lying in his bed in an upper chamber of his house . . . accompanied only with Mr. Howse and Mrs. Franklyn, his the said testators wife, and after this deponent came unto him the testator aforenamed told this deponent that he had sent for him of purpose to be a witnes of his will which Mr. Howse had then written as yt seemed for he the said Mr. Howse had the same will in his hand and asked the testator whether he should read it unto him agayne or noe, who presentlie made answer, noe said he (being the testator) what need you to read it agayne I have heard it read unto me and it is very well and as I would have and so calling for penn and inck did write somewhat unto yt and affixed his seale unto yt and then delivered the same unto the said Mr. Howse and said yt was his last will and Testament entreating this deponent withall to sett to his hand as a witnes of the same which this deponent at his entreaty accordingly did at the lower end of the first page or sheet of paper being contained in seaven small sheets.'[41]

The oft-repeated phrase 'my well-beloved wife' cannot have been a scrivener's formality every time. But, in addition to the bonds of love and affection, the wife had the protection of custom, which extended even more widely in her widowhood. According to the custom of gavelkind, the Kentish widow was entitled to hold and enjoy one-half of the lands and tenements of inheritance of her late husband provided that she remained a widow or did not bear another's child. Also, the widow was entitled to one half of the goods and chattels of the deceased, if there were no children of the marriage and to one-third if there were.[42] The lands and tenements with which a wife became endowed at the time of her marriage were inalienable without her consent. They were her dower and they should not be confused with her dowry which she might bring to the marriage.

[41] CALC., X.II.13.154b.

[42] T. Robinson, *The Common Law of Kent; or the Custom of Gavelkind* (1858), 95–113.

39 of the 67 males referred to wives in their wills. The remaining 28 were either widowers, one was so described, bachelors, or and this seems unlikely, they totally ignored their wives. In two-thirds of the 39 wills, the widow was made the sole executrix of her husband's estate. With few exceptions the widow was made the guardian of her children and sometimes of her step-children, with the responsibility for their education or apprenticeship. Apart from one instance in a nun-cupative will, the widow always received some share of the household goods and chattels and sometimes a share of her husband's other personal estate. In one-quarter of the wills the husband specified what house or in what part of the house his widow should continue to live. Some widows did not have to surrender this privilege of 'free bench', even when they remarried.

Only one yeoman threatened his wife with disinheritance, if she attempted to claim her dower. Richard Everidge gave to his wife Susan, her bed, two chairs and a chest and a rent charge of £8 per annum during her natural life, 'but if my said wife shall at any time after my decease goe about by suite either in Law or in Equitie to recover any Dower or other interest or estate whatsoever then and from thenceforth I will that the said annuities of eight pounds shall cease' (89). He did not make his wife executrix of his will and he cut off his son's second wife and her daughter with the proverbial shilling 'to be paid on demand'. His farm and lands were left to three grandsons, the children of his son's first marriage.

John Coggar treated his wife a little better leaving her one half of his household goods, but the annuity of £10 was 'in liew and satisfaction of hir Right of Dower to my said lands' (40). All his houses, lands and tenements, subject to the rent charge, were left to his son John. His estate was considerable, for when his son John married Elizabeth, one of the daughters of Francis Best, landlord of the Crown Inn at Sevenoaks, she brought a dowry of £200 and John made her a marriage settlement, which comprised seven houses, including the family farm of Dibden, two coppices, 17 acres of land and five acres of hops.[43]

Some yeomen who had no surviving sons left their widows in charge of their farms. John Everest left his lands in Pembury to his wife Ann for her natural life with no proviso about her remarriage. 'Also, my will is that she shall have the use of the farm wherein I live called Elses and all my stock thereon together with all my household goods during her natural life, she paying the rent for the farm and making no wilful waste or destruction' (87). After her death, the

[43] SL., Gordon Ward Notebooks, SXIII. 88.

lease, stock and household goods were to go to his nephew, Peter Everest. When Ann died five years later in 1677, she made no mention in her will of the farm, which she had held in reversion, and her inventory showed that her furniture was worth less than £4 (101. 102). Neither will nor inventory gave a true indication of her previous life style – a cautionary tale for those of us who would attempt to deduce living standards from probate records.

The majority of the yeomen made a life-long provision for their widows and showed some concern for their comfort. Most widows received their half of the household goods and chattels – Richard Everidge's allowance of furniture to his wife is noticeably mean. If it were not specified, it appears to have been taken for granted that the widow should share part of the house, at least until the son had come of age or the term of the lease had expired. John Hayns, who described himself as a cordwainer but who had far more farm stock than he had leather goods, divided all his goods, chattels and stock equally between his wife and his son and made them join executors of his will. His son had the lease of the farm but 'My wife shall have her biding in the house during the time of the lease and the paller wholly to herself to log in' (47).

Without exception the widows of the craftsmen and shopkeepers were made the executrices of their late husbands' estates, but they were saddled with much responsibility for bringing up and educating the children and for finding capital sums for daughters and sons when they married or came of age. David Jeffery, clothworker, who died in 1666, left all his goods, chattels and lands to his wife, with instructions to pay certain sums to three of his daughters. The payment of legacies to his other daughters he left to his wife's discretion. His son John, also a clothworker, who died in 1679, left £20 to each of his six children. After other small legacies had been paid, his wife and executrix, Bridget, was left the whole of his personal and real estate with instructions to sell immediately the corn mill which he owned. The rents and profits of the dwelling house, fulling mill and its land were to be reserved for the bringing up of his children. When the youngest was ten years old the widow was to sell the fulling mill and the land (122). One might surmise that John Jeffery had foreseen that the decline of the cloth industry in Kent was irreversible. His mills at Greatness were later converted to silk spinning.[44]

The two Richard Bosses, father and son, were vicars of Sevenoaks during this period. Both made their wives their sole executrices. The

[44] E. Hasted, *The History and Topographical Survey of the County of Kent* (1797), vol. iii, 61.

elder Bosse left large dowries to his daughters which necessitated felling the timber and wood on his land (19). The younger Bosse thought it prudent to charge his wife 'to take care as she by law and nature is bound of all my children and to take care with the profits of my said personal and also my real estate . . . for their education' (117). His real estate of 40 acres was to go to his eldest son when he was 25 years of age but, if he died before that time, it was to be divided equally between his three younger sons. This mixture of primogeniture and partible inheritance may be explained as an inducement to his elder son to enter the ministry.

Widows' wills like widows' weeds hide more than they reveal: but they are intriguing and are distinguished by certain features. Widows were circumscribed by estates that were entailed or held in reversion and, therefore, they could devise less than they had enjoyed. Because their sons and grandsons had usually inherited under their husbands' wills, the majority of their bequests tend to be to women relatives and to friends. As they invariably have had a share of the family's goods and chattels and often the first choice, widows tended to accumulate the best furniture, the silver plate and the family heirlooms.

Dame Margaret Boswell's heir in land was her cousin, William Bosville, but in her will she gave the largest legacies to six women and left the remainder of her personal estate to Elizabeth and Ann Worsley (141). Mary Beardsworth 'being desirous to make provision for my three daughters' gave 2*s*. 6*d*. to each of her five sons and the rest of their goods and chattels to her daughters, whom she made her executrices (28). Alice Gill left small legacies to other widows, a ring to Miss Bosse and her wearing apparel to her nurse (58). Parnell Hunt left the remainder of her very considerable estate to a kinswoman (35). Elizabeth Everest left all her goods, plate and money for the use of her daughter (151). Joan Fremling left her house and land to her daughter Mary, and the rest of her real and personal estate to her daughters, Mary and Ann (120). Ann Swaine gave the lease of her property in Broad Street, London, to her daughter (16).

Family treasures rarely remain long in the house of the deceased even today and many items mentioned in the wills are not recorded in the accompanying inventories. Margery Burgess left to her daughter a bed with green curtains, a green rug of worsted, two green cloth chairs and stools, one great yellow satin chair, one pair of grey curtains, a table carpet and a cupboard cloth. To her granddaughter she gave a silver tankard (63). The appraisers of her inventory recorded just two items: £1 in her purse and her clothing valued at £10. The inventory was made 33 weeks after her burial (64). Dorothy Everidge gave her daughter-in-law Mary, a silver bowl and two pairs of her best hempen sheets, and to her other daughter-in-law,

Elizabeth, she gave her wedding ring and two more pairs of hempen sheets. To Anne Jessup she gave her wedding gown and petticoat, and to Mary Jessup her biggest piece of gold (124). The silver bowl, ring and sheets were noted in the inventory, which was made eight days after her burial, but not the wedding dress and the gold (125).

Widows tended to be more careful than men in the descriptions of the goods they bequeathed. Some part of the furnishing of Mary Pierrepoint's house could be reconstructed from the details given in her will. She gave to her son 'two feather beds, the hangings in the hall chamber and the hangings in the next chamber to it, and the hanging in his own chamber where he now lieth and the table in the hall and the two tables in the two parlours and the tables and dressers in the kitchen and the carpet in the parlour . . . and I give him more all the Turkeyworke chaires and stooles which formerly did belong to the little parlour and the red leather chaires in the hall' (148). Wives, who spent more time in the home than their husbands, had a better memory for such things. One can only marvel at the retentive memories of the female witnesses to the nun-cupative will of Frances Jermine. In the longest of the nun-cupative wills is recorded the greatest amount of plate in the Sevenoaks wills. To four of her seven grandchildren mentioned in her will she gave a silver basin and all her linen, one silver gilt bowl and cover and all her silver spoons, one silver drinking pot with cover, her wedding ring and forty shillings in gold (8).

It has been tiresomely repeated, but no doubt, it is true that imminent death concentrates a man's mind wonderfully. The victualler, Thomas Wood's non-cupative will is worth quoting in full because it illustrates the priorities and obligations facing a man with short notice:

'He said he would give his daughter Joane halfe a skore lambes and to his sonne John he gave one great chist which was his grandfathers and the part of a tenement and land lying below Baylies Hill which were his mothers and to his sonne Thomas he gave a cow and a yong bud or heyfor which he willed to be sold and put out for his use, and being asked what he would give to his daughter Anne he said he would give hir nothing for that shee had allredy more than hir share. All the rest and residue of his estate he gave to Elizabeth his wyfe and hir daughter Susan' (78).

It would appear that Thomas had married twice and he gives to his elder son, John, land which may have been part of his first wife's dowry. The younger son gets stock which can be converted to cash, perhaps for an apprenticeship. His unmarried daughter receives her dowry of ten lambs. Anne's dowry reflected a time when Thomas's fortunes stood higher. His second wife, Elizabeth, who also had been married before, and her daughter receive as is customary the remainder of his estate. We do not know what Elizabeth brought to him with her widowhood, but it must have been more than the financial liability of Susan, for widows, particularly Kentish widows, were an attractive marital proposition.[45]

Servants

The most obvious gap in the list is the servant class. Gregory King supposed that about 14 per cent of the population of Sevenoaks parish were servants. Presumably, he included farm servants and perhaps the servants of craftsmen. Some information of the servants' lot can be inferred directly from the wills and inventories. In three inventories servants' rooms are listed. At The Crown, the largest inn at Sevenoaks, there was a Maid's Chamber furnished with two bedsteads, two feather beds, one flockbed and a joined chest (69). The Man's Chamber in the farm of Richard Everidge contained one bedstead, one trundle bedstead, two chaff beds, a chaff bolster, a flock bolster, one blanket and a coverlet (90). The Servant's Chamber in Joan Fremling's house had a flock bed and bolster, an old blanket and a chest – no bedstead (121). One might hazard a guess that at Edward Courthop's house the chamber over the entry in which there was a bed filled with cloth shreds, a cradle, cradle rug and blanket, was a servant's room (29). Some servants may have slept on the numerous truckle or trundle bedsteads, which when not in use could be pushed out of the way under the high bedsteads used by other members of the household.

Six testators left sums of money of between five and forty shillings to their servants. Richard Peake left small sums of money to five of the servants, including the 'fotboy' of Ralph Petley, Esquire (136). In addition to twenty shillings, Alice Gill left Goodwife Murchin her nurse 'my ordinary wearing apparrel as one westcoate and two petticoats' (58) Elizabeth Pierrepoint gave her mother's maid mourning to be worn at her, Elizabeth's, funeral (134). The best provision was to Rachel Craft, servant to the innkeeper John Thornton for she was given a house and garden for the remainder of her life (53).

The greatest number of domestic servants were at Knole, where Richard, the fifth Earl of Dorset kept a diary of servants' faults and

[45] For a fuller account of Sevenoaks widows at this time see H.C.F. Lansberry, 'Free Bench See-saw: Sevenoaks Widows in the late seventeenth Century', *Arch. Cant.*, c (1985), 281–93.

recorded the fines that he imposed for their misdemeanours.[46] William Loe was fined two shillings 'for running out of doors from Morning to Midnight without leave' and Henry Mattock was fined one shilling 'for not doing what he is bidden and 3*d.* a day until he does.' Some bullying went on within the servants' hierarchy and inspired the following letter revealing the state of affairs at Knole:[47]

Aug 16 1676 Knoll

My Lord

I am glad your Lordship is come home, for to take my part against my enimy Margery, for I did want your Lordship for to take my part, for she does abuse me most sadly and bet me, and call my Mother whore, and me Bastard and whoremaster and Roach belly, which affront I cannot endure it. I hop your Lordship will bet her, because I am too little for to bet her. And I desire your Lordship to bet William because he threw me down against the stones and had allmost broken my head, for there is a great bump in my head still, for I thought I should ner rose againe. So I rest.

Your Lordship very humble servant
Thomas Ireland

Under Charles, the easy-going sixth earl, the servant's life at Knole may have improved. An account for apothecary's items, which totalled £600 in ten years, included a bill 'For your servants', specifying plasters for the footman and purging pills for the coachman.[48] Sir Edward Dering complained in 1670 about the 'insolence and carelessness of servants requiring more wages and doing less work here [Kent] than any county in England.[49]

The siting of the great mansion of Knole within the boundaries of the parish broadened and fudged the status of servant making it difficult to generalise about the economic and social position of servants in Sevenoaks at this time. Among the Sackville papers there is a bond dated 1677 for £500 'for the performance of the true and faithful service of Walter Parkinson in the place of Buttler' to the Earl of Middlesex.[50] Even allowing that commonly bonds were made for twice the value of the obligation and that Middlesex had been Treasurer to James I and had acquired a great deal of plate, this was a large sum of money. The highest annual wage for a servant set by

46 V. Sackville-West, *Knole and the Sackvilles* (1948), 112–13.
47 KAO., Sackville MS., U.269 C.95/23.
48 *Ibid.*, A215. The bill was from John Chase, Charles II's apothecary.
49 (Eds.) J. Thirsk and J.C. Cooper, *op. cit.*, 85.
50 KAO., Sackville MS., U.269 E.80/1 (71).

magistrates at Maidstone in 1673 was £6 a year for 'a baylif taking charge.'[51]

Perhaps the most prosperous servants in Sevenoaks were the Blomes, father and son. The family originated from Penshurst and from the beginning of the seventeenth century they had been acquiring property in the market area of Sevenoaks.[52] William Blome was for many years steward at Knole.[53] No office of profit was beneath his grasp, it could always be improved, sometimes much to the annoyance of the Earl:[54]

7 Nov 1653 Dorset House

Bloome,

I doe very much wonder at your continual murmuring and disputing my agreements and conditions with you concerning my allowance of your wages for woodreeveship which I will not alter from or add one penny too otherwise than what I offered you in my letter.

William's son, John, followed closely in his father's footsteps by screwing the maximum financial advantage out of every situation he occupied. In 1662, Goodwife Mirrium petitioned the Earl:

'That I live in a little house which standeth upon your ground and that Mr. Bloome hath caused me to pay the rent to him as being steward to Mr. Goodwin, and I doe know that he hath no right to it therefore do desire that your Honour would take it into your hands that I may turn tennant to you, for he makes me pay him twice as much as the house is worth and unleethes it, and thretens to throw me in prison in case I will not pay him.'[55]

An advantageous marriage brought John considerable property in the Isle of Oxney and when he died, a 'gentleman', in 1684 he was able to leave a farm or a share of a farm to each of his four sons and £800 to one daughter and £500 each to three other daughters and still feel confident of a 'joyful resurrection with the Rightious' (138).

The Poor

Though their needs were few and basic, yet they offended. Many were so poor that they were obliged to drink water instead of beer.[56]

[51] BL., Egerton 2985, *op. cit.*, f.146.
[52] Gordon Ward, *op. cit.*, 193–5.
[53] KAO., Sackville MS., U.269 A41/1–2. Account books of William Blome 1629–30, 1647–52.
[54] *Ibid.*, U.269 C.(61).
[55] *Ibid.*, U.269 C. 95/5 (61). For a distraint on her goods, C. 95/4 (61).
[56] J. Larking, *Proceedings in Kent* (1862), 184–5.

The town had three public springs, the most convenient one on rectorial glebe. Dr Gibbon, rector from 1631 to 1644, blocked off this spring with a high stone wall. The magistrates ordered a pipe to be laid from the spring through the wall, but the supply often failed, and the well water, which the poor resorted to, made them 'more infirm and subject to infection and sickness.'[57]

During the Interregnum circumstances changed for the poor – and for the rich. William Blome, while acting as woodreeve for the Earl of Dorset, excused the unproductiveness of the woods in his care because the poor had grown 'so theevish and unconscionable' that 'I have made many journeys to one poor old Justice and he dwells six miles from me, but to little purpose. The poore of Senoke are grown so insolent that they spare not to tell me they have as much to do there as I have or any man that I emploie. We have no waie but force to curb them. I wish it were otherwise.'[58]

A contemporary indication of the numbers of the poor in Sevenoaks is contained in the Hearth Tax returns of 1664. The tax of two shillings per hearth or stove was extracted from every householder unless exempted by poverty, i.e., those who did not pay poor or church rates, or those who occupied a house or land worth less than twenty shillings per annum, or those who possessed property worth less than ten pounds. The 1664 return listed for the first time those who were 'not chargeable' as well as those who were 'chargeable'.[59] The number of households for the whole parish can be broken down as follows:

	not chargeable	chargeable	total	% not chargeable
Sevenoaks town	79	106	185	42
Sevenoaks weald	41	44	85	48
Riverhead	13	43	56	23
Sevenoaks parish	133	193	326	40

Using the mutiplier of 4.5 to convert households into persons, this would imply that out of a total population of 1467 persons about 600 were paupers and about 350 of these were concentrated in the town of Sevenoaks. If these figures appear high, one might compare them

[57] J. Rooker, *Notes on the Parish Church of Sevenoaks* (1910), 31–2.

[58] KAO., Sackville MS., U.269 C(61). William Blome to Richard, fifth Earl of Dorset, no date but *c.* 1653.

[59] See Appendix A.

to those of Exeter where in 1671 70 per cent of the population were considered to be paupers.[60] No doubt, there were evasions of the tax by people who were able to pay, though this became less easy in 1664 when the newly created 'chimney men' took over the responsibility for the assessments. The return shows that the number of hearths in a household is not a guide to wealth. 20 households which had a single hearth were taxed, whereas 57 which had two and four that had three hearths were not.

Occasionally, funerals were still accompanied by the medieval custom of a dole. Thomas Beecher, yeoman, left ten shillings to be laid out on bread to be distributed at his funeral – sufficient for 240 loaves (107). John Blome, after leaving £5 to the sixteen poor inhabitants of the Almshouse, to be laid out by the Wardens and Assistants for coats and gowns, left 4*d*. a piece to forty of the poorest people, married or single, living in the parish, and 2*d*. a piece to forty of the poorest children (138). Lambarde in his *Perambulation of Kent*, first published in 1570, noted that there was an endowed almshouse at Sevenoaks,[61] but Professor Jordan says that the almshouse was built between 1583 and 1585 and received its first endowment in 1599 by a rent charge of £5 per annum made by John Pett, gentleman.[62] By the 1660s, the almshouses were receiving modest benefactions. Six of the nineteen testators, who left money to the poor, specified that it should go to the Almsrowe or Almshouses, the sums of money ranging from ten shillings given by John Hooper (2), to £5 given by Dame Margaret Boswell (141). One of the most generous benefactors was Edward Lampard, yeoman, who left £20 to one widow living in the Almsrowe and a further £8 to the poor of Sevenoaks, £10 to the poor of Sundridge and £1 to the poor of Leigh (91). The largest single bequest in this period was made by Frances, the Dowager Countess, who by will dated 28 January, 1684, at Knole gave £100 to the poor of Sevenoaks parish to be laid out in the purchase of land or rent, the revenue of which was to be paid to the poor each year in the parish vestry.[63]

Finally to 'honest Hodge', the labourer (73). Unmarried? Lodging with a spinster? Capital out on bond? Friend of the Blomes? 'We know so little about these people. As we stir these cold ashes, a tongue of flame seems to dart out and flicker and die. We cannot feel sure of very much.[64]

[60] W.B. Stephens, *Seventeenth Century Exeter* (1958), 147.
[61] William Lambarde, *Perambulation of Kent* (1570), 57.
[62] W.K. Jordan, *Social Institutions in Kent, Arch. Cant.*, lxxv (1961), 41.
[63] C.J. Phillips, *History of the Sackville Family* (1930), vol. i., 425.
[64] Quoted by my tutor, K.B. McFarlane, *John Wyclif and the Beginnings of English Nonconformity* (1952), 9.

WILLS AND INVENTORIES, 1660–1685

1

WIMBLE Robert	Innholder	bur. 24 Mar. 1661
W. 29 Feb. 1660	prov. 28 May 1661	Prob. 11.304 f.90

In the name of God Amen I Robert Wimble of Seavenoke in the Countie of Kent Inholder being at this present in good health and of perfect memory (praysed be God for it) but being of greate yeares and not knowing how suddenly it may please the Almighty to call me out of this world doe this nine and twentieth day of February in the yeare of our Lord one Thousand sixhundred Fifty and 1659 [sic] make this my last will and testament in manner and forme following videlicet Imprimis I bequeath my soule into the hands of Almighty god that gave it hopeing and trusting through his mercys in and for the merritts of Christ my Saviour to have the same eternally saved my body I bequeath to the earth whereof it is made to be buried in a decent manner according to the discrecion of my overseer herein after named And I do hereby appoint that five pounds shall be expended for the charge of my said funerall and for my worldly goods wherewith it hath pleased god to blesse me I dispose of them as followeth That is to say First I give unto my daughter in lawe Jane late the wife of my sonne Robert Wimble deceased the yearely summe of forty shillings to be paid to her half yearely at the feast of St Michael the Archangell And the Annunciacion of the blessed Virgin Mary by equall porcons for and towards the education of Robert Wimble my grandsonne untill he shall attayne the age of fowerteene yeares The first of the said payments to beguine at the next of the said feasts comeing after my decease Item I give to my grand-daughter Anne the wife of Thomas Cooper the summe of five pounds of lawful English money And to him the said Thomas Cowper I give all my wearing apparrell Item I give to my three grand-children Alice Anne and Jane Cronke daughters of my sonne in law Richard Cronke of Seavenoke tenne shillings a peece And to my godson George Johnson the younger tenne shillings which said Annuity of forty shillings per annum together with the severall summes aforesaid I doe order and appoint shalbe paid by my overseer hereafter named out of the proffitts or yearely rents of my messuage tenement or Inne scituate in Seavenoke aforesaid with the appurtenances called or known by the name or Signe of the Swan as the same Annuity and Sommes of money shall or may arise from thence Item I give to my grand-daughter Anne the wife of Richard Cronke of Tonbridge one halfe headed bedsteddle one Fetherbed one Fether bolster one blankett one Joyned Chest and a brasse Skillett Item I do order and directe that my funerall expences and what debts I shall justly owe at the tyme of my decease other then such debts as I have already given security for by mortgage shalbe paid and discharged by my overseers hereafter named out of my goods Chattells money and other personall estate Then I doe give the same overplus to my said grandson Robert Wimble And I do make and ordayne my said grand sonne Robert Wimble sole executor of this my present last will and testament And I doe nominate and appoint my said sonne in lawe Richard Cronke of Seavenoke mercer to be overseer of this my present will whome I entreat to see the same performed in all things according to the true intent thereof And as touching the disposicion of the inheritance of my Messuage or tenement called the Swan with the appurtenances I doe give divise and dispose thereof as followeth Vizt I doe give and devise the same Messuage Tenement or Inne together with all the barnes stables edificies buildings yardes backsides and appurtenences whatsoever thereunto belonging unto my said grandsonne Robert Wimble and to the heires of his body lawfully begotten forever And in default of such issue then I give and devise three full parts of the whole into fower parts to be devided of and in the same messuage tenement or Inne and premises with the appurtenences unto my said three grandchildren Alice Anne and Jane Cronke or to such and soe many of them as shall survive and be living at the tyme of my death and to the heires and assignes of any said three grandchildren or the survivor or the survivors of them or eyther And then after the decease of my said grandsonne Robert Wimble without heires of his body as aforesaid I doe give and devise the other fowerth parte of my said messuage tenement or Inne and premises with the appurtenences unto my granddaughter Anne the wife of Thomas Cowper and to her heires and assignes forever Provided alwayes whereas the said messuage or Inne called or knowne by the name of the Swan is mortgaged to Richard Cronke of Tonbridge yeoman for fiftie pounds principal money I doe therefore hereby order and direct that my said overseer shall from tyme to tyme pay and discharge out of the rents and proffitts of the said Swan Inn all such interest money as from tyme to tyme shall growe due for or by reason of the same mortgage And after the time lymitted in the said mortgage for the payment of the said fifty poundes to the said Richard Cronke the mortgagee or in case of any forfayture for the nonpayment of the moneyes conteyned in the said mortgage or any part thereof then I doe hereby authorize my said overseer to enter into the said messuage tenement or Inne and premises with the appurtenences or to take any legal or equitable course to redeeme the same And the same to mortgage againe to any person or persons whatsoever for the like somme of fiftie poundes and likewise for the payment of all expenses of my funerall and of such debts remayning due at the tyme of my death which my personall estate will not be sufficient to pay and discharge (if my said personall estate shall fall short to discharge the same) and so to continue the same messuage and tenement and premises with the appurtenences mortgaged from tyme to tyme until my said grandsonne Robert Wimble shall have attayned the age of one and twenty yeares or be marryed dureing all which tyme I will that the interest money accrewing by reason of such mortgage as aforesaid be from tyme to tyme paid by my overseer out of the proffitts of the said messuage or Inne and the principall money to be paid by my said grandsonne at such his age or marriage as aforesaid And I doe further will and appointe that for the payment of the said interest money and also of such Annuity legacies and charges as are before in this my will appointed to be paid and discharged out of my said Inne and premises with the appurtenences until such age or marriage of my said grandsonne Robert Wimble as aforesaid And if any remainder or overplus shall happen to be of the said rents and proffitts after the payment and dischargeing of such interest money Annuity legacies and charges aforesaid I doe give and bequeath all such remainder and overplus to my said sonne in lawe Richard Cronke of Seavenoke as a gratuite for his care and paines to bee taken in the discharge of the trust in him reposed by this my present will And I doe desire and appoint that my said sonne in lawe Richard Cronke of Seavenoke shalbe tutor and guardian of my said grandsonne Robert Wimble dureing the minority of my said grandsonne In Witnes whereof to this my present last will and testament written in two sheets of paper (revoking all other wills by me heretofore made) I have set my hande and seale the day and yeare first above written

Robert Wimble his marke

Signed sealed delivered and as his last will and testament published and declared the day and yeare abovesaid after theis words (And I doe hereby appoint that five poundes shall be expended for the charge of my said funerall) Ten) were interlined in the first sheete of this will in the presence of us

Geo Gilbourne   James Porter   John Groombride his marke

2

HOOPER John   Schoolmaster

W. 18 Oct. 1661   prov. 8 Jan. 1662   Prob. 11. 307 f.6

In Nomine Dei Patris Filii et Spiritus Sancti Amen Decimo Octavo Die Octobris Anno Domini Millimo Six Centisimo Sexagesimo Primo Annoque Regni Regis Caroli Secundi Angliae etc. Decimo Tertio I John Hooper of Seavenoke in the County of Kent servant of Almighty God who blesse mee now herein And in the residue of my life doe make and ordaine this my Testament and last will in manner and forme following To the poore people dwelling in the Almeshouses of Seavenok I will Tenn shillings And the like summe to the poore people dwelling in and about Mill Lane in Tunbridge To my daughter Alice the wife of William Allen (already preferred) I will as a token of my love Tenn shillings And to her little daughter a silver spoone To the foure children of my Deare Brother Hooper (vizt) Jane Sarah John and George to each a silver spoone And the like to the three children of my Deare Sister Piper And to my Deare Sister herselfe I will as a token of my love Fifty shillings To my Deare and loveing wife for and towards her livelyhood and the education of my son George I will and give Forty pounds to be paid her within Three Moneths after my Decease To her also I will the use of such and soe much of my goods and household stuff of all sorts as shall be needful for the furnishing a little Dwelling house for her the same not exceeding at an indifferent apprisement the worth and value of Thirty pounds to be taken with the approbation of my Executor in Trust hereafter named And if he think good to be inventaried to her Att her death to be left to my three sonns John Thomas and George Hooper equally To her I also will the Rents and proffitt of my Tenements and lands in Tunbridge during her life for the better enabling her to maintaine and Educate my sonne George untill he shall be fitt to be put out an apprentize The revercion of which said tenements and lands I will shall descend equally to my three sonns John Thomas and George Hooper And as for the residue of my goods Householdstuffe Plate wood and Chattells whatsoever (except my Lybrary and such other things as my Executor in Trust shall thinke fitt to preserve for my three sonns or any of them) I will they shall be put to sale by my Executor in trust with the assistance of my Deare wife and the moneys thereout arising and made from tyme to tyme I will shall be received and taken into the Custody of my Executor in Trust together with all such redy moneys bonds and Bills as shall belong unto mee att the tyme of my decease The which said moneys I will shalbe imployed in paying my debts funerall charges and Legacies As also in placing out my sonne George when his abilities shall require it. And the placing out of my sonns John and Thomas or either if there should be cause of soe doeing And the overplus I entreate my Executor in Trust either to put to interest or else to lay out in lands to be purchased in my said three sonns names and to their uses equally enjoyed by them at their ages of one and twenty yeares And I doe make and ordaine my onely Deare and loveing Brother Mr George Hooper of Tonbridge the full and sole Executor in Trust of this my Testament and last will Earnestly intreating him to take upon him the execution thereof for the use and benefitt of my said three [sonns] John Thomas and George Hooper And in token of my most indeared affection to my said Brother my Executor in Trust I will and give unto him my Clock with the furniture thereto beseeching him to accept thereof And it is my very will and mind that my said Executor in trust shall from tyme to tyme be allowed and paid not onely all such costs and charges as shalbe occasioned to him by this my will but also that he be recompensed for the losse and expence of his tyme and the service of his horse etc. And whereas there may be att the tyme of my death severall small summs of money owing to me for the boarding and teaching of Schollers It is my desire that my said wife doe not only assist my said Executor in trust in gathering in and receiving the said Arrearages but also doe herself take some paines in the gathering in thereof And for such moneys as she shall receive her acquitiance shall be a sufficient discharge And I doe hereby declare it to be my will and desire that my said loving wife shall at no tyme in her life nor att the tyme of her Death will or give away above Twenty Marks worth of her estate wherewith she shall be possessed But doe distribute it amongst my Three sonnes Lastly I doe entreat my loveing Brother in Law Mr Robert Parker and my loveing sonne in law Mr William Allen to be overseers of this my last Will and Testament And to assist in selling my goods And for a remembrance of my loveing respects for them I will to each of them to buy them a Ring Tenn shillings In Witnes whereof to this my testament and last will written with my owne hand I the said John Hooper have subscribed my name and put to my seale the day and yeare first above written

John Hooper

sealed published and declared in the presence of

Tho Lambert William Richardson

3

HOOPER John Gentleman
I. 3 Dec. 1661 prov. 8 Jan. 1662 Prob. 4. 6806

A true Inventary indented of all and singuler the goods household stuff debts and chattles late of John Hooper late of Seavenock in the County of Kent gent deceased taken valued and aprized the Third day of December in the Thirtenth yeare of the reigne of our Sovereigne Lord Charles the second by the grace of God King of England etc. Anno Domini 1661 by Thomas Lambard Esq. John Cooper gent William Allen and Giles Law as followeth

	£	*s.*	*d.*
Inprimis the said deceased ready money	54	14	00
Item his apparrell of all sorts	5	00	00
In the Parlor of his late dwelling house			
One presse one Court Cupbord a nest of Boxes one long table and frame one carpett and cupbord cloth xii stooles of Russhy leather one old leather elbow chayer one other leather chayer one leather stole two turkyworke stooles two turky work chayers one joyned chayer a cupbord with two drawers vi greene Quisshions one paier of cast Andirons one paier of Andirons with brasse knobbs one fier shovell and tongs and two window curtens and Rodds	07	13	00
Item one clock with the furniture	05	00	00
Item one hand bell	00	03	00
In the Kitchen next the Parlor			
one Table two formes one little Table and forme a joyned stool one new safe cupbord one lesser cupbord a glasse cage a cradle to carry cloths in two Andirons a wooden Peele and fower dozen of candles	02	05	08
Item one little Table in the Entry	00	02	06
In the little Buttry under the Stayers			
fower Rundlets one stalder a lock and key and certaine bottles	00	06	08
In the Hall			
One fur table frame and forme 1 short table and forme 1 other forme a dresser boord one yron Jack with the appertenances a paier of yron Racks a paier of Andirons a payer of creepers a paier of Tongs a fier slice an yron to lay before the fier 2 paier of pothangers and a tosting yron	03	06	08
In the Milkehouse			
1 table and frame 2 powdring tubs 7 milke trayes			

one large Tray 2 crock with Butter	02	16	01
In the Boulting house			
1 boulting hutch a meale box 2 leather meale baggs and 2 sacks	02	03	00
Item one skreene to hang cloths on	00	03	00
In the 2 Sellers			
6 stalders 8 barrells 3 hogsheads	02	07	08
Item the Buckett chaine and Rope at the Well and 2 hog tubs there	00	08	08
In the old Kitchen			
4 hogsheds and a barrell	00	16	04
Item one large furnace one little Furnace 1 new Tonne 1 long keeler 4 Spitts 1 Smoke Jack 3 chains a large turne spitt and an yron forke	07	09	00
Item one Whelebarrow	00	06	08
Item one morter and pestle a gridiron 2 dripping pans two frying pans one large yron pott and cover one kettle one table one stalder and 2 dresser boords	02	00	06
Item 9 Tubbs and Keelers 4 pailes and a large Tonnell	01	10	00
In the Man servants Roome			
1 little bedsteddle 1 forme and 3 boords	00	06	00
Item a paier of garden shares 2 yron wedges 2 spades 1 shovell a pitchforke an Axe a hand bill a hammer a peas hooke and certaine other tooles	00	12	00
In the Hayloft			
4 new barrells 3 little vessells and lumber	01	00	00
Item one Large yron dripping pan 5 yron potts 1 brasse pudding pan 3 brasse kettles 2 little pot brasse skilletts 2 other brasse postnetts and a brasse ladle	02	15	00
Item 1 large brasse Kettle one other brasse kettle one pott brasse pott 2 kettle brasse skilletts 1 old pott brasse skillett 1 skummer a brasse ladle and a Cleaver	01	08	00
In the Chamber over the Milkehouse			
one cabonett with a carpet 1 Trunck 1 joyned bedsteddle with matt and cord curtens and valence and rodds 1 trundle bedsted with matt and cord one high bedsteddle 2 feather beds and bolsters 1 greene Rug 2 blanketts 1 coverlett 2 little Andirons with brasse knobbs	09	19	00
In the chamber over the Boulting house			
2 half hedded bedsteds with matts and cords 1 featherbed 1 flockbed two feather bolsters and a pillow 1 tapestry coverlett 2 other old coverletts 2 blancketts and 1 joyned Chist	05	06	08
In Linnen 60 paier of sheets 22 table cloths 15 pillow coates 8 dozen and a half of napkins 30 Ells of new cloth	38	15	08

In the Chamber over the Entry one bedsteddle with a matt and cord a buckrome top and curtens and valence 1 halfhedded bedsted with cord 2 feather bedds 1 feather bolster 3 pillows 2 green Rugs 4 blanketts 2 little tables a paier of Andirons with fier shovell and tongs a turkyworke cowch and a Wicker chayer	10	06	00
Item a Little Cabonett	[?]	04	00
In the chamber next the stayers one joyned bedstadle with matt and cord curtens rods and valence one other bedsted with a buckrome head curtens valence and rodds one other bedsted with say curtens one trundle bedsted with mat and cord one downe bed 3 feather beds 1 downe bolster 3 feather bolsters 4 pillows one halfhedded bedsted 2 greene Rugs 1 red rug 2 coverletts 9 blancketts 2 presses one trunck one deske and a close stoole	18	08	00
In the Little Study 1 halfhedded bedsted 1 feather bed and bolster 1 blanckett one Rugg with a canopy and a curten and a hanging table	03	15	00
In the chamber over the kitchen 3 halfhedded bedsteddles and one trundle bedsted with matts and cords 3 feather beds 1 flockbed 3 feather bolsters 1 flock bolster 3 rugs 1 coverlett 6 blancketts and one studylate set up of fir boords	13	10	00
In the middle chamber over the parlor 3 halfhedded bedsteddles 1 trundle bedsted with matts and cords 3 feather bedds 3 feather bolsters 2 blancketts 1 blew Rug and 3 coverletts	07	15	00
In the chamber over the Parlor 1 halfhedded bedsted with a canopy one other bedsted with a buckrome top 1 trundle bedsted 1 little halfhedded bedsted 3 featherbeds 3 flockbeds 4 feather bolsters 1 Rug 2 coverletts 3 curten rods 6 blancketts 1 wooden shovell 1 ladder	10	06	00
In the Garrett 23 fir boords an old court cupbord and certaine earthen bottles	01	04	00
Item in Pewter 199 lbs in weight 8 chamber potts and 3 candlesticks	09	13	04
Item 2 chists at the top of the Stayers	00	10	00
Item in silver Plate 96 Spoones 1 Tankard 1 salt 2 porrengers 2 cups	30	00	00
Item 8 halfhedded bedsteddles and a trundle bedsted with matts and cords over the Schoole	03	00	00
Item 3 Swine	03	10	00
Item Cordwood and Fagotts	35	00	00

Item one Beehouse and a house of office late set up	01	00	00
Item owing to the deceased in desperate debts	440	00	00
Item Lumber and things of small value	00	06	08
Summa totalis huius inventarii	747	02	09

4

BECKETT John	Yeoman	bur. 19. Nov. 1660
W. 15 Nov. 1660	prov. 13 Feb. 1662	Prob. 11. 303 f. 18

In the name of God Amen this fifteenth day of November in the yeare of our Lord God one thousand six hundred and sixty I John Beckett of Seavenokes in the county of Kent yeoman being weake of body but of perfect memory praysed be god therefore doe make and ordaine this my last will and testament as followeth first and principally I bequeath my soule into the hands of Almighty god my Creator stedfastly trusting through the merritts death and passion of Jesus Christ to have free forgiveness of my sinnes and to inheritt eternal life And my body to the earth to be decently buryed according to the discretion of my Executrex Item my mind and will is and by this my last will and testament I doe Impower and authorize Mary beckett my loveing wife whome I make sole Executrix to sell and convey and make sale of those three pieces of land of mine called by the name or names of Upper Gawthderds Lower Gawthderds and Brawd feild conteyning by estimacion eighteene Acres lying betweene Seaven nokes towne and Riverhead in Kent whereby to pay and discharge a Mortgage of one hundred pownds which I owe to Mr John Culpepper upon Ingagement of other Lands and to pay and discharge all other debts whatsoever which I owe Item I will and bequeath unto my two daughters Mary Beckett and Jane Beckett and unto their heyres for ever equally to be divided one peece or parcell of land called Greate Stony Croft lying between Seavenokes towne and Riverhead in the county of Kent aforesaid when they or either of them shall attaine to the age of one and twenty yeares and in case either of them should dy before they do attaine the age aforesaid that then the survivor shall inherritt the whole Item I will and bequeath to my two sonnes John Beckett and Edward Beckett all the rest of my lands unbequeathed and unto their heyres for ever lying in the parish of Seavenokes in Kent when they or either of them shall attain to the age of one and twenty yeares they or either of them or either of their heyres or executors paying out of the rent of the said lands unto Mary Beckett their Mother Forty shillings a quarter during her natural life Item all the rest of my goods Cattells and Chattells I will and bequeath unto Mary my loveing wife whome I make sole Executrix to see my funerall Duties and Debts discharged In Witness whereof I hereunto sett my hand and seale the day and yeare first above written

John Beckett

Sealed and delivered in the presence of
John Fremlin John Coulard Edward Besbeech

5

ALLEN Thomas	Warrener	bur. Mar. 1661
W. 21 Mar. 1661	prov. 6 Nov. 1662	Prob. 11. 309 f. 136

In the name of God Amen I Thomas Allen of Seavenocke in the County of Kent warriner being at this present sickly in body but of good and perfect memory all laud and praise be given unto the Almighty God for the same I doe by the permission of God make and declare this my present testament wherein is contained my last will in manner and forme following That is to say first I commend my Soule into the hands of Almighty god hopeing and assuredly beleeving through the death and passion of Jesus Christ his onely sonne my Saviour to obtayne remission and forgiveness of all my sinnes and to be made pertaker of life everlasting my body I committ to the earth from whence it came to be decently buried in such place and manner as my Executor hereafter named shall think fit And as concerning all such worldly goods and Chattells as it hath pleased God to endue me withall I will demyse give and bequeath the same in manner and forme following vizt Inprimis I give and bequeath my tenement and lands in the parish of Chelsfield in the county aforesaid and in the occupation of Thomas Heath husbandman unto my sonne Thomas Allen and his heires for ever when he shall attaine unto the age of one and twenty yeares And if the said Thomas shall happen to dye before he shall attaine unto the said age then my will and desire is that the said tenement and lands be equally divided betweene my three daughters Sarah Barbara and Mary Allen or to such of them as shall be liveing and their heires for ever Item [I] give and bequeath unto the said Sarah Barbara and Mary my daughters the summe of tenne pounds a peece to be paid unto them by my sonne Thomas Allen within six months after he the said Thomas Allen shall attain unto the age of one and twenty yeares And if it shall happen that any of my said daughters doe dye before the abovesaid tyme of payment that then her or their parts soe dying to be paid to her or them which shall survive and be lyving to be equally devided The rest of all and singuler my goods Chattells and personal estate whatsoever to me incident and belonging and also the rent of the said tenement and lands abovesaid untill he shall attaine unto the yeares abovesaid I do give and bequeath unto my loveing brother in lawe Henry Soane of Seavenoake aforesaid warriner to enable him to disburse my funerall charges and discharge all my just and true debts and towards the education of my children in such a decent manner as he shall think fit and convenient And to dispose of whatsoever shall remayne (my children being brought up my debts and funerall charges being satisfied) out of the said goods and chattells unto my three daughters or such of them as shall survive equally to be divided The which Henry Soane my brother in law I doe make full and Sole executor of this my last will and testament And for his paynes I doe allow unto him the somme of twenty shillings desireing him to see this my last will and testament duely and truely performed according to my true intent and meaning And I doe hereby revoke all other former wills and bequests by me heretofore in any wise made And this to stand for and as my last will In witnesse whereof I the said Thomas Allen have hereunto sett

my hand and seale the one and twentieth day of March in the thirteenth yeare of the raigne of our Soveraigne Lord Charles by the grace of God of England Scotland France and Ireland King defendor of the Fayth etc Annoque Domini 1660
The marke of Thomas Allen
sealed and published by the said Thomas Allen for and as his last will and testament the day and yeare aforesaid in the presence of
Edward Courthop Alexander Fowle Thomas Platt

6

ALLEN Thomas	Husbandman	bur. Mar. 1661
I. 5 Feb. 1662	prov. 6 Nov. 1662	Prob. 4. 165/9

An Inventary of all and singular the goods Chattells and creditts of Thomas Allen late of the parish of Sevenoake in the County of Kent Husbandman decesed Taken & praysed the Fifth day of February Anno Domini Stilo Anglie 1661 by Richard Evridge and Richard Cackott as followeth vizt.

Inprimis the deceseds Purse and ready Money		xxx^s	
Item the deceseds Weareing Apparell undisposed of by himself not expressed in his will		xx^s	
Item one Lease of West Wood	£x	iii^s	iiii^d
Item one Lease of Seale Chart for his part	£vii		
Item xx Cords of Wood	£x		
Item 6 Thowsand of Faggotts	£xv	x^s	
Item due from Henry Soane the Executor for share of Stock	£C		
Item one Obligation for the sum of	£xx		
Suma	£CLXV	iii^s	x^d
In the Hall			
Item one plaine Table a Forme & 2 joyned Stooles		x^s	
Item one old Joyned Cubberd with a Desk & a Striped Cubberd Cloath		x^s	
Item one other small Joyned Table & a forme		vi^s	
Item a Table Chaire		iiii^s	
Item one old Warmeing Pan		i^s	vi^d
Item 2 old Crossebowes & a Glasse Case		v^s	
Suma		xxxvi^s	vi^d
In the Cheesehowse			
Item 2 Table Chaires & a Cheesepresse		vi^s	viii^d
Item one Powdring Tub & one Gallon		vi^s	vi^d
Item 2 Small Drink Tubs & 24er old quart bottells		vii^s	
Item one Salting Trough 2 Planks & one Churne		iiii^s	vi^d
Item other Glasse Bottells		i^s	

Item one Planke small Shelves & other Lumber		ii^{s}	vi^{d}
Suma		xxviii^{s}	ii^{d}
In the Chamber over the Kitchen			
Item 20 pieces of Pewter of the biggest sort 12 pieces of a smaler sort 2 basins 7 candlesticks 4 Salts 3 Chamberpots one Pint pot one Aquavite bottle one Porringer one Cup Six Spoones in all waying 120 lbs.	£vi		
Item one Hutch & 10 dozen of Trenchers		viii^{s}	iiii^{d}
Item one old Joyned Bedsteadle & Cord one Fetherbed 2 Featherbolsters 5 Pillowes 2 litle Pillowes 2 Blankets one Coverlet Curtens Vallence & Curten Rods	£vii	xiii^{s}	iiii^{d}
Item one old set of Curtens & Valence		v^{s}	
Item one Trundlebedstead Matt & Cord one Fetherbed & 2 flockbolsters 2 blankets & 2 old Coverlets		xxx^{s}	ii^{d}
Item 4 Leather Chayres 5 Cushins & a Childs Chaire		xiiii^{s}	vi^{d}
Item 2 Joyned Chists & 2 Borded Chists		xxxvii^{s}	
Item one litle Table & Glasse Shelf		ii^{s}	
Item one Flaxen sheete & 4er Holland Pillowbeeres		xxvi^{s}	viii^{d}
Item 8 paire of fine Hempen Sheets 4 paire of a second sort 5 pair of course one Fine Tablecloth 2 course 12 Diaper Napkins one fine Towell & 7 other pieces of course Linnen	£x	v^{s}	
Suma	£xxx		
In the Closett			
Item 15 new Milk Trugs		xiiii^{s}	
Item 10 other Trugs		v^{s}	
Item other Wodden Vessells & 6 old Locks		vii^{s}	
Suma		xxvi^{s}	
In the Chamber over the Hall			
Item one litle halfheaded Bedstead Cord & Matt one small flockbed & Bolster		x^{s}	
Item 1 old Borded Bedsteadle one Flockbed & Bolster 2 old Blankets & one Settle		xv^{s}	
Item one small Court Cubbert one Chist old one plaine litle Box & 3 Shelves		viii^{s}	ii^{d}
Suma		xxxiii^{s}	ii^{d}
In the Kitchen			
Item one Fowleing Peice		xv^{s}	
Item 3 Shovell Woods & a Shaule		ii^{s}	ii^{d}
Item one great brasse Pott one great brasse kettle 2 small brasse Kettells one Potbrasse Skillet one brasse Mortar & Pestle one brasse Chafing Dish one brasse Skummer & brasse Candlestick		liiii^{s}	

Item one paire of Iron Cobirons 3 Spits one Dripping Pan one Gridiron one old pair of Tongs 2 smoothing Irons			xi^{s}	
Item one old Iron Pott one Iron Ketle one Iron to lay before the Fire			v^{s}	
Item one old Cubberd				xii^{d}
	Suma	£iiii	viii^{s}	vi^{d}
In the Buttery				
Item 2 Hogsheads 4er old Hogsheads and three Keelers			xxii^{s}	
Item one Grindstone and other Lumber			v^{s}	vi^{d}
			xxvii^{s}	vi^{d}
	Summa totalis	£CCvii	xv^{s}	viii^{d}

7

ROWETT John Linnen weaver bur. 29 Mar. 1663
W. 26 Mar. 1661 prov. 29 Sep. 1666 PRS/W/14/70

In the name of god amen the twentie Six day of march 1661: I John Rowet of Sevenoaks in the Countie of Kent Linien wever beinge sick of bodie but of good and perfect memorie and understandinge praysed be god doe make and ordaine this my Last will and Testament in maner and forme following, that is to say First I Comend my Soule into the Handes of god my maker; Hopeinge assuredly throughe the onlie merritts of Jesus Christ my Saiviour to be made partaker of everlasting Life and my bodie I Commed to the earth wher of it is made:
Item I give to my sonn John Rowet one plaine table and forme & one Joyne Chest: Item I give to my sonn Thomas Rowet the stedle and bed wher on I lie; but my wife to have the use of it soe longe as shee doth Live and the Linnen Lome that he works in to have presently within three dayes after my decease by my Excecutrix deliverd unto him
Item I give more to my sonn John Rowet one wollen Lombe to be deliverd him within three dayes after my wives decease: Item I give to my loveinge wife Alice Rowet all the rest of my goodes and moveables and doe mak hir excecutrix of this my Last will and testament in Wittness wher unto I set my hand
the marke of John Rowet
Wittnesse by us
Richard Hackesup
David Jeffery
the mark of
Ann Smyth

8

JERMINE Francis Widow
NW. 30 Apr. 1661 prov. 29 July 1661 Prob. 11.305 f. 112

Memorandum That [on] or about the Thirtieth day of Aprill One Thousand Six Hundred Sixtie One Francis Jermine late of Seavenoakes in the Countie of Kent Widdowe deceased beinge of perfect myude and memory and haveinge a full intent and purpose to make and Declare her last Will and Testament Nuncupative did utter and speake theese or the very like wordes in Effect and Substance followinge (vizt) shee gave to her graundchild Mistress Francis Harler Fiftie pound and One Silver Bason with all her lynnen And to her grandchild Mistress Margaret Harler Fiftie Pound more with one silver gilt boule and Cover with all her silver spoones To her Grandchild Mistress Katharine Harler Fiftie Pound and one silver drinking pot with a cover To her Grandchild Mistress Elizabeth Harler Fiftie Pound To her Grandchildren Mrs Francis and Mr John Theobald To each of them Twentie shillinges in Gold To her Grandchild Mrs Frances Gregorye her weddinge ringe which her first husband gave her To the Children of Mistress Frances Gregorye tenn shillings a peece To her grandchild Mistress Elizabeth Lambe Fiftie Pound And to the poore of the parishe where she lived in Lincolnshire Five Pound To the Parish of Seaven Oakes Fourtie Shillings To the poore of the parish of Kemsing Fortie Shillinges where she desired to be buryed To her Daughter Katharine Harler and her heyres for ever she gave her land in Lyncolnshire Lyeing and being in the parish [?] afield being two Parcells One called Eight Acres and the other Norther Wood or Norther Close containeing Fourteene Acres And itt was her Will and desire That Mr Davyes the Minister should Preach her Funerall Sermon for which she gave him Twentie Shillings And all the rest and residue of her Estate both Reall and Personall she gave and bequeathed to her daughter Katharine Harler whom she made full and whole Executrix of this her last Will and Testament Nuncupative All which wordes or the like in effect she the said Frances Jermine being then in Perfect mynde and memory uttered and declared for as her last Will and Testament Nuncupative in the presence and heareinge of Anne Bloare and Sarah Blake and other credible witnesses

9

SEWER Henry Yeoman
W. 13 Sep. 1661 prov. 3 Apr. 1667 Prob. 11. 323 f. 50

In the name of God Amen The thirteenth day of September in the yeare of our Lord God 1661 and in the Thirteenth yeare of the Raigne of our Soveraigne Lord Charles the second by the grace of God of England Scotland France & Ireland King Defendor of the Faith etc. I Henry Sewer of Sevenocke in the County of Kent Yeoman being in perfect health of body and sound mind and memory thankes be therefore rendered unto Almighty God but being farr stricken in yeares and well knoweing that it is appointed for all men to Die and the tyme place and manner altogether unknown And being Desirous to prevent all Differences which may happen to arise amongst my friends and kindred after my decease touching the small estate the Lord of his mercy hath heere lent me doe make and declare this my last will and Testament in manner and forme following First and principally I bequeath my soule into the hands of almighty God my Creator and Jesus Christ my Redeemer by whose merritts only I trust to be saved and my Body from the Earth from whence it was taken to be interred at the discretion of mine Execotors hereafter named Item I will give and bequeath unto my sister Elizabeth Acourte alias Gardner Widdowe the sume of Fifty shillings of lawful money of England to be paid within six moneths next after my decease And to my sisters daughter Elizabeth Whitehead and her husband Fifty shillings a piece to be paid them in like manner within six moneths after my decease Item I give will and bequeath unto the Thirteene children of the said Elizabeth Whitehead my Neese the like sume of Fiftie shillings a peece to bee respectively payed to such of them as shalbe of competent age to give a sufficient discharge thereof to myne Executors hereafter named within six moneths after myne decease And for such of the said Thirteene Children male and female as shall not have attayned such age at the tyme before expressed my will and mind is and soe I do bequeath that the Legacy or Legacies of such Child or Children of the said Thirteene Children soe under age and uncapable to give a discharge as aforesaid shalbe then delivered and paid unto the said Elizabeth their Mother my Neese and her husband Whitehead to be by them imployed to and for the best benefitt of such Child or Children until he she or they shalbe respectively capable to receive and manage the same themselves acording to the true intent and meaning of this my present will And if any of the said Thirteene Children happen to Die before he she or they shall have received and had their respective Legacie or Legacies in manner as aforesaid then the legacy or legacies of him her or them soe Dyeing to be equally divided among the Survivors of them share and share like Item I give and bequeath unto my two kinswomen Elizabeth Sewer daughter of Peter Sewer deceased and Elizabeth Sewer daughter of Richard Sewer also deceased the sume of Tenn pounds a peece to be severally paid them within six moneths after my decease and if either of the said two Elizabeth Sewers shall happen to Die before she of them two soe Dyeing shall have received her Legacies of Tenn pounds then the Survivor of them to have the Legacie of her soe Dyeing All the rest and residue of myne Estate goods Chattells Bills bonds Specialtyes and other personal estate whatsoever After my funerall decently performed and discharged I give Will and Bequeath to my Kinsman John Sewer Citizen and Haberdasher of London Sonne of the said Peter Sewer and Henry Sewer of London Grocer sonne of the said Richard Sewer to be equally and indifferently parted and divided betweene them the aforesaid John and Henry And I make and Constitute the said John Sewer and Henry Sewer Executors of this my last Will and Testament and my loveing friends John Round and Israell Round both of Dartford in the said County of Kent Overseers of the same my will

and testament to see the same duely performed And revokeing all former wills by me made In Witnes hereof I have hereunto put my hand and Seale the Day and yeare first above written
Henry Sewer
Sealed signed Read published and
declared in the presence of
John Round
William Gamons
Elizabeth Gamons

10

PORTER Edward Yeoman
W. 30 Dec. 1661 prov. 4 Feb. 1670 Prob. 11. 332 f. 26

In the name of God Amen I Edward Porter of the parish of Seavenoke in the County of Kent yeoman being sick and weak in body but of sound and perfect mind and memory (Praysed be God therefore) And being mindful of my last end And desirous to settle that estate as it hath pleased God in mercy to lend me do make and ordaine this my last Will and Testament in manner and form following (vizt) First and principally I committ and commend my soule into the hands of Almighty God my Creator hopeing assuredly through the merritts death and passion of Jesus Christ my only Saviour and Redeemer to obtain a full and free pardon and remission of all my sins And my body to be interred by the discretion of myne Executrix herein after named Item I give and bequeath unto Amy my beloved wife All my personal estate whatsoever moveable and immoveable of what nature or condition soever the same are or be my debts and funerall expences being first paid and discharged Whom I make and ordaine sole Executrix of this my last will and testament And revokeing and adnulling all former wills by me made either in word or writing In witness whereof I have hereunto sett my hand and seale the thirtieth day of December in the Thirtieth year of King Charles the Second and in the year of our Lord God one thousand six hundred sixty and one
Edward Porter
Signed sealed and published to be the last will and testament of the abovesaid Edward Porter in the presence of us
Allen Pope his mark
James Walker his mark
Robert Newman

11

PORTER Edward — Yeoman
I. 15 Nov. 1669 — prov. 4 Feb. 1670 — Prob. 4. 855

An Inventory of all and Singuler the Goods and Chattells and Credits of Edward Porter late of Skinehill in the parish of Seavenoke in the County of Kent yeoman decesed Taken and praysed the Fifteenth day of November In the yeere of our Lord 1669 By Richard Everidge Humfry Couchman and John Porter Senior as followeth vizt.

In the Hall			
Inprimis a Table a Forme and an old Cubberd		xxiii^{s}	viii^{d}
Item the Money in his Purse and his Wearing Apparell		xl^{s}	
Suma	£iii	iiii^{s}	viii^{d}
In the Kitchen			
Item a Table a Forme a Fly Cubberd a great Cubberd litle Table a dresser Board one Wicker Chayre one great Chayre Six small Chaires one pair of Brandirons one pair of Tongs 2 fireslices one Bloome Back one Iron Pott one Iron Kettle one pair of Bellowes 2 Spitts one Iron Dripping Pan one Basting Ladle one Warmeing Pan one Tinne Dripping Pan 2 Wire Candlesticks 2 pair of Potthangers 4er Earthen Dishes one Bin cloth one Flich and a piece of Bacon one Creeper	£iiii	xviii^{s}	vi^{d}
Suma patet			
In the Buttery			
Item 2 Drink vessells one Joyned Stoole one dozen of Trenchers one Gridiron 4er Earthen dishes one Dresser Board one Crock one Pastry Peele one Brasse Pott 9 Woodden Dishes and a pair of Potthooks		xii^{s}	
Suma patet			
In the Milkhowse			
Item 13 Milktrayes 12 crocks one frying pan certaine Wayts and Skales		xxii^{s}	
Suma patet			
In the Bakehouse			
Item one Bakeing Keeler one Bunting Hutch Two Brasse Kettles one litle Brasse Pott 2 Sives a Lanthorne one Woodden Bowle one Chopping Block		xiiii^{s}	
Item Nine Cheeses		xv^{s}	
Suma		xxix^{s}	
In the Brewhouse			
Item one Brewing Tub one Bucking Tub one Fatt 4 Keelers 2 Churnes one Powdring Tub one Trough			

one Querne 2 Linnen Wheles one Cheese presse and 3 Payles one Tunnell 2 Shales		xxxi^{s}	vi^{d}
Item 2 Brasse Skillets		iii^{s}	
Item 13 pieces of Pewter		xviii^{s}	
Item one Pewter Chamber Pott and one Porringer		ii^{s}	vi^{d}
Item one Brasse Candlestick			vi^{d}
Item 6 Pewter Spoones			viii^{d}
Suma		lvi^{s}	ii^{d}
In the Chamber over the Hall			
Item one Bedstedle one Flockbed 2 Bolsters 2 Blankets one Coverlet a set of Curtens and valence		li^{s}	
Item one Drawing Table		xx^{s}	
Item one Joyned Chest one borded Chest 2 Joyned stooles		xi^{s}	
Item 5 Fine Sheets and 4er pair of Course Sheets		xlix^{s}	
Item 3 Napkins and 2 Pillowbeers		vii^{s}	
Item 22 lbs of Hempe		xi^{s}	
Suma £vii		ix^{s}	
In the Chamber over the Kitchen			
Item one Bedstedle one Flockbed 2 Bolsters Two Blankets a Sett of Curtens and Valence one Trundle Bedsted Matt and Cord one Coverlett		xliii^{s}	viii^{d}
Item one Fetherbed one Fether Pillow one Flock pillow 2 Blankets and one Coverlett	£iiii		
Item one Joyned Chest one plaine Chist one Joyned box and one litle Box		xv^{s}	
Item one Lookeing Glasse			vi^{d}
Item 5 Sheets 4er Napkins 2 Towells		xvi^{s}	vi^{d}
Item 30 Bushells of Apples and Peares		xv^{s}	
Item xxv Sheepe	£viii	v^{s}	
Item one Cow and one Bullock	£iiii		
Item 4er small Hogs	£iii	xv^{s}	
Item one Mare		xxxv^{s}	
Item 3 Akers of Wheate and Rye	£iiii	x^{s}	
Item for oates in the Barne	£iii		
Item for Wheate in the Barne		xlviii^{s}	
Item Corne in the Howse		xxx^{s}	
Item 7 loads of Hay	£vi	x^{s}	
Item Hoppoles in the Hopgarden	£iiii	x^{s}	
Item one Oasthare		x^{s}	
Item one Cart one Court one Harrow and other Husbandry tacklings		xxx^{s}	
Item one Cord and a half of Wood		x^{s}	
Item certaine other things owt of sight and forgotten		xxx^{s}	iiii^{d}
Item Principal Money owing upon 3 Bondes by John Porter Senior of Seale	£l		
Suma	£ciii	vii^{s}	
Suma totalis	£cxxii	xviii^{s}	iiii^{d}

12

WITHERS John Tailor
W. 24 Mar. 1662 prov. 24 Jun. 1665 PRS/W/17/207

In the name of god Amen the foure and twentieth day of March in the yeare of our lord god One thousand six hundred sixty and one I John Withers of Rethered in the parish of Seavenoke in the County of Kent Tailor being sicke and weake in body but of perfect memory and understanding thankes be given to Almighty god doe make and ordayne this my last will and testament in manner following First I commend my soule into the hands of Almighty god my Creator assuring myselfe through the onely merritts of my blessed Saviour Jesus Christ to receive pardon and remission of all my sinns and that my soule shall be made partaker of life everlasting my body I appoint to be buryed at the discreccion of my Executor hereafter named. Whereas my sonne in Law John Christopher of Kemsing in the said County of Kent yeoman is and stands indebted unto me in the somme of two hundred pounds of lawfull money of England to be paid within one yeare after my decease by virtue of one paire of Indentures of mortgage beareing date the eighteenth day of September one thousand six hundred fifty and foure and made betweene him the said John Christopher of the one parte and me the said John Withers of the second parte My will and meaneing is and I doe here by give and bequeath unto my sonne in Law Richard Everest and Lydea his wife the some of threescore and six pounds thirteene shillings and foure pence parte of the said somme of two hundred pounds Item I give and bequeath unto my said sonne in Law John Christopher and Tymothy his wife the like some of threescore and six pounds thirteene shillings and foure pence other parte of the said some of two hundred pounds Item I give and bequeath unto my sonne in Law John Fowle and Sarah his wife the some of six pounds thirteene shillings and foure pence parte of the said some of two hundred pounds which severall sommes before by me given I appoint shall be paid by my sonne Christopher within one yeare after my decease And for the remaynder of the said somme of two hundred pounds which is owing by my sonne Christopher as aforesaid amounting to the somme of threescore pounds my will and meaneing is that the same shall remayne in the hands of the said John Christopher on the security which is by him given unto me by his Indentures of mortgage aforesaid But in trust notwithstanding that he the said John Christopher shall from and after the expiracion of one yeare after my decease pay or cause to be paid the somme of three pounds yearely and every yeare unto my said daughter Sarah the wife of John Fowle dureing her naturall life for and in respect of the interest of the said somme of threescore pounds and after her decease my will and meaneing is that the said John Christopher shall equally devide and pay the said somme of threescore pounds to and amongest the children of her the said Sarah that shall be liveing at the tyme of her death and in case shee happen to dye without issue my will and meaneing is that the said somme of threescore pounds be equally devided amongest such of the children of my said daughters Lydia and Tymothy as shall be then liveing But in case my said sonne John Christopher

shall refuse to take upon him the charge and trouble of the trust aforesaid then my will and meaneing is that he shall pay the said three score pounds unto my overseer hereafter named who I request to putt the same out upon good security to be ymployed according to my intencion and meaneing aforesaid The rest of all my goods and Chattells not before bequeathed my debts legacyes and funerall charges being paid I give and bequeath unto my said sonne Richard Everest and Lydia his wife John Christopher and Tymothy his wife and John Fowle and Sarah his wife equally to be devided between them And I nominate and make the said Richard Everest and Lydia his wife John Christopher and Tymothy his wife and John Fowle and Sarah his wife Executors of this my will And I hereby revoke all former wills by me made whatsoever And I make and ordayne Richard Rigsbey of Rethered aforesaid my overseer of this my will and doe give unto him five shillings for his paynes and care to be taken herein In wittnesse whereof I have to this my present will sett my hand and seale the day and yeare first above written
The marke of John Withers
Signed sealed and published by the said John Wythers to be his last will and testament in the presence of us
John Blome Richard Rigsbe
the marke of Thomas Ward

13

BESBEECH Edward	Gentleman	bur. 21 Apr. 1662
W. 25 Mar. 1662	prov. 11 Jun. 1662	Prob. 11. 308 f. 80

In the name of God Amen the Five and Twentieth day of March in the Fowerteenth yeare of the Reigne of our Sovereigne Lord Charles the Second by the Grace of God King of England etc Anno Domini 1662 I Edward Besbeech of Seavenocke in the County of Kent gent being at this present of perfect mind and memory praysed be God for the ordering and settleing of that Estate as well Reall as personall which God hath lent me hereon Earth doe make and ordeine this to be my Testament and last will in manner and forme following That is to say First and principally I will and resigne my Soule into the hands and gracious acceptance of Almighty God my Maker hopeing and stedfastly beleeveing to have the pardon and remission of all my sinns and eternall Salvacion by the only merritts death and passion of his deerly beloved sonne Jesus Christ my alone Saviour and Redeemer and my body I committ to the Earth in a decent manner to be buried as mine executor hereafternamed shall think fitt Item I will and bequeath to the poor of Seavenocke aforesaid fifty shillings to be paid by mine Executor into the hands of the Churchwardens of the same parish and by them to be distributed amongst the same poor within short time after my decease Item I will and give to Richard Besbeech sonne of Richard Besbeech gent my brother deceased my gold Ring which I usually weare Item I will and give to Elizabeth Besbeech my sister all my Linnen and Pewter whatsoever and also my best bedsteddle with the curtens and valence featherbed and bolster covering and blancketts and other furniture thereto belonging and the hangings in the Rome I now lodge Item I will and bequeeth to the said Elizabeth Besbeech my sister and to her Heires and Assignes for ever All that my messuage tenements Lands and Hereditaments whatsoever with their appurtenants scituate being and lyeing in Staplehurst in the said County of Kent To hold to her the said Elizabeth Besbeech my sister her Heires and Assignes for ever Item I will and give to Arthur Children of Tonbridge in the said County Yeoman my Brother in Lawe and to his heires and Assignes for ever All my moyety or half of and in one annuity or yearly Rent of Fower pounds issueing out of certaine Lands called the George Lands in Seavenock aforesaid and all my power to enter and destreine in and uppon the same lands for want of paymant thereof and all other my interest Estate Title clayme and demand out of in and to the same lands and premisses Item I will devise and give to Rachel my sister for and dureing the term of her naturall life One Annuity or yearly Rent of Twenty pounds of lawful English money to be issueing goeing forth and annually to be perceaved receaved had and taken out of and in all that Capital Messuage or Tenement wherein I now dwell and out of and in all and singuler the barnes edifices and buildings Closes Yards Gardens Orchards Lands Meadowes Pastures and Wood-grounds thereto belonging in Seavenock aforesaid and all other my Lands Tenements and Hereditaments in Seavenock aforesaid To be paid unto her on the feasts of St Michael Tharchangell and the Annunciation of the blessed Virgin Mary by equal and even portions and the first payment thereof to beguine and to be made at the feast of the feasts aforesaid that shall next come and be from and after the end of fower yeares next after my decease if the said Rachel my sister shallbe then liveing and if and as often as the said annuity or yearly Rent of Twenty pounds or any parte thereof shallbe behind and unpaid by the space of one and twenty daies next over or after either or any of the Feast daies aforesaid whereon the same ought to be paid being lawfully demanded at or in my said Capital Messuage Then and soe often I will it shall and may be lawful to and for the said Rachel my Sister and her Assignes into all and singuler my said Messuage lands tenements and premisses with the appurtenances to enter and distreigne and the distresse and distresses there taken and found lawfully from thence to beare leade drive carry away impound determine and keepe until the said Annuity or Yearly Rent and all arrerages thereof and all costs charges and damages occasioned by takeing impounding and keeping of such distresse and distresses shallbee to her the said Rachel my Sister fully paid or satisfied Item I will devise and give to Arthur Children (Eldest sonne of the aforesaid Arthur Children by the said Rachel my sister) and to his heires and Assignes for ever All my said Capital Messuage and all my Lands Tenements and Hereditaments whatsoever in Seavenock aforesaid with their appurtenences (soe charged with the said annuity) to hold to the said Arthur Children the sonne his Heires and Assignes for ever Provided alwaies and my will and minde is that myne Executor his Executors Administrators and Assigns shall or may have hold receive take and deteine the use occupacion Rents Issues and profits of all my said Messuage Lands Tenements and Hereditaments

with the appurtenences in Seavenock aforesaid (soe charged with the said Annuity) from my death until the age of five and Twenty yeares to be atteined by the said Arthur Children the Sonne and shall imploy the fower first yeares of profitts and Rents made thereof from and after my decease in about and towards the raysing and satisfying of the mortgages by me made of the said Tenements and Lands and other my debts and from and after the end of the same four yeares until the said Arthur Children the Sonne shall attaine his said age of Five and Twenty yeares I will the rents issues and profitts of all my said tenements and lands in Seavenock (soe charged with the said Annuity) shallbe soe recived by mine Executor for the use of Richard John Rachell and Jane the fower younger children of myne Executor by the said Rachel my sister equally to be devided betweene them and to be paid unto them at their several ages of One and Twenty yeares Item I give and bequeath to James Hunt my Tennant my white Cowe Item I make and ordeine the said Arthur Children my brother in lawe the full and sole Executor of this my Testament and last will and for the better raysing of my Debts and the defraying my Funerall chardges and the chardges in probacion of this my Testament and last will I give and leave to the said Arthur Children mine Executor all goods household stuff Debts and Chattles not formerly disposed of In Witnes whereof I the said Edward Besbeech have to this my Testament and last Will set my hand and seale the day and yeare first above written
Edward Besbeech
sealed published and declared in the presence of
Sign Jacobi Hunt Sign Elizabeth Duke & George Hooper

14

SOANE John Carpenter
W. 9 April 1662 prov. 24 Jun. 1662 Prob. 11. 308 f. 90

In the name of God Amen I John Soane of the parish of Seavenock in the County of Kent Carpenter being sick and weake in body but of perfect memory and understanding and being desirous to setle and dispose of such temporall Estate as it hath pleased God to blesse me withall Doe make and ordaine this my last will and testament in manner and forme following First I give and bequeath unto my loveing brother Edward Soane the sume of forty shillings to be paid unto him at the end of twelve moneths after my decease if he shall be then liveing and not otherwise Item I give and bequeath unto Mary and Sara Soan children of my said brother Edward Soane the summe of foure pounds a peece to be paid unto them at their respective ages of One and Twenty yeares and if either of them happen to dye before they shall attain such their age of one and twenty yeares Then my will and meaning is that the survivor of them shall have and receive the part or share of her soe dying Item I give and bequeath unto my loveing Mother Elizabeth Soane the summe of Eight pounds to be paid unto her at the end of one moneth next after my decease if she shall be then liveing and not otherwise Item I give and bequeath unto my sister Elizabeth now the wife of Thomas Johnson the somme of forty shillings to be paid at the end of two yeares next after my decease if she shall be then liveing and not otherwise And I doe also give and bequeath unto Thomas and Abraham Johnson children of her my said sister Elizabeth the somme of five pounds a peece to be paid unto them at the end of twelve yeares next ensueing my decease and if either of them happen to dye before the same shall be payable as aforesaid Then my will and meaning is that the Survivor of them shall have and receive the part and share of him soe dyeing and in case they happen to both be dead before the expiration of the said term of twelve yeares Then my will and meaning is that the said somme of tenn pounds soe to them given as aforesaid shall be equally devided amongst and paid unto such other child or children as my said sister Elizabeth shall have then liveing Item I give and bequeath unto my loveing sisters Mary and Ann Soane Tenn pounds a peece to be paid them at the end of tenn yeares next after my decease and my will and meaneing is that if either of them happen to dye before the expiracion of the said term of tenn yeares That then the Survivor of them shall have and receive the whole sume of Twenty pounds And lastly I doe give and bequeath unto my loveing brother Thomas Soane all that my messuage or tenement commonly called the old messuage being now devided into two tenements with the garden plots thereunto belonging with the yard or backside and barn therein standing togeather with all that peece or parcel of land lyeing above the said barne called Bramley Croft containing by estimacion two acres be the same more or less which said messuage lands or premisses are scituate lyeing and being in Seavenock aforesaid and now are or late were in the occupacion of Edward Pattenden and me the said John Soane To hold the said Messuage lands and premisses unto him the said Thomas Soane his Heires and Assignes for ever this specyall trust and confidence notwithstanding that he the said Thomas Soane shall out of the Rents and Profitts of my said Tenements and Lands or by sale thereof or otherwise pay and discharge all and every the legacys by this my Will given at such tymes and in such manner and forme and according to the true intent and meaneing of this my will And of this my will I nominate and appoint my said loveing brother Thomas Soane my Executor hereby revoking all former and other wills by me made In Witnes whereof I the said John Soane have hereunto set my hand and seale this nynth day of April in the fourteenth yeare of the Raigne of our Soveraigne Lord Charles the second of England Scotland France and Ireland King defendor of the faith etc Annoque Domini 1662

John Soane

Signed sealed and published by the said John Soane to be his last will and testament in the presence of us

John Blome John Amason

15

HALL Thomas Husbandman bur. 23 May 1662
W. 8 May 1662 prov. 16 Jun. 1662 PRS/W/99

In the name of god amen I Thomas Hall of the parish of Seavenoke in the Countie of Kent husbanman beeing sicke in bodie but parfict in mind and of good remembrance Thankes therefore be giveen to Almightie god doe at this time ordaine and make this my last Will and Testament in maner and forme Folowing And First and princepallie I give Commend and beueath my Sowle into the handes of Almightie god trusting by an assuered faith which I have in the merits death and blood sheding of his deare and onely Soone my Savyour Jesus Christ that the same shall be presented pure and without spott before the Throne of his majestie and my bodie to earth decently to be buered in the parish Churchyard of Seavenoke and as for my personall estate which it hath pleased god to blesse me withall I give and bequeve as Followeth Inprimas I give and bequeve unto my sister Joane Champes teene shillings ayeare to be paid hir halfe yearly after my decease out of my house and Tenement lieing at Ide hill in the parish of Sunderish in Kent duering hir natuerall life and Item I give unto my brothers Stephen Hall and John Hall all the reast of the reentes of the same house equally to be devided betwne them duering there natuerall lifes and after there decease I give the same house and land to Thomas hall the soone of my brother Stephen hall and unto Thomas hall the soone of my brother John Hall to them and there heiers for ever to be equally devided betwne them Item I give and bequeve unto prudence Taylor the summe of Eight poundes of good and Corant money of England and my gould rings to be paid hir by my executore within twlefe months after my deceace Item I give unto my two kindswomen the dafters of my sister Joane Susana and Marie Champes the summe of thirtie shillings apeace to be paid unto them by my executor when they shall ataine to the age of eighteene years of Age all the rest of my landes goodes debtes Catell Chatells I give unto my Brother John hall paying my debtes legesces and funarall Charges to him and his heiers for ever Whome I ordaine and make my sole Executor of this my last will and Testament in witnes whereof I have hereunto seet my hand and seale This eight day of may in the yeare of our lord one thousand six hundred sixtie and two
The marke of Thomas hall
Read sigened an sealed in the presences of
Will Wall thomas taylar

16

SWAINE Anne Widow
W. 27 Jun. 1662 prov. 12 Aug. 1672 Prob. 11. 39 f. 104

In the name of God Amen the Twenty Seaventh day of June in the Foureteenth yeare of the Reigne of our Soveraigne Lord Charles the Second by the Grace of God of England Scotland France and Ireland King defender

of the Faith etc Annoque Domine 1662 I Anne Swaine of Seavenoke in the County of Kent Widdow Being att this present somewhat weake in body But of perfect memory Doe for certaine good reasons me hereunto moveing make ordaine and declare this my present last will and Testament in manner and forme following (That is to say) First and principally I commend my Soule to God that gave it hopeing and assuredly believing through the onely merritts death and passion of Jesus Christ to have free remission and pardon of all my sinnes and to inheritt Eternal life And my body I committ to the Earth from whence it was taken to receive Christian Buriall where it shall please God to appoint Item I give and bequeath unto my daughter Anne Adam All my Lease Interest and Terme of yeares to come of and in Certaine Messuages and Tenements with their appurtenences Lying and being in Broad Street London which I hold of the Deane and Commons of Windsor willing and desireing her therewith to discharge and defray the charge of Proveing this my last Will and Testament and all my Funerall Expences And to satisfy and pay all the debts which I shall owe att the tyme of my death Item I give and bequeath unto my daughter Anne Adam and my daughter Elizabeth Smith All my Plate Lynnen and Householdstuffe To be equally devided between them part and portion like Item I do ordaine and make and by these presents have ordained and made my daughter Anne Adam my full and sole Executrix of this my last will and Testament In Witnes whereof I have hereunto put my hand and seale the day and yeare first above written
Anne Swayne
Sealed subscribed pronounced and
declared in the presence of
John Conyer
Mary Pierrepoint
Anna Wilkes

17

HILLS Henry — Mealman
W. 10 Mar. 1663 — prov. 8 May 1668 — PRS/W/8/116

In the name of God Amen I Henry Hills of the parish of Seavenoke in the County of Kent mealeman being in sound and perfect mynd and memory prase be given to God for the same Doe make and ordaine this my last will and testament in manner and forme following First I give and bequeath my soule into the hands of Almighty god my merciful creator resting in an assured hope of Eternall Salvacion in the world to come through the onely meritts of Jesus Christ my ever blessed redeemer my body I dispose to the earth to be decently buried according to the discreccion of my Executrix hereafter named And touching and concerning such temporall estate as it hath pleased god to blesse my endeavors to possesse and enjoy which is some few goods and howsehold stuffe and the some of one hundred and threescore pounds principall money which is now in the hands of Edward Walsingham of Ryarsh in the said County of Kent yeoman and by him secured by his deed of mortgage dated the six and twentieth day of December last past And also the some of fifty pounds principall money which is now in my sonne Thomas his hands and by him secured by his bond of the penalty of one hundred pounds beareing date the five and Twentieth day of February 1660 My will and meaneing is that my Loveing wife Mary shall have receive and take unto her owne use for her support and livelyhood the yearly interest and benefitt of the said one hundred and threescore pounds soe remayneing in the hands of the said Edward Walsingham to her best advantage for and dureing the tearme of her naturall life and after her decease my will and meaneing is that the Executors administrators or assignes of her my said wife shall within one moneth after her decease pay or cause to be paid unto my Loving sonne John Hills or unto his Executors or assignes one hundred pounds part of the said principall somme of one hundred and threescore pounds and alsoe that the threescore pounds remaynder thereof shall be by them or some of them within the said space of one moneth after her decease paid unto my Loving sonne Henry Hills his Executors or assignes Provided alwaies and my will and meaneing is and is hereby declared to be that if my said sonne John happen before the tyme appointed for payment unto him of the said one hundred pounds to depart this life sole and unmarried that then the said somme of one hundred pounds shall be equally devided betweene my said other sonnes Henry and Thomas or in case they or either of them happen to dye before that tyme then my will and meaneing is that the child or Children that shall be then liveing of him or them soe dyeing shall have and enjoy the part or share of him or them soe dyeing equally to be devided amoungest them Item I give and bequeath unto my said loving wife Mary all such interest at the tyme of my death shall be due and payable unto me from my said sonne Thomas on the bond aforesaid by him to me entred into And also I give and bequeath unto her the somme of tenn pounds parte of the principall somme of fifty pounds to me by him owing on the said bond to be paid in unto her by my said sonne Thomas within one moneth after my decease and on payment thereof and on giveing unto my said wife good security such as she shall approve of to pay unto her yearely by quarterly payments dureing her life the somme of Forty eight shillings I doe will and appoint that thereupon she my said wife shall deliver up unto my said sonne Thomas the said bond to be cancelled and that my said sonne shall be freed and discharged from any farther payments thereon And lastly I hereby give and bequeath unto my said wife all the rest and residue of my personall estate whatsoever or wheresoever and doe constitute and appoint her the sole Executrix of this my will In witness whereof I have hereunto sett my hand and seale this tenth day of March in the Fifteenth yeare of the Raigne of our Soveraigne Lord Charles the second of England Scotland France & Ireland king defendor of the faith etc. Annoque Domini 1662

the marke of Henry Hills

Signed sealed and published by the said
Henry Hills to be his last will and
testament in the presence of us
John Blome
Timothy Stone

18

COLVIN Ann Widow
W. 10 Apr. 1663 prov.. 12 Dec. 1663 PRS/W/3/228

In the Name of God Amen The Tenth Day of April in the Fifteenth yeare of the Reigne of our Soveraigne Lord Charles the Second by the grace of God of England Scotland France and Ireland King, Defendor of the faith etc. Annoque Domini 1663 I Ann Colvin of Seavenoake in the County of Kent Widdow being of a sickly and weak Constitution in Body, but in good and perfect memorie, thanks therefore be ascribed to Almighty God, I doe by the permission of God make and declare this my present Testament wherein is Conteyned my Last Will, In manner and forme followeing, That is to say First I Commend my soule into the hands of Almightie God hopeing and assuredly beleeveing, through the Death and passion of Jesus Christ his onely sonn my saviour, to obtaine remission and forgivenesse of all my sinns, and to be made partaker of life everlasting, My Body I Committ to the earth from whence it Came to bee decently buried as beneath expressed And as Concerning all such worldly goods and Chattells as it hath pleased God to blesse me withall I will, Demise, give and bequeath the same in forme following vizt. Inprimis I give and bequeath unto my sonn George Colvin and to my Daughter Elizabeth the wife of Edward Latter the summe of five shillings a peece Item I give and bequeath unto my Daughter Joane the wife of William Thistleton the summe of Five pounds, of good and Lawfull money of England. Item I give and bequeath unto my Daughter Ann wife of Robert Chapman the summe of Tenn Pounds of the like money, And my Two best petticoates & best wastcoates, my best hatt, my scarfe and one fine Hempen Table Cloath. Item I give and bequeath unto my Daughter Mary Colvin Spinster the summe of Fifteene Pounds of the like English money, my silver spoone and one fine hempen Table Cloath. Item I give and bequeath unto my sonn John Colvin the summe of Five Pounds of the like English money And one pair of Hempen sheetes which were my Uncle Cranes All which said Legacies I appoint to bee paid by myne Executor and Executrix hereafter named within Eight and Twenty Dayes after my Decease, it being the money and goods left unto me by my Uncle William Crane, all the rest of my Linnen and woollen not formerly disposed of or bequeathed my will and desire is to have it equally divided beetweene my daughters Ann, Mary & Elizabeth abovenamed And all myne other goods left unto me by my husband I give and bequeath them to bee equally distributed amongst all my Children according unto his last will and Testament. And I doe appoint my sonn John Colvin and my daughter Mary Colvin joint Executor and Executrix of this my last will and Testament And I doe make and ordaine my Loveing friend James Pelsett of Seale in the said County my Overseer of this my Last Will and Testament Desireing him to see this my Last will and Testament duely and truly performed according to my true intent & meaneing And for his paines taken therein I doe give unto him the summe of Five shillings fir a remembrance. And I doe hereby revoake all other former Wills by me heretofore in any wise made, and this to stand for and as my Last will and

Testament. In Witnes whereof to this my last Will and Testament I the said Ann Colvin have sett my hand and Seale the Day & yeare first abovewritten.
the marke of Ann Colvin
Memorandum before the sealeing publishing and Delivery of this my last will, it is my desire that my Executor or Executrix or both shall bestow a decent buriall as to him or them shall seeme fitt out of the goods and Chattells left by my husband and to be divided, laying my Corps in Plaxtoll Church yard, and also I give my pillion & pillion Cloath unto Elizabeth wife of Edward Latter, my riding hood unto Mary Colvin and my safeguard unto Ann abovesaid. Published Sealed and Delivered as the last will and Testament of the abovenamed Ann Colvin in the presence of us
Thomas Greene   Alex: Fowle

19

BOSSE Richard   Vicar
W. 17 May 1663   prov. 7 Mar. 1665   PRS/W/1/270

In the name of god Amen I Richard Bosse viccar of the parish Church of Seavenoke in the County of Kent being sicke and weake in body but of perfect mynd and understand praised be given to god for the same doe make and ordaine this my last will and testament in manner and forme following First I give and bequeath my soule in to the hands of god my Creator resting in an assured hope of eternall salvacion in the world to come through the onely meritts of Jesus Christ my redeemer my body I dispose to the earth to be decently buryed according to the discrecion of my Executrix hereafter named. Item I give and bequeath unto my Loving sonne Richard all my Library of Bookes sermon notes and other papers concerneing my studdy and my Deske on which I usually write and my Deathes head seale ring Alsoe I give unto my said sonne the some of Tenn pounds to be paid unto him within one moneth after my Decease Item I give and bequeath unto my Daughter Mary Bosse the some of one hundred pounds to be paid unto her within one moneth after my Decease Item I give and bequeath unto my Daughter Margarett Bosse the some of one hundred pounds to be paid unto her within three monethes after my Decease. Item I give and bequeath unto my Daughter Elizabeth the some of one hundred pounds to be paid unto her at her age of one and twenty yeares or day of marriage which shall first happen my mynd and meaneing being that if shee shall dye before that tyme that then this Legacy to her given shall be void. Item my will and meaneing is and I Doe hereby Declare that my intencions are that the some of one hundred pounds shall be by my Executrix hereafter named raised out of the sale of the tymber and wood now growing upon my land now in the occupacion of William Whitehead the better to enable her to pay and Discharge the aforesaid legacyes by me given and in case either by the Death of my Executrix or upon any other occasion or accident shee be prevented in raiseing of the said one hundred pounds out of the said timber and wood that

then and in such case my said sonne and Daughters aforesaid shall out of theire said legacyes hereby to them by me given abate the said one hundred pounds every one of them proporcionably according to the Legacy to them by me given as aforesaid. Item my will is that if my Grandchild William Ducke shall attaine to yeares fitt to be placed out to an apprentize or to any other ymployement that then my Executrix shall bestowe in placeing out my said Grandchild the some of fifteene pounds Item I give and bequeath unto my Brother John Bosse and to my two sisters Rebecca and Frances to each of them tenn shillings a peece to buy them rings to weare in remembrance of me All the rest and residue of my personall estate either in goods Chattelles Debts securityes for Debts or otherwise howsoever or wheresoever I give and bequeath unto my Loving wife Margarett Bosse whom I make sole Executrix of this my last will and testament In wittnesse whereof I have hereunto sett my hand and seale this seaventeenth day of May in the fiveteenth yeare of the raigne of our Soveraigne Lord Charles the second of England Scotland France and Ireland King Defender of the faith etc Annoque Domini 1663
Richard Bosse
Signed sealed and published by the said Richard Bosse to be his Last will in the presence of
John Blome
The marke of Edward Baker
Dorothy Groome

20

STILEMAN Thomas Innholder
W. 6 Nov. 1664 prov. 15 Jan. 1665 PRS/W/15/58

In The Name of god amen I Thomas Stileman of Sevenoke In the County of Kent Inhoulder being secke in body but of whole and parfet mind Thanks be to the allmity god doe make publish and Decleare this my Last will and Testament In maner and Forme Followeing first I bequeth my sowle Into the hands of allmity god In sure hope of Sowlevation In by and through the merets of our Lord Jesus Christ and my body two be decently buried at the Descretion of my executrex here after mentioned and as for my worldly Goods First I give and bequeth unto my Daster Sarah now wife of Robert Staple five shillings becids and over and above what is allredy setelled upon hur by Deed in writeing under my hand and seale Item all the rest of my Goods Catell and Chatels Moveable and unmovable whatsoever my funerall expences and Debts being satesfied I give unto my Loveing wife Grace whome I doe make my hole and sole executrex of theis My Last will and testament and I Doe Nominat and apoynt my Brother John Stileman and my Loveing Freind Leonard Gale to be my overseers of this my Last will and testament earnestly Intreateing them to be Aideing and asisteing unto my Loveing wife and to Doe For hur what In them Lyeth In allthings and my will is that my Loveing wif shall in all things take there advice & for there pains I

Give them twelve pence apece In witnes hereof I have set my hand and seale the sixt day of November In the sixteenth yere of our sovereign Lord Chorls the second by the grace of god King of England Scotland France and Ireland defender of the Faith etc. Anoque Domini 1664
Tho: Stileman
Sealled and published in the presence of
John Stileman Robert Staple

21

COUPER John Gentleman
W. 16 Dec. 1664 prov. 10 Mar. 1666 PRS/W/3/235

In the name of God Amen: The sixteene day of December one thousand six hundred sixty and Foure: According to the computation of the Church of England: I John Couper of Seavenoakes in the County of Kent gent; being of perfitt Memory, and remembrance, praysed be God, doe make and ordaine this my last will and Testament in manner and forme Following, Viz First I bequeath my soule into the Hands of Almighty God my maker, hoping that through the Meritorious Death and Passion of Jesus Christ my onely Saviour, and Redeemer to receive Free pardon and Forgivenesse of all my sinnes: and as For my Body to bee buried in Christian Buriall att the discretion of my Executor hereafter nominated. Item I give unto my Eldest daughter Jane Wickenden, the wife of Thomas Wickenden the sum of Forty shillins. Item I give unto my youngest Daughter Elizabeth Olliver the Wife of Mr Richard Olliver the Sume of forty shillins: Item all the rest of my Houses, Leases, Tenements, and Goods whatsoever: I give unto my youngest sonne Thomas Couper, upon Condition that he shall pay all my Legacies, and make him sole executor of this my Last Will and Testament, revoking all other Wills and Testaments: In Wittness whereof I have hereunto sett my Hand and Seale the day and yeare First above written
John Couper
Sealed in the presence of us:
Edward Courthope Wa: Smith

22

COUPER John
I. 12 Mar. 1666 prov. 13 Mar. 1666 PRS/I/3/88

An Inventary of all & singuler the goods Chattles and Debts of John Couper late of Seavenoke in the County of Kent Deceased Taken and appraysed the 12th day of March Anno Domini 1665 by Walter Smith and Bartholomew Wood as followeth vizt

Inprimis 2 old feather beds with some Curtaines and vallences thereto	))	£iii	
Item One Table a greate chaire with some other Chaires			x^{s}
Item i paire of Andirons with other smale Irons aboute the fire	))		iii^{s}
Item halfe a Dozen of Napkins and some Towells			vi^{s}
Item 2 pewter dishes with a brasse Chaffine Dish			iiii^{s}
Item some old Hop pooles		£ii	
Suma totallis hujus Inventarii		£vi	iii^{s}

23

SMITH Robert Gentleman
W. 13 Mar. 1665 prov. 30 Jun. 1665 prob. 11. 317 f. 68

In the name of God Amen I Robert Smith of Seavenocke in the County of Kent gentleman being weak in body but of sound and perfect mind and memory thanks be given to Almighty God therefore Doe make and declare this my last will and testament in manner and form following First I bequeath my soule into the hands of Almighty God that gave it trusting through the merritts of my only Saviour Jesus Christ to obtain remission of all my sins And my body I committ to the earth from whence it was taken to be decently buried hopeing for a joyful resurrection unto life everlasting Item I do give and bequeath unto my Grandchild Joane Smith One Silver Can and Six Silver Spoones and a double Gilt Salt Item I give and devise unto my said Grandchild Joane Smith and to the heires of her body lawfully begotten All my lands messuages tenements and hereditaments whatsoever and wheresoever Except such lands and tenements as I have formerly given to my son in law Walter Smith by deedes And if my said Grandchild Joane Smith shall happen to dye without heires of her body laefully begotten Then I give and devise all my said lands tenements and hereditaments whatsoever unto Francis Lennard Esquire my Godson his heires and assignes forever Item I do hereby make constitute and ordaine my trusty and well beloved friends Thomas Lennard Esquire and Thomas Crompe gentleman the Executors of this my last Will and Testament in Trust only for the said Joane Smith my Grandchild And my will and mind is that the said Thomas Lennard and Thomas Crompe shall receive the rents issues and profits of all my said lands tenements and hereditaments until the said Joane Smith my Grandchild shall accomplish her age of one and twenty years to and for her only use benefit and behoof desireing them to have a care of my said Grandchild Joane Smith And I do hereby revoke all former wills In witness whereof I have hereunto set my hand and seale the thirteenth day of March Anno Domini One Thousand Six Hundred Sixty Four in the Seaventeenth year of the reign of

our Sovereign Lord Charles the Second by the Grace of God of England Scotland France and Ireland King defendor of the Faith etc.
Robert Smith
Read signed sealed and published and declared by the said Robert Smith in the presence of us
George Toller   Wa: Smith
The First day of April One Thousand Six Hundred Sixty and Five I Robert Smith of Seavenoke in the County of Kent gent Doe will and ordaine this present writing and the bequests and legacies herein contayned to be annexed to my will which I made in March last past by Thomas Lennard esq. and Thomas Crompe gent my Executors in the said will nominated and appointed (vizt) I give and bequeath unto Walter Smith my son in law One annuity or yearly rent of eighteen pounds per annum for and during his natural life only to be issueing and going out of all those my lands and tenements with the appurtenances in Sundridge in the occupation of my brother Owtrem and Gervase Watts to be paid quarterly That is to say at Midsummer Michaelmas Christmas and our Lady Day by equal portions the first payment to begin at that feast of the feasts aforesaid which shall first happen after my decease with powers of distress for not payment thereof And I desire the said Thomas Lennard Esqr. and Thomas Crompe to see this annuity truely paid unto my said son in law William Smith to fulfill and augment the portion which I promised him with my daughter Joane his first wife And for the great care he hath had of me in my sickness
Item I give unto all the children of Nicholas Brattle gent deceased Twenty Shillings a piece And further I will that the said Thomas Lennard Esqr and Thomas Crompe my Executors in my said will shall make a new lease of my lands in Halstowe unto William Bridge of Hedcorn Taylor to commence from our Lady Day last past for twenty one years at the rent of – pounds per annum And to allow the said tennant fourteen pounds for reparations of the house and buildings out of the said rent as it shall come due And I also will that my said Executors Mr. Thomas Lennard and Thomas Crompe shall make a lease to Richard Styles of Chevening to commence from our Lady Day last past for twenty one years at the rent of eighteen pounds per annum In witness whereof I the said Robert Smith have hereunto set my hand and seale the day and year above written
Robert Smith his mark
This was read sealed published and declared by the said Robert Smith And by him willed to be added and annexed to his said will in the presence of us
George Toller   Jane Marten her mark   Margaret Smith

24

FRENCH John   Carpenter
N.W. 10 Jun. 1665   prov. 4 Aug. 1665   PRS/W/6/58

Memorandum that John French of the parish of Seavenoke in the County of Kent Carpenter On or about the Tenth day of June Anno Domini 1665 last

past being sick in Body but of sownd and perfect memory made his last Will and Testament Nuncupative, vizt: being asked by Timothy Stone then present how he would dispose of his Estate said I give all my Goods whatsoever to my loveing Wyfe Jane and my Daughter Dorathy to be equally divided betweene them, Excepting only all my Workeing Tooles which I give to my Sonne John, Theis words or to the selfsame effect he spake in the presence and heareing of Timothy Stone and William Floate both of Seavenoke aforesaid
Timothy Stone William Flot

25

FRENCH John Carpenter
I. 24 Jul. 1665 prov. 23 Feb. 1666 PRS/I/6/45

An Inventory of all and singuler the Goods Chattells & Credits of John French late of Seavenoke in the County of Kent Carpenter decesed Taken and prized the 24th day of July Anno Domini 1665 By Thomas Chorley and Timothy Stone as followeth vizt.//

Inprimis in ready Money	£ v		
Item his Weareing Apparell		xx^s^	
Item in the Hall One Presse Cubberd one Table 3 Joyned Stooles & 3 old Chayres		xiii^s^	iiii^d^
Item one Kneading Trough and 3 Spinning Wheeles		v^s^	
Item one litle Brasse Furnace one Brasse Pot one small Warmeing Pan & 2 Kettles		xxv^s^	
Item 9 small Pewter Dishes 4er litle Pewter Salts & one Porrenger		xii^s^	
Item 3 small Iron Pots one Iron Kettle one Pestle and Mortar two paire of Pothangers one Gridiron a Fire Pan & Tongs		xi^s^	
Item 4er litle Beere Tubs one Stalder 2 Payles & 4er old Trayes		vii^s^	
Item 2 Tubs		v^s^	
Item in the Chamber over the Hall 2 halfheaded Bedsteads Mats and Cords		xii^s^	
Item 2 Flockbeds 2 Flockbolsters one Flock pillow & 3 Fether Pillowes		xv^s^	
Item 2 Coverlets & 3 old Blankets		vi^s^	
Item 7 paire & one od Sheete		xxx^s^	
Item Hemp yarne & pownd of Flax		xviii^s^	
Item 5 Chests & 2 Boxes		xxiii^s^	
Item 2 old Sives			viii^d^
Item in a litle Inner Chamber one old Flockbed		iii^s^	
Item his workeing Tooles		xxvi^s^	viii^d^
Item Lumber in & about the Howse		x^s^	
Suma totalis	£ xvii	ii^s^	viii^d^

26

TAYLOR Thomas Butcher
W. 7 Oct. 1665 prov. 9 Jan. 1669 PRS/W/16/188

In the name of God Amen the Seaventh day of October in the Seaventeenth yeare of the Raigne of our Soveraigne Lord Charles the Second by the grace of God of England Scotland France and Ireland Kinge Defender of the faith etc Annoque Domini 1665 I Thomas Taylor of the parish of Seavenoke in the County of Kent Butcher being at this present (God be praysed therefore) in good health of Body and of perfect mind and memory but caling to mind the uncertainty of this Life Doe make and ordaine this my Last Will and Testament First and principally I comitt my Sowle to God my Creator whoe infused the same And my Body to the earth to be decently interred by my Executor hereafter named trusting and assuredly beleiveing thorough the Merrits of my blessed Saviour Christ Jesus to obtaine Remission of my Sinnes and to be made partaker of life everlasting, And as touching the disposition of that worldly Estate wherewith God hath blessed mee my Will is as followeth First I will and bequeath unto my Eldest Sonne Thomas and his Heires for ever All that my Messuage or Tenement wherein I now live Comonly caled Westlands and Rowles Pownd with thappurtenances and Seaven peices or parcells of Land therewith all used conteyning by estimation Eighteene Akers more or lesse Scituat in Seavenoks Weild with in the said parish of Seavenoke, Also I give unto my said Sonne Thomas my Two best Beds with the Bedsteadles and all the Furniture to them belonging Item I will and bequeath to my Sonne Edward and his Heires for ever, All those Five peices or parcells of Land caled Croch Lands Conteyning by estimation Two and Twenty Akers more or lesse, lying and being in the parishes of Seavenoke and Leigh in the said County of Kent, which Lands I lately purchased of Thomas Lambert Esq Item I will and bequeath unto my loveing Father Nicholas Taylor and Dorathy his Wyfe my Mother and the longer liver of them, One Annuity of Forty Shillings a yeere owt of my said Lands, That is to say Twenty Shillings a yeere owt of the Messuage and lands hereby given to my Sonne Thomas, and Twenty Shillings a yeere owt of the Lands herein given to my Sonne Edward, To be payed unto them and the longer liver of them the said Nicholas and Dorothy half yeerely viz: At the Feasts of Thanuntiacon of the Blessed Virgin Mary and St Michaell Tharchangell by even and equal portions, Provided allwayes that yf default be made of payment of the said Sume of Forty Shillings, That in such Case it shall and may be lawfull to and for the said Nicholas and Dorathy their Assigne or Assignes to enter into the premises therewith chargeable, and to distreyne therefore, and to detaine the same distresses untill they shalbe satisfied the same with all Damages for nonpayment thereof And my desire is that my Executor hereafter named shall within convenient time after my decease Sell All the rest and residue of my Goods Cattle and chattells whatsoever not herein bequeathed for the best value he can, And that also my Executor shall receave have and take the Products Rents yssues and profitts aswell of my Messuage or Tenement and Lands formerly herein devised to my Sonne

Thomas as of all my Lands herein devised to my Sonne Edware untill such time as my said Sonne Edward shall attaine to his Age of One and Twenty yeeres and shall therewith mainetaine educate and bringe up all my Children, And whatsoever Sume or Sumes of Money can be saved or spared aswell owt of the Money made owt of the Sale of my said Goods Cattle and chattells as also owt of the said Rents and profitts of my said Messuage and Lands untill my said Sonne Edward shall attaine his said Age of One and Twenty yeeres, My Debts Legacyes and Funerall expenses being first satisfyed and discharged, and all necessary expenses being allowed to my Executor which he shall expend about the premisses, My Will and meaneing is that all the rest and residue shalbe equally divided by my Executor and Overseer hereafter named Betweene my Three Daughters Mary, Elizabeth and Hannah the Survivers or Surviver of them, And I nominate appoint and desire my kind and loveing freind John Childrens of Lower Street in the parish of Tunbridge in the said County of Kent yeoman sole Executor of this my Last Will and Testament, And I give unto him as a token of Remembrance Forty Shillings of Lawfull English Money, And I nominate Overseer of this my Will my Loveing Brother Richard Taylor desireing him to see this my Will performed And I give him for his paines therein Twenty Shillings of like Money In witnesse whereof I have to this my Last Will and Testament set to my hand and Seale the day and yeere first before written Revokeing all former Wills
Thomas Taylor
Sealed and delivered and
Declared for his Last Will and Testament In presence of
John Thornton   Chris: Thomas Notary Public

27

TAYLOR Thomas   Butcher
I. 14 Dec. 1668   prov. 8 Jan. 1669   PRS/I/20/4

An Inventary of all and singuler the Goods chattells and Credits of Thomas Taylor late whilst he lived of the parish of Seavenoke in the County of Kent Butcher deceased Taken and prized the Fourteenth day of December Anno Domini 1668 by Williams Wall and Richard Children as followeth vizt/.

Inprimis the deceseds Purse Girdle and redy Money	£iiii	xvi^s
Item his Apparell of all sorts		xl^s
Item in the Hall of the said late deceseds dwelling howse one Table & Frame one Forme one Joyned Settle one Joyned Stole 4 Chayres 4 Cushins 1 paire of Andirons one Fireshovell and Tongs)		xxxvi^s
Item in the Kitchen one old Table with Tressells 4er Chayres one Cubbord 3 Spits one Tin pan one litle)		

Andiron one Gridiron a pair of Potthangers a pair of Bellowes a Tosting Iron a pair of Tongs a litle Iron to lay before the Fire & a litle Box 1 Forme an old Pudding pan)		xxvi^{s}	vi^{d}
Item one Bible & 2 other litle Books		viii^{s}	
Item 16 peices of Pewter great & small weying 43 pounds, 2 Flaggons 2 Candlesticks 2 Salts 1 Porrenger one Bason an Aquavite Bottle 17 Spoones & a pack Candlestick)	£iii	vii^{s}	
Item in Brasse 2 pots 2 litle Ketles one great Buck Ketle 3 Skilletts one Basting Ladle 2 Skamers one Warmeing pan & an old Brasse Mortar)		xxiiii^{s}	
Item one Fowleing peice		vi^{s}	
Item 4er Iron pots 2 pair of Pothooks & a litle Trevet to warme Beere)		xvi^{s}	vi^{d}
Item in the Milkhowse 14 Milktrayes one Churne 2 Frying pans one Table with Tressels one Forme 4er Bords one Earthen pan 8 Crocks)		xvii	iiii^{d}
Item 33 Cheess		xx^{s}	
Item 2 Drink Vessels under the Stayres		vi^{s}	
Item in the Buttery adjoyning to the Hall 3 Drinke Vessells 2 powdring Tubs one long Keeler 2 old Tressels 2 Mealebags a Bord & a Planke)		xxix^{s}	
Item in the Cheesepresse howse one Cheese presse i Wicker Chaire 5 Tubs i Keeler one Trevet one Forme one Seedcorne one Sith one Spade 4er pitchforks 4er Rakes 3 Cheesebayles & a matthook)		xxvii^{s}	
Item in the Shoppe a paire of Skales & 7 wayts & 3 Sacks		xiii^{s}	
Item in the Corne loft about a Quarter of Beanes		xvi^{s}	
Item 8 Bushels of Oats		viii^{s}	
Item 15 Fleecs of Woll		xv^{s}	
Item one Scry		vi^{s}	viii^{d}

Item one boarded Bedstedle i Flockbed one Bolster 2 Blankets & a Coverlet		x^{s}	
Item an old Trundle bedstedle			xii^{d}
Item 2 Linnen Wheeles & Lanthorne		iiii^{s}	
Item in the 2 other Chambers of the said deceised 2 best Beds with the Bedstedles & the Furniture belonging to them given by his will to Thomas his Sonne standing in the Inner Chamber	£vi		
Item one Trundle Bedsted 3 Chests 1 Box		xviii^{s}	
Item one Flockbed		vi^{s}	
Item in the Owter Chamber i borded Bedstedle a Flock bed a Chaffe bed 2 pillowes 1 Bolster one Blanket i coverlet one Curten 3 Chests one Box one hanging Cubberd		xxix^{s}	
Item in the Garret one new Flasket a Basket 12 pownds of Tow		v^{s}	
Item 10 paire of Sheets 2 dozen of Napkins 2 paire of Pillowcots 2 Tablecloths 5 peics of New cloth for Napkins	£iiii	v^{s}	vi^{d}
Item 10 Fleshclothes & 5 Aprons		xviii^{s}	
Item in the Barne certaine Wheate	£xiii	x^{s}	
Item certaine Oats	£vi	v^{s}	
Item certaine Tares in a Stack	£iiii	x^{s}	
Item certen Hay in Stack & Clover in a Stack	£xiiii		
Item 3 Fatling Steeres	£xx		
Item 4er workeing Oxen & 3 Steeres	£xx		
Item 15 Sheepe	£vi	xvii^{s}	
Item one Gelding one Mare & 2 Colts	£xii		
Item 1 Fatting Hogge & 5 other Swyne	£iii	xv^{s}	

Item Waghorne with 4er Shod Wheeles one Plow 3 yokes 3 Tights 2 Coarts with 2 pair of Chowlwheeles 2 Horsharrowes one Ox Harrow 2 Whippletrees	£vii	ix^{s}	iiii^{d}
Item a paire of Swippes 3 Sives 4 Pitchforks in the Barne and two Waggon Ropes		vi^{s}	
Item in the Shop at Seavenoke Towne Two Course & a Beame & Skales & Wayts		xv^{s}	
Item the Seed & plowing & Sowing & Harrowing of about 4er akers of Wheate upon the Ground		lviii^{s}	
Suma	£clxii	xii^{s}	viii^{d}

Sperat Debts owing to the deceased at the time of his death

Item owing by Sir Bernard Hyde	£xlix	xiiii^{s}	
Item owing by John Taylor		xl^{s}	
Item owing by John Arnold		xx^{s}	
Item owing by Thomas Vyne		x^{s}	viii^{d}
Item by Widdow Wallis		xxiiii^{s}	viii^{d}
Item by Thomas Huggins		iiii^{s}	
Item owing by John Goodhue		vii^{s}	iii^{d}
Item owing by the parishioners of Sevenoke	£viii	iii^{s}	iiii^{d}
Suma	£lxiii	iii^{s}	xi^{d}
Suma Totalis	£ccxxv	xvi^{s}	vii^{d}

Desperat Debts

Item owing to the deceased by Wickenden	£x	xi^{s}	ix^{d}
Item owing by William Saunders		xii^{s}	
Item owing by Richard Goodhue		ii^{s}	iiii^{d}
Item owing by Edward Yonge		xiii^{s}	x^{d}
Suma	£xi	xix^{s}	xi^{d}

28

BEARDSWORTH Mary Widow
W. 2 Nov. 1665 prov. 12 Oct. 1667 PRS/W/1/227

In the name of God Amen the second day of November in the Seaventeenth yeare of the raigne of our Soveraigne Lord Charles the Second of England Scotland Fraunce and Ireland King Defendor of the faith etc: Mary Beardsworth of Seavenoke in the County of Kent widdow being praised be god in good health perfect memory and understanding but considering the mortalitie of man kind and being desirous to make some provision for my three daughters who are yett unprovided for I doe Declare this my last will and testament in manner and forme following And first I commend my Soule into the hands of my God and Saviour Jesus Christ hopeing through his merritts to have a joyfull resurreccion with the righteous and to be partaker of the heavenly kingdome by him prepared for those that love him And for my body I leave the burieing thereof to the discreccion of my Executrixes hereafter named onely desireing that the same may be with as little charge and expence as may be reasonably contrived Item I give and bequeath unto my five sonnes Nicholas John Thomas William and Richard Beardsworth to each and every of them that shall be liveing at the tyme of my decease two shillings and six pence which I appoint shall be paid unto them respectively within one moneth after my decease And to the intent and purpose to avoid all controversy which may happen betweene my Executrixes hereafter named and my sonne John Beardsworth who hath purchased to him and his heires the inheritance of the messuage or tenement wherein I now dwell I doe hereby declare my mind and meaneing to be that my said sonne John and his heires shall have and enjoy to his and theire owne proper use and behoofe all such doores lockes keyes setles wainscott shelves dressers & benches and other things as are or att the tyme of my death shall be fixed nailed or fastned to my now dwelling house alsoe all such window shutters as belong unto the same And my farther will and desire is that in respect my said sonne John by his deed under his hand and seale hath impowred me in my life tyme or my Executrixes after my death to pull up take carry away sell and dispose of my two furnaces which are now fixed and sett upp in my Brewhouse That my Executrixes hereafter named shall after my death accomodate the said John Beardsworth with the said furnaces at an easier rate and price than otherwise they may sell the same for to any other person if he my said sonne John shall desire to buy the same. Item I give and bequeath the aforesaid furnaces and all other my goods chattells cattell ready moneys and personall estate whatsoever unto my daughters Mary Beardsworth Grace Beardsworth & Prudence Beardsworth to be equally devided amonngest such of them as shall be liveing at the tyme of my death they my said daughters as shall bee then liveing beareing and paying an equall share of my funerall and of such debts as I shall then owe and of the legacies hereby by me bequeathed And if any difference shall happen or arise monngest them touching the equall shareing and devideing of my said personall estate in such case I desire my loveing freinds Mr John Blome of Seavenoke and Mr William Allen and my said sonne John Beardosworth according to theire best skill and judgement to determine and end the same controversies to and with whose determinacion and judgement I require my said Daughters to submitt and rest satisfied And I make ordaine and appoint my said three Daughters Mary Grace and Prudence the joynt Executrixes of this my will In wittnesse whereof I have hereunto sett my hand and seale the day and yeare first above written Annoque Domini 1665

the marke of Mary Beardsworth

Signed sealed and published by the said Mary Beardsworth
to be her last will in the present of us
John Blome W. Allen

29

COURTHOP Edward Gentleman
I. 29 Dec. 1665 prov. 15 Sep. 1666 PRS/I/3/102

A true and perfect Inventorie of all and singuler the goods and chattells of Edward Courthopp late of Seavenoke in the County of Kent gentleman had appraised and taken by Walter Smith of Seavenoke aforesaid gentleman and William Allen of Seavenoke aforesaid Mercer the nine & twentieth Day of December in the seaventeenth yeare of the Raigne of our Soveraigne Lord Charles the second of England Scotland France and Ireland King Defendor of the faith etc Annoque Domini 1665

	£	*s.*	*d.*
Imprimis ready money in his purse	0 –	2 –	0
Item his weareing apparrell	2 –	0 –	0
In the entry			
Item severall glasse bottles old Gally potts and an old Chest	0 –	6 –	0
In the Shopp			
Item eight & twenty white potts with Tynn covers	0 –	6 –	8
Item nine and fifty Gally potts of severall sizes	0 –	9 –	10
Item severall other Glasse bottles and old Gally potts of severall sorts	0 –	10 –	0
Item an old sadle	0 –	3 –	4
Item an old Turkyworke Carpett	0 –	5 –	0
Item foure cases of Shelves	0 –	13 –	4
Item two peeces of Beeswax weight seaven pounds	0 –	7 –	0
Item two bottles of stilled waters and two bottles of surrupps and some few old Druggs	0 –	6 –	8
Item a paire of brasse skayles & two setts of weights	0 –	6 –	8
In the Buttery			
Item one powdring Tubb	0 –	5 –	0
Item one other smale powdring Tubb	0 –	4 –	0
In the Brewhowse			
Item foure smale Drincke Tubbs	0 –	8 –	0
Item one new Keeler	0 –	5 –	0
Item one bucking Tubb and one Keeler	0 –	7 –	0
Item one old brewing fate and two halfe Tubbs	0 –	5 –	6
Item a Standard a Jett and other lumber there	0 –	1 –	8
In the Buttery			
Item three smale Drincke Tubbs	0 –	7 –	0
Item one old friing pann and an old ax	0 –	1 –	6
Item two Drincke potts and other lumber	0 –	2 –	0
In the kitchin			
Item one paire Andirons & a paire of Creepers two smale spitts & two paire of old Tongs	0 –	6 –	8

Item two old Gridirons & two tosting irons		0	2	0
Item a potthanger and a hearth iron		0	3	0
Item an Iron hand Jack a cord & two weights		0	6	6
Item three wooden platters & other woodenware		0	1	0
Item a paile and three old low chaires and a paire of Bellowes	)	0	2	0
In the Parlour	)			
Item six Turkyworke Chaires		1	16	0
Item foure low leather Chaires		0	10	0
Item a window Curtaine and Curtaine rood and the hangeing of the roome & three Carpetts all of old striped stuffe	)	1	15	0
Item a little Table		0	2	0
In the Closett over the Parlour				
Item six pewter Dishes a pasty plate a pye plate & severall peeces of old pewter	)	2	0	0
Item three smale brasse Morters with pestles a Chaffing Dish & severall peeces of Tynn ware	)	0	10	0
In the Parlour Chamber				
Item two kettles and foure Skylletts		0	16	0
Item two smale Iron potts and a paire of potthangers		0	10	0
Item an old pewter still and bottome and a close pann		0	12	0
Item a warming pann		0	2	0
Item two paire of Bellowes with wooden noses		0	1	0
Item three old Trunckes		0	4	6
Item one old Chaire		0	1	6
Item one table Cloath & tenn napkins of Damaske worne very thyn	)	0	6	8
Item foure paire of old sheets and foure pillow beares and six towells and foure table Cloathes and twelve napkins	)	1	10	0
Item a Bedstead & curtaines and valance matt cord and Curtaines roods	)	1	10	0
Item a feather bed boulster & pillow		3	0	0
Item three old blancketts & a Rugg		0	13	4
In the Chamber over the shop				
Item a wheele and a Reele and three earthen potts		0	3	0
In the Chamber over the entry				
Item an old bed filled with cloath shreds a feather boulster a coverlett one blanckett and an old Rugg	)	1	10	0
Item a cradle & a cradle Rugg & blanckett		0	3	6
Item a hamper		0	1	0
In the Chamber over the Buttery				
Item two old Trunckes two old Deale boxes and a sive		0	5	0

In the Kitchin Chamber			
Item one bedstead Curtaines & Valance matt & cord & curtaine roods	1	10	0
Item one featherbed one boulster and three pillowes	3	13	4
Item one old Rugg and two blancketts	0	15	0
Item one old elbow chaire & two stooles	0	8	0
Item a Close stoole two stands a nest of Drawers and an old Truncke	0	5	0
Item one old table	0	0	6
Item an old Turkyworke Carpett	0	5	0
Item a paire of Andirons fire shovell & Tongs	0	2	6
Without Doores			
Item one wheelebarrow	0	1	0
Item a Coope	0	2	0
Item severall parcells of wood	0	13	4
Instruments of Chirurgery and the Lybrary of bookes in the shopp			
Item one case of silver instruments	1	4	0
Item one case of steele instruments	0	5	0
Item a smale case with three tortishell Lanncetts	0	4	6
Item severall other instruments of Chirurgery	1	0	0
Item twenty bookes infolio	5	0	0
Item tenn bookes in large quarto	1	10	0
Item thirty bookes in smale quarto	2	5	0
Item thirty bookes more of a lesser quarto	1	10	0
Item sixty bookes in octavo	1	5	0
Item thirty more bookes in octavo and lesse	0	7	6
Summae totalis	39	13	6

30

SPILSTEAD Richard Butcher
I. 12 Jan. 1666 prov. 7 Apr. 1666 PRS/I/19.106

A true and perfect Inventory of all and Singuler the Goods Cattell Chattells and Debts of Richard Spilstead Late whilst he Lived of the Parish of Seavenoakes in the County of Kent butcher Deceased taken and Prized the twelfth Day of January in the Yeare of our Lord God One thousand Six Hundred sixty and Five by Timothy Stone and William Everest as followeth, to witt,

	£	s	d
Inprimis Ready mony in his Purse	10	0	0
Item his Apparell	02	0	0

Item in the Halle one Table to formes and an other Little table)	01	0	0
Item one settle and a Cubboard	0	10	0
Item Five Chaires and two Stooles	0	3	6
Item one Jacke two Spitts a paire of Andirons one fire Pan and tongues)	01	0	0
Item three Bibles and other Bookes	00	5	6
Item in the Buttery two brasse Cettles two brasse Skillets)	02	0	0
Item two Iron Potts and Iron Skillet	00	8	0
Item one Bucking tube one Powdering tub and other brewing Vessell)	01	2	0
Item in the Chamber over the Hall, one Joyne Bedsted one halfe heded Bedsted a feather bed one Boalster two Pillowes two Blancketts one Coverlett one Payre of Curtaines and Rods Fower Matts)	08	5	0
Item two Chests and a boxe	00	10	6
Item one Mare and horse and Furniture	05	0	0
Item for scales and weights and other thing belonging to them)	01	15	0
Item Lumber and things forgotten	01	5	0
The sume is	53	7	6

31

MASTERS Thomas Yeoman
I. 15 Jan. 1666 prov. 15 Sep. 1666 PRS/I/13/3

A true and perfect Inventorie of all the goods and chattells of Thomas Masters late of Seavenoke in the County of Kent yeoman Deceased taken and appraised by John Willson and Henry Swaisland the fifteenth Day of January in the seventeenth yeare of the Raigne of our Soveraigne Lord Charles the second of England Scotland France and Ireland King Defendor of the faith etc Annoque Domini 1665 as followeth

	£	s	d
Imprimis his weareing apparrell and ready money in his purse)	0	10	0
Item one Jointe bedstead with matt and cord	0	9	6
Item one old feather bed	1	0	0
Item two old flocke beds	0	9	6
Item two flocke boulsters and two old Pillowes	0	2	6
Item two old rugges & one coverlett	0	15	6
Item one blanckett	0	2	6
Item a paire of Curtaines & valence	0	6	0

Item two joynt Chests and one Joynt boxe		0	10	0
Item six old Joynt stooles		0	3	6
Item two paire of hemppen sheetes and an odd one and six paire of towen sheetes	))	1	9	0
Item six pillow coates one dozen of napkins and one table cloath	))	0	14	0
Item Three old table Cloathes and other smale linnen		0	6	0
Item one wastcoate three old petty Coates		0	14	0
Item one old hat		0	4	6
Item one paire of Andirons and one paire of tongs		0	3	4
Item one old wicker Caire		0	1	6
Item one old courte Cupboard		0	2	4
In the Hale				
Item one joint Cupboard & one old plancke table & frame & two old wooden chaires	))	0	17	6
Item foure old Chaires		0	2	0
Item a Jacke two spitts & a old tynn Dripping pann		0	6	8
Item a paire of old Andirons a fire shovell and a paire of Tongs	))	0	3	0
Item one old Friing pann and one old gridiron		0	1	4
Item one brasse pott and an Iron pott		0	6	0
Item one old Iron kettle & two old Trivetts		0	3	4
Item two paire of pott hangers		0	1	2
Item five old brasse kettles one pot and a brasse skillett one old warmeing pann one old Iron Morter and one pessle	)))	0	12	6
Item two old buckeing tubes and one baking keeler & three smale old Drincke tubes	))	0	9	0
Item five smale pewter Dishes one basin one Colen-der one old Chamber pott and one quarte pott	))	0	11	6
In the Barne				
Item thirty Copp of Barley		5	5	0
Item thirty Copp of Rye & some gleaned wheat		0	18	0
Upon the Ground				
Item one Cow		2	0	0
Item one hogg		1	10	0
Item a parcell of Dunge		1	13	0
Item five thousand of old hopp poles		10	0	0
Item a parcell of Charcoale and severall parcells of old lumber	))	0	12	0
Item a parcell of hopps		30	0	0
Sumae Totalis		63	15	8

32

PAYNE Simon Butcher
W. 28 Jan. 1666 prov. 25 Feb. 1666 PRS/W/13/4

In the name of God Amen: In the yeare of our Lord God one thousand six hundred sixty and six January the Eight and Twentyeth and in the seventeenth yeare of the Raygne of our Soveraygne Lord Charles the second by the Grace of God Kinge of England Scotland France and Ireland defender of the fayth etc.: I Simon Payne of Ryverhead in the parish of Sevenoke in the County of Kent Butcher beinge sick and weake in body but of perfect minde and Memory doe make and ordeyne this my last will and Testament in Manner and forme Followinge: Viz: First of all and Cheifly I commend my soule into the hands of God whoe gave itt assuredly Trustinge to bee saved by the onely merritts of Jesus Xt my onely Saviour and Redeemer and I bequeath my body to the Earth from whence it came to bee decently buryed by the discretion of my Executrix and overseers: first I doe make Mary Payne my Lovinge wife my whole and onely Executrix of this my Last Will and Testament: Item I doe give to my sonne Thomas Payne one shillinge to bee payd hime one moneth after my decease: Item I doe give unto my daughter Anne Holdstock five pounds after her mothers decease one moneth: Item I give and bequeath unto my sonne John Payne twenty pounds seven yeares after my decease to bee payd hime by my Executrix aforesayd: Item I give unto my sonne Joseph five pounds to binde hime out apprentise and five pounds when hee shall come to the age of one and twenty yeares. Item I give to my Daughter Sarah twenty pounds to bee payd her att the age of one and twenty yeares and if shee shall dye before she come the age of one and twenty yeares the said Sarah's twenty pounds given to her shall bee payd to John Payne her brother within one yeare after her decease. Item My will and pleasure is that Mary my wife is and shall be my sole Executrix as aforesaid, soe longe as she keepes her selfe a widdowe or bee unmarryed, but if in Case shee bee marryed that than my sonne John I make and ordeyne to bee the Executor of this my Last Will and Testament: and that then Mary my said wife shall have twenty pounds payd to her by my son John or the overseers of this my Last will hereunder mencioned: and also my sayd wife shall have one bed bedstead and all thinges belonging to itt which is in the hall Chamber and all the Linnen brasse and peuter with the wicker Chayre Jack and 2 payre of brandirons Item I give to my son John all my weareing Clothes Excepte one Cloth Coate: and all my Knives and axes belonginge to the trade: Item I doe finally make constitute and Ordeine Edward Clements of Nockholt and Richard Rigsbye of Riverhead to bee my overseers of This my Last will and Testament and doe give them full power leave and authority if in case my sayd wife marry before my Children come of age for their porcions to Cease and secure the sayd porcions in their hands till they come to age and to see it payd to them as they shall come of age. In witnesse hereof I have sett my hand & seale the day and yeare above Written
Simon Payn
Sealed and delivered in
the presence of Tho: Broad Paul Payne

33

JEFFRY David | Clothworker
W. 3 May 1666 | prov. 29 June 1666 | PRS/W/9/178

In the name of god amen the thurd day of may one thousand sixe hundered sixty an sex I david Jeffry being sick in body but of good and perfect memery thankes be to allmighty god and Calling to rememberance the unsertain estate of this transitory life and that all flesh must dy when it shall pleace god to Call: doe make Constitute ordaine and declare this my last will and testament in manner and form following revoking and anulling by these presents all and every testament and testaments will and wills heretofore by me made and declared either by word or writing and this is to be taken only for my last will and testament and none other: and furst being sorri for all my sins past most humbly desiring forgiveness for the same I commit my spirit to god and my body to be buried in such a place as shall please my executor hereafter named and now as tuching my temporal estate I doe order give and dispose the same in manner and forme following that is to say furst I give to my well loved wife bridgett Jeffery all my lands goods and Chatels to be at her disposing only I will that shee pay all the deates an legases that I owe first I give to my dautheer mary the sume of twenty shilling to be payd within two yeares 2 ly to my dauther bridgett I give the full sume of thirty pounds to be payed ten pound a yeare. 3 to my dauther elizabeth the full sume of fiftine pounds to be payde next micmilmase following as for my other daughters I leav to my wifes dispousing I make my wife full and solle executor and I mak John Jeffer of Wadharst and John Jeffery of sevenoaks my overseers
David Jeffery
sealed in the presents of John Inge John Jeffery Welliam Jeffery

34

JEFFREY DAVID | Clothworker
I. 15 May 1666 | prov. 3 Jul. 1666 | PRS/I/10/9

An Inventary of all and singuler the goods chattells and Credits of David Jeffery late whilst he lived of the parish of Seavenoke in the County of Kent Cloath Worker decesed Taken and praysed the Fifteenth day of May In the yeere of our Lord 1666 By John Jeffery John Inge and John Jeffery as followeth vizt.

Inprimis the deceseds weareing Apparell and redy Money	£v	
Item 3 Cowes	£xii	
Item one Horse a Mare & a Colt	£xiii	
Item 2 Akers & 3 yards of Wheate and Rye	£iiii	xv^s
Item 3 yards of Oats		xx^s

Item one Aker & a half of Pease and Barley			xl^{s}	
Item 4er Akers & a halfe of Hopgrownd with the	)	£xlviii	x^{s}	
Stock of Hoppoles	)			
Item Hemp Flax & Beanes			xx^{s}	
Item Faggots & Wood in the yard and Hogtubs and	)	£iiii	xv^{s}	
Troughes & one Court & a Grinstone	)			
Item Tainters & v Akers of Grasse		£viii		
Item 2 Beds in the Mill Two Bolsters 2 Blankets &	)		xl^{s}	
Flocks & other things in the Mill	)			
Item 8 paire of Sheares and Handells and Stainge &	)			
2 Sherebords & Wayts and Skrues and Brushes and	)	£v	xv^{s}	
other things in the Shoppe	)			
Item in the Hall one Cubberd one Table one Forme,	)			
Two Iron Pots 2 joyned Stooles a Jack Six Chayres	)			
and 3 Fliches of Bacon & 16 peices of Pewter	)	£x	ii^{s}	vi^{d}
2 Pewter Candlesticks with the Brasse & all other	)			
things in the Hall				
Item in the Kitchen one Copper 2 Fatts one Hott	)			
Presse one Table Papers and the Pumpe & Skales &	)	£xv	vii^{s}	vi^{d}
Beames & other things & wayts	)			
Item in the Flockloft with other things			xliii^{s}	
Item in the Butteryes one Cheesepresse & 5	)	£iii	iii^{s}	vi^{d}
Drinkevessells 2 Pitchers 4er Tubs with other things	)			
Item in the Milkhowse one Table one Bacon Trough	)		xl^{s}	vi^{d}
14 Trayes & other things	)			
Item in the Oasthowse 2 Haires one Wheelborow	)		xxvi^{s}	
2 Braks & other things	)			
Item in the Hall Chamber one Bedstedle one Feth-	)			
erbed one Coverlett 2 Blankets 4er paire of Fine	)			
Sheets & one sheete 4er Fine Tableclothes 4er paire	)	£xi	xv^{s}	vi^{d}
of course Sheets 2 course Tablecloths one Cub-	)			
bardcloth 14 Napkins 4er Pillowbeeres	)			
Item in the Closets 8 pownds of Flax one paire	)		xxxv^{s}	vi^{d}
of stockcards with other things	)			
Item in the Owter Chamber 3 bedstedles 2 Chists	)	£v	iii^{s}	
with the Furniture belonging to the 3 Beds	)			
Item in the Inner Chamber one Bed with the	)	£iiii	ii^{s}	vi^{d}
Furniture thereunto belonging one Chist & 2 Boxes	)			
with Tow yarne				

Item the Lease & 2 Sacks & one Chist at the Towne & other things unseene & forgotten	£x		
Suma totalis	£ clxxiiii	xiiii^{s}	vi^{d}
Item owing to the decesed at the time of his death in doubtfull & desperat debts	£x		
Suma patet			

35

HUNT Parnell Widow
W. 30 Jul. 1666 prov. 15 Sep. 1666 PRS/W/8/108

Instructions given by Parnell Hunt of Seavenoakes widdow for the making of her last Will and Testament this 30th of July 1666
Item I doe make & ordain my loving Kingswoman Joane Hope Executrix of this my last will & Testament whom I desire to dispose of all my goods Stock & Estate whatsoever & to pay out foure score & tenn pounds to Henry Sewers being a debt upon bond & the residue to bee disposed of in manner & forme following
Item I doe give & devise unto my three Kinsmen John Hope James Hope & Thomas Hope sonnes unto my sayd Executrix ten pounds a peice to bee payd unto them within twelve months after my decease.
Item I give & bequeathe unto Penelope Hope daughter to my sayd Executrix ten pounds to bee payd unto her in like manner
Item I give and bequeathe unto Parnell Hye of Seale wife of Richard Hye the sume of fowrty shillings to bee payd unto her in like manner
Item I give & bequeath to Sarah Everest wife to Foll Everest of Chipsted the sume of twenty shillings to be payd her in like manner and I doe by this my will discharge her from a debt of fourty shillings which shee now oweth mee
Item I give & bequeath unto my brother Thomas Whitehead the sume of twenty shillings to bee payd unto him in like manner
Item I give & bequeath unto Joane Whitehead daughter to my brother Thomas Whitehead the sum of twenty shillings to bee payd to her in like manner
Item I give & bequeathe unto Thomas Whitehead & William Whitehead sonnes to my brother Thomas Whitehead the sume of twelve pence a peece to bee payd to them in like manner
Item I give unto Mary Parnell & Elizabeth & Forathy Daughters to my sayd Brother Tho. Whitehead twelve pence a peece to bee payd as above
Item I give unto Dorothy Daulton twelve pence to be paid in [like manner]
Item I give & bequeathe unto John Thomas Ann and Grace Sonnes and Daughters unto John Haynes of black Hall the sume of twelve pence to bee payd to each of them in like manner
Item I give & bequeath unto Margaret Raines & James Raines her sonne &

Joane Raines & Ann Raines her daughters the sume of twelve pence a peece to bee payd to them in like manner
Item I give & bequeath unto Ann Haynes wife to John Haynes the sume of twelve pence to bee payd to her in like manner
It. I doe give & devise to my sayd Executrix Joane Hope all the rest of my goods chattells cattels Stock moveables household stuff & utensells & debts whatsoever together with all my right title interest & terme of yeares yet to come & unexpired in that farme which I now use in lease from Right Worshipfull Dame Margarett Boswell towards the defraying my funerall charges & other debts & the Legacyes above mentioned.
Item I doe make & ordaine my two loveing friends Godhelp Couper of Grillins & Edmund Weston of Seavenoake overseers of this my last will & testament & doe desire them to see it performed in all poynts according to the true intent & meaning of it
That this is the true will of the Testatrix taken from her owne mouth the day & yeare above written & signed by her is Attested by us whose names are underwritten
The mark of Parnell Hunt
Margaret Boswell   Anthoine Fuller   Edm. Weston

36

HUNT Parnell   Widow
I. 14 Aug. 1666   prov. 15 Sep. 1666   PRS/I/8/120

A true and perfect Inventory of all and singuler the goods Cattell and Chattells of Parnel Hunt late of Blackhall in the parish of Sevenokes in the County of Kent widdow deceased taken and appaysed by Francis Hills of Seale in the said Countie of Kent yeoman and Godhelp Cooper of Seavenoke aforesaid yeoman the foureteenth day of August in the eighteenth yeare of the Raigne of our Soveraigne Lord Charles the second of England Scotland France and Ireland King Defendor of the faith etc. vizt.

	£	*s.*	*d.*
Inprimis in ready money	0.	2.	6.
In the Hall			
Item one greate Cupboard	1.	0.	0.
Item seaventeene dishes of pewter	1.	4.	0.
Item Two candlesticks and three dripping panns and foure spitts)	0.	12.	0.
Item one brasse pott thre brasse kettles and two Skilletts)	2.	0.	0.
Item two paire of Andirons a paire of potthookes and tonges)	0.	6.	0.

Item a Jacke and a fowling peece		0.	16.	8.
Item a table forme and thre chaires		0.	8.	0.
In the Buttery				
Item one Ironpott and a frying pan		0.	8.	0.
In the Milkehouse				
Item seaven milke bowles one great Iron pott two churnes and a Cooler	)	1.	0.	0.
In the other Buttery				
Item five drincke tubbs a cheese presse and an old halfe tubb	)	1.	0.	0.
In the Brewhouse and washhouse				
Item six tubs a little old furnace and three old payles		1.	10.	0.
Item two Iron kettles and a little pott		0.	15.	0.
In the low lodgeing roome				
Item two flockbeds and steddles with blancketts sheets and a Chest	)	2.	0.	0.
In the Parlour				
Item two small feather bedds with the Steddles sheetes blancketts and furniture	)	5.	0.	0.
Item six silver spoons & a silver bowle		4.	10.	0.
Item six paire of sheetes		2.	5.	0.
Item Two and Twenty peaces of linnen a Chest a Truncke a chaire and other things	)	2.	0.	0.
In the chamber over the entry				
Item one feather bedd and two boulsters and Steddle one flockbedd and blancketts	)	4.	0.	0.
Item seaven turkyworke Cushions		0.	14.	0.
Item a sideboard and a Carpett		0.	5.	0.
Item a presse and a Rugg		1.	0.	0.
Item two Joyntstooles foure leather chaires one other chaire and two Chests	)	1.	5.	0.
Item one Chest of lynnen		4.	0.	0.
In the Chamber over the little Parlour				
Item Twenty Stone of wooll		5.	0.	0.
Item a flockbedd and Steddle etc.		1.	0.	0.
In the Corne loft				
Item wheat mault oates and measures		3.	5.	0.
In the woodhowse				
Item one old Tubb		0.	10.	0.
In the Barnes				
Item Two hundred and Thirteene cop of oates at 3^s		31.	19.	0.
Item Fiftie five copp of wheate		13.	15.	0.
Item Thirtie six copp of oates & tears		4.	0.	0.

Item seaven load of Hay	7.	0.	0.
Item three load of Pease	3.	0.	0.
Item a waggon two ploughes three Harrowes and two old courts)	6.	0.	0.
Item nyne Hoggs	6.	10.	0.
Item six oxen	28.	00.	0.
Item nyne Cowes at fiftie shillings a peece	22.	10.	0.
Item three Colts and one Mare	11.	0.	0.
Item eight young bullocks	12.	0.	0.
Item one Hundred and sixteene sheep and lambs	40.	0.	0.
Item for old lumbar	1.	0.	0.
The sume is	234.	10.	2.

37

HARLING Richard Labourer
I. 20 Jun. 1666 prov. 30 Apr. 1666 [sic] PRS/I/8/18

An Inventary of all and singuler the Goods of Richard Harling late whilst he lived of the parish of Seavenoke in the County of Kent Labourer decesed Taken and prized the Twentieth day of June Anno Domini 1666 as followeth vizt.

Inprimis his weareing Apparell xxx^{s}.

Suma patet

38

TURK Robert
NW. 12 Aug. 1666 PRS/W/20/43

My mind and will is and I give unto my Two Brothers Thomas Turke and John Turke and to my Sister Phillip Ward Ten Pownds a peice And to the Children of my Brother Joseph Turke deceased And to all the Children of my said Brothers and Sister Twenty Shillings a peice, To be payd by my Wyfe whome I make Executrix of this my last Will and Testament.

39

RYGSBY Thomas Yeoman
NW. 30 Aug. 1666 prov. 29 Sep. 1666 PRS/W/14/69

Memorandum that on or about the Thirtieth day of August Ano Domini 1666 Thomas Rygsby the Elder of the parish of Seavenoke in the County of Kent yeoman being sicke in Body but of perfect mind and memory with an intent and purpose to dispose of his Estate spake theis words following vizt: I give unto my Sonne Thomas, All my Landes Goods and Estate whatsoever (He giveing Bond to pay to my Wyfe Jane his Mother Seaven Pownds a yeere dureing hir life) And also I give to the said Jane my Wyfe the Bed whereon I usually lye with all the Furniture thereto belonging. Theis words or the selfsame in effect he spake in the presence and heareing of William Wall yeoman and Thomas Tayler Butcher.
Will Wall Thomas Taylar

40

COGGAR John Yeoman
W. 23 Sep. 1666 prov. 27 Oct. 1666 PRS/W/3/236

In the Name of God Amen I John Coggar of the parish of Seavenoke in the Count of Kent yeoman being Sicke in Body but of perfect Mind and Memory (praysed be God therefore) Doe make and declare this my last Will and Testament In manner and forme following vizt: Inprimis I bequeath my Sowle to Allmight God whoe infused the same trusting thorough the Meritts and passion of Christ Jesus my blessed Redeemer to obtaine pardon for my Sinnes and of a Joyfull resurrection to life everlasting My Body I comitt to the Earth to be decently interred by my Executor hereafter named And as touching that Estate wherewith God hath blessed mee I dispose thereof as followeth Inprimis I nominate and appoint my Sonne John Executor of this my Last Will and Testament Item I give unto my Loveing wyfe Margaret the Moyety of all my Howshold goods whatsoever More I give unto hir Tenne Pownds a yeere dureing hir naturall life owt of the profits of my Messuages and Lands to be payed unto hir by my Executor half yeerly by equall porcions in liew and satisfaction of hir Right of Dower to my Said Lands and Tenements And for default of payment thereof within Fowerteene dayes after any halfe yeere after my decease It shalbe lawfull for hir to enter into any and every of my Messuages or Tenements or Lands and thereon to distreyne and the distresses there taken to retaine and keepe untill payment thereof be made togeither with all expences and charges More I give unto hir One Cow, Item I give unto my Grandchild John Berdsworth Sonne of my Daughter Edy Berdsworth Tenne Pownds of Lawfull Money of England to be payed unto him at his Age of Fifteene yeeres (yf he soe long live) Item to Thomas Berdsworth one other of hir Sonnes Five Pownds at his Age of

Fifteene yeeres (yf he soe long live) Item I give unto my Grandsonne John Hawes Sonne of my Daughter Mary One Annuity of Forty Shillings a yeere owt of my Lands and Tenements at Dibdin in the parish of Seavenoke to be payed unto him half yeerly by my sayd Executor, the first payment to beginne next half yeere after my Wife Margaret decease for and dureing the terme of his naturall life, Item I give unto my Five Grandchildren Mary, Anne Elizabeth Edy and Margaret Daughters of my Said Daughter Mary Five Pownds a peice at their severall Ages of Fifteene yeeres yf they soe long live, Item I give unto my Said Daughters Mary Hawse and Edy Berdsworth Tenne Pownds a peice to be payed unto them by my Executor within Twelve Moneths after my decease The rest and residue of all and singuler my Messuages and Tenements Lands and Hereditaments and All my Goods Cattle and Chattells whatsoever my Debts Legacyes and Funerall expences being payed I wholy give to my said Sonne and Executor desireing him to fullfill this my Will in all respects In witnesse whereof I have hereunto sett my hand and Seale (revokeing all former Wills by me made) and declareing this for my Last Will and Testament the Three and Twentieth day of September In the yeere of our Lord God One Thowsand Six Hundred Sixty and Six.
John Coggar his marke
Sealed and delivered and published and declared for his last Will and Testament in the presence of Chris Thomas
Thomas Playston his marke Thomas Giles his marke

41

FULLER Mary — Spinster
I. 22 Oct. 1666 — prov. 22 Oct. 1666 — PRS/I/6/62

An Inventary of the goods and Chattells of Mary Fuller late whilst shee lived of the parish of Seavenoke in the County of Kent Spinster decesed Taken the Two and Twentieth day of October Anno Domini 1666 as followeth vizt

Inprimis one Legacy Given hir by Thomas Fuller decesed	£xx
Suma patet	

42

COSIER Edward — Gentleman
W. 22 Jan. 1667 — prov. 18 June 1667 — PRS/W/3/237

In the name of God Amen I Edward Cosier of the parish of Seavenoke in the County of Kent, gent being weake in body but I praise god of perfect memory and understanding (revokeing all former wills) doe make and ordaine this my last will and testament in manner and forme following first I

give my soule into the hands of my blessed saviour Jesus Christ trusting in his meritts for eternall Salvacion my body I dispose to the earth to be buried by my Executor hereafter named with as little charge and Expence as cann be reasonably contrived Item I give and bequeath to the poore people of the Almesrow in Seavenoke tenn shillings to be by my Executor devided amoungest them all the rest of my estate both reall and personall whatsoever I give and bequeath unto my Loveing freind Mr. John Blome of Seavenoke aforesaid whom I make Executor of this my will in wittnesse whereof I have hereunto sett my hand and seale this two & twentieth Day of January Anno Domini 1666.
E.D.W. Cosier
Sealed signed and published by the said Edward Cosier to be his last will in the presence of Thomas Weston
The marke of John Staple

Memorandum before the sealeing and publishing of this will Mr. Edward Cosier did declare that his will and mind was that Mr George Bruere should have his purple Gowne and Mr. Thomas Weston his darke gray coate with Gold buttons and that Giles Law should have another coate and a paire of New shooes.
Wittnesse hereto Thomas Weston
The marke of John Staple

COSIER Edward Gentleman
I. 20 Mar. 1667 prov. 20 June 1667 PRS/I/3/99

An Inventary of all and singuler the goods and Chattelles of Edward Cosier late of Seavenoke in the Countie of Kent gent Deceased taken and appraised by William Allen aforesaid Mercer and Thomas Allen of the same Sadler the twentieth Day of March in the nyneteenth yeare of the raigne of our Soveraigne Lord Charles the second of England Scotland Fraunce and Ireland king Defendor of the faith etc Annoque Domini 1666

	£	*s.*	*d.*
Inprimis his weareing apparell and ready money in his purse	1:	10:	0
In his Bedchamber			
Item one Bedsteadle matt & cord	0:	10:	0
one featherbed two boulsters & two pillowes	3:	0:	0
three blanketts and one greene Rug	1:	4:	0
Curtaines and Vallance of Dorinx and Curtine roods	0:	10:	0
two joyned stooles a trunck and a Little table	0:	4:	0
one other sett of Curtaines and vallance of old striped stuff	0:	6:	8
one silver Cupp	0:	6:	0
a pewter Chamber pott	0:	2:	0

In his Dyning roome			
Item six leather Chaires	1:	4:	0
foure Chaires and foure stooles	0:	8:	0
one table and old cloath	0:	4:	0
Earthen weare	0:	1:	0
Two Andirons one Fire shovell a paire of tongs one slice one tosting iron one Gridiron and two peeces of iron and a paire of Bellowes	0:	5:	0
Two pictures and severall Escutchions	0:	6:	8
foure Cushions	0:	1:	4
one box with severall peeces of old Lynnen	0:	12:	0
one Deale Box	0:	2:	0
Seaven Cushions more	0:	7:	0
one paire of sheets and other parcells of Lynnen and two Chests	1:	15:	0
a Pott a Kettle & Bouldish	0:	3:	0
some old Lumber	0:	3:	4
Some total	13:	5:	0

44

STRINGER Edward Husbandman
W. 20 Apr. 1667 prov. 13 Jul. 1667 PRS/W/15/68

In the name of God Amen this seaven & twentieth day of May in the yeare of our Lord God one thousand six hundred sixtie & seaven I Edward Stringer of Seavenoke in the Countie of Kent Husbandman beeing sicke in Boddy but of perfect minde & memory thancks bee to Almighty God doe make and ordaine this my last will and Testament in manner and forme following first I commit my soule into the hands of Almightie God that gave it, And my body to bee decentlie buried according to the discretion of my Executrix Item I give and bequeath to my sonne Edward ten pounds to bee payd within foure years after my decease Item I give and bequeath to my sonne Thomas five pound to putt him out Apprentice and five pounds to bee payed him when hee shall ataine the age of one and twentie years Item I give and bequeath to my daughter Sara ten pounds to bee payed when shee shall ataine the age of one and twentie years or uppon her day of marriage which shall first happen, Item I give and bequeath to my daughter Margrett the wife of George Wood five shillings alsoe my will is that if any of my fore named Children dye before theire severall portions groe due then his or her portion (soe dyeing) to bee equally divided amongst the rest of my surviveing Children, Item all the rest of my goods Chattells & personall Estate I give and beequeath to Mary my beloved wife (she paying my debts and legacyes) whom I make and ordaine full and whole Executrix of this my last Will and Testament in witnes hereof I sett my hand & seale the day and yeare above written.
Edward Stringer
Witnes hereunto Tho: Chorley John Thornton Richard Cakott

45

STRINGER Edward — Husbandman
I. 20 June 1667 — prov. 21 Jul. 1667 — PRS/I/19/146

An Inventary of all and singuler the Goods & Chattells of Edward Stringer late whilst he lived of the parish of Seavenoke in the County of Kent husbandman decesed Taken and prized the Twentieth day of June Anno Domini 1667 By John Thornton and Richard Cackot as followeth vizt.

In the Hall			
Inprimis his weareing Apparell		xvi^{s}	
Item one old Joyned Table a forme a Settle a little Table & an old Cubbord		vi^{s}	viii^{d}
Item one litle paire of Andirons one Firepan a paire of Tongs & a paire of Pothangers		iii^{s}	
Item on Spitt one Dripping pan one Ketle one Chafing dish and some other small things		vi^{s}	iiii^{d}
Item 2 Pewter Dishes with other small peics of Pewter		v^{s}	
Suma		xxxvii^{s}	
In the Buttery			
Item 4er Beere Tubs one Bucking Tub & a Watertubb		x^{s}	
Suma patet			
In the Hall Chamber			
Item one Flockbed one Bolster one Straw bed one Coverlet & Blanket & an old paire of Curtens & Vallence		xii^{s}	vi^{d}
Item 6 paire of Towne Sheets one Tablecloth with other small peics of Linnen		xxx^{s}	
Item one Joyned Table & forme one Joyned Chest & a Joyned Presse		xx^{s}	
Suma	£iii	ii^{s}	vi^{d}
In the Chamber over the Shoppe			
Item one Flockbed & Bolster one Bedstead Matt & Cord & one old Chest & Box		xi^{s}	
Suma patet			
Withowt Dores			
Item 2 yong Hogs		xvi^{s}	
Item one Horse & 2 Mares	£iiii	iii^{s}	iiii^{d}
Item some Corne	£xv		

Item things unseene & forgotten			ii^s^	iiii^d^
Item an old Court			xvi^s^	
	Suma	£xx	i^s^	viii^d^
	Suma totalis)	£xxvi	viii^s^	ii^d^

46

SMITH Walter Gentleman

I. prov. 20 June 1667 prob. 4. 17293

An Inventary of all and singular the goods, chattells and credits of Walter Smith of Sevenoke in the county of Kent Gentleman deceased taken and appraised by William Allen of Sevenoaks aforesaid Mercer & Richard Rundall of the same Gardener Thomas Allen of the same. . .

	£	*s.*	*d.*
Inprimis his weareing apparell and ready money in his purse	10.	0.	0.
In the Parlor			
Item seaven Turky work chaires and six Turky worke stooles	5.	0.	0.
Item one old Turky worke Carpett	0.	15.	0.
Item six Cushions	0.	3.	0.
In the [? roome] behinde the Parlor			
Item one old Truncke and a greate deale Box	0.	4.	0.
Item one leaden Cistern weighes 26 lbs.	0.	13.	0.
In the Parlor Chamber			
Item one sett of purple Curtaines and valance with silke fring and lace and seaven knobs	4.	0.	0.
Item one feather Bedd one boulster twoe pillowes twoe blancketts and one Rugg	6.	0.	0.
Item twoe Sarge carpetts and six low Chaires of purple with covers to them and hangings to the roome of striped stuffe	3.	10.	0.
Item six greene purpetuany low chaires with covers and a sett of Curtaines and valance of the same	2.	15.	0.
Item a lookeing glass and a side table	0.	7.	0.
Item one low greene foote stoole a paire of Brasse Andirons a paire of Creepers fire shovell and Tongs	1.	2.	6
In the Chamber within the Parlor Chamber			
Item two feather bedds one feather boulster and two feather pillowes a Bedsteadle cord and matt and Curtaines roods two blancketts one coverlett one green Rugg with Curtaines and valance of old silke	9.	0.	0

Item Six greate peeces and two smale peeces of Verders hangings	1.	2.	6
Item one high Turky worke chaire and two high stooles of the same	0.	8.	0
Item twoe greate Trunckes	0.	13.	4
Item two paire of fine sheets and foure paire of other sheets	4.	10.	0
Item three flazen table cloathes and two dozen of flazen Napkins	3.	10.	0.
Item twoe towells three paire of pillowe beares one table cloath and one side board cloath and three course table cloathes and one dozen of Diaper Napkins	3.	5.	0.
In the Hall Chamber			
Item twoe chests one Chests of Drawers	1.	0.	0.
In the Chamber over the entry			
Item one Beddsteedle matt and cord and one little Chest	0.	12.	6.
In the Kitchin			
Item three spitts two Iron driping panns one iron Trencher knife two Iron forkes one Iron basting ladle and one Iron pott	1.	5.	0.
Item one greate brasse pott a little brasse pott a brasse pott chafer two brasse skillets one brasse kettle one brasse pann and a brasse chafing dish	2.	2.	6.
Item severall peeces of pewter weighes fourescore and five pounds at 12d per lb	4.	5.	0.
In the Hall			
Item one Turky worke stoole and twoe joynt stooles and one old wooden chaire a paire of iron Andirons and creepers & fireshovell and Tongs	0.	18.	0.
Item one Presse and in it a library of bookes	5.	0.	0.
In the Studdy within the Hall			
Item two cases of Drawers & one Deske	0.	10.	0.
Item two silver Tankerds one silver plate two silver sugar dishes one silver porringer thirteene silver spoones and one paire of silver snuffers	25.	0.	0.
Item six Bagges of Hopps weighes 15C 3 quarters at 50s per Cent	39.	7.	0.
Item one old Trunck	0.	3.	0.
In the Hopp Kilne			
Item Twenty Busshells of Cloverseed	10.	0.	0.
Item Three basketts for coales	0.	3.	0.

Item a parcell of Rough Hempe		0.	10.	0.
Without Doores				
Item one plow with a coulter and share one dunge court and one waggon one Harrow and one oxe yoke	)	2.	10.	0.
Item one Stack of Hay about eight load		10.	0.	0.
Item twoe young Hoggs		1.	0.	0.
Item twoe sadles with bridles and other furniture for horses	)	0.	10.	0.
In the Barne				
Item one parcell of Rye in the sheafe about foure copps	)	1.	10.	0.
Item one parcell of Oate straw		0.	6.	0.
Item a lease of the howse and lands late in the occupacion of Mr Walter Smith and the stack of Hoppoles on the ground and about the howse with several parcells of dung	)	80.	0.	0.
Item severall parcells of lumber about the howse		1.	3.	4.
The summe is		243.	11.	08.

J. Richardson

47

HAYNS John　　Cordwainer
W. 13 Jun. 1667　　prov. 13 Jul. 1667　　PRS/W/8/112

In the Name of god Amen I John Hayns of Seavenoke Cordwiner doe make & ordaine this My Last will & Testament as followeth I bequeth my Soule in to the hands of All-mitey god my maker & to Jesus Christ my Redemer Trusting in his merrits to be saved & my bodey to the erth to be berid in desent maner by my execeters Item I give unto my sonn Thomas Hayns Twenty pounds of Lawfull money to be paid by my exectters within ayer & aday after my deces Item I give unto my dafter Ann Hayns of Tenn pounds of Lafull mony to be paid hur within a Twelfmont & aday after my deceas by my executers

Item I give unto my dafter grace Hayns Twenty pounds of Lick Lawfull mony to be paid hur with in a twelfmont & a day by my executtors Allso I doe give unto my Loving wife Ann Haynes & to my sonn Johne Haynes All my stockes & goods excepting on bedstedell & bed & All that belongeth to it which I doe give unto my dafter grace to be delivered to hur forthwith after my decease by my execcuttors which is the bed that she ueseall layeth oupon & doe make & ordaine my Loving wife & my sonn Johne my hole execcattors of All my goods & Chattells equalley to be devided betwen them

Item my will Is that my sonn John shall have the lease of my farme holley to

hemselfe & All the monis upon band paying the legacis to his brother Thomas & his tow sisters as above expressed with in the tim set for the payment ther of Allso my will is that my wife shall have hur biding In the house during the tim of the leas & the paller holley to hursellf to log in this I doe make & ordaine to be my last will & Testement to which I have her unto set my hand & seall the thertenth day of June & in the yer of our Lord Chirst one Thowsand Six hundered Sixtey & Seven 1667
the marke of John Hayns the elder
Sealled & sined in the presents of Thomas Greene Daved Durtnall

48

HAYNS John — Cordwainer
I. 25 June 1667 — prov. 21 Jul. 1667 — PRS/I/8/50

An Inventary of all and singuler the Goods chattells and Credits of John Haynes thelder late of the parish of Seavenoke in the County of Kent Cordwyner decesed Taken and prized the Five and Twentieth day of June Anno Domini 1667 By Frances Hills thelder and David Durtnoll as followeth vizt:

In the Parlor		
Inprimis one Bedstedle with the Bed and all belongs thereto	£iii	
Item 3 Joyned Chists one plaine one a Cubberd a Table a Carpet & 4er Joyned Stooles		xL^{s}
Item 10 Pewter Dishes		xx^{s}
Suma	£vi	
In the Roome over the parlor		
Item 2 Bedstedles & one Truckle Bed with all the furniture thereto belonging	£iiii	
Suma patet		
In the Chamber over the Hall		
Item for Woll & Hempe		xxx^{s}
Item for Linen in the Chests	£iii	
Suma	£iiii.	x^{s}
In the Hall		
Item 2 Brasse Pots one Ketle two Chafers one Iron pot one Furnace		xxx^{s}
Item one Table 4er Chayres 4er Cushins one Jack 2 Spits one paire Pothooks 1 paire of Brand-irons		xx^{s}
Suma		L^{s}
In the Milkhowse and Brewhowse		
Item 3 Drinke Tubs 2 Keelers 12 Bowles one Cheese		

presse one Churne & 3 Brewing Tubs	)		xL^{s}
Item for Wheate Ry & Pease in the Howse			L^{s}
Suma £iiii	x^{s}		
In the Shoppe			
Item Leather Shoos & other Materials belonging to	)		
the Shop	)	£v	
Suma pate			
In the Barne			
Item the Corne in the Barne			xL^{s}
Item for the stock of hoppoles		£vi	
Item for 3 Akers of Wheate & rye		£vi	
Item for 7 Akers of oats		£vii	
Item for 2 Akers of Pease & one of Barley		£iii	x^{s}
Item for halfe an Aker of Teares & 4er Akers & a	)		
half of Buck	)	£v	
Item redy money in his Purse & for the deceseds	)		
wearing Apparel	)	£iii	
Item for 5 Milch Cowes		£xx	
Item one Mare		£iii	
Item 20 Shepe		£vi	
Item 9 Lambs			xxvii^{s}
Item 1 Sow 7 Pigs			xxiiii^{s}
Item 2 Barrow hogs			xxx^{s}
Item old Lumber within dores & without			xxx^{s}
Suma		£Lxvii	
Suma Totalis		£Lxxxiii	x^{s}

49

HARMON Samuel Weaver
NW. 14 Nov. 1667 prov. 29 June 1668 PRS/W/8/117

Memorandum that on or about the Foureteenth day of November Anno Domini 1667 Samuell Harman of the parish of Seavenoke in the County of Kent Weaver being of perfect mind and memory with an intent and purpose to dispose of his Estate and make his Will spake theis words following vizt he gave his Loome and all that belongd to it To Thomas Harman his Eldest Sonne And that all the residue of his estate should be equally divided amongest all his Children Theis words or the self same in effect he spake in the presence and heareing of Thomas Haynes and Edward Gybbins.

50

HARMON Samuel Weaver
I. 20 Nov. 1667 PRS/I/8/21

An Inventary of all & singuler the goods and chattells & Credits of Samuell Harman late whilst he lived of the parish of Seavenoke in the County of Kent Weaver decesed Taken & prized the xxth day of November Anno Domini 1667 By Thomas Haynes and Edward Gybbons as followeth vizt.

Inprimis the deceseds Wearing Apparell		x^{s}	
Item 3 old Beds with the furniture	£iiii	v^{s}	
Item 2 Joyned Chists & a Trunke		xx^{s}	
Item one Box		v^{s}	
Item a Bunting Hutch & a Table		xi^{s}	
Item a Cubberd		xviii^{s}	
Item a Table		xii^{s}	
Item one Pewter Dish & a Saltseller		ii^{s}	
Item i Spit a Pan & a Chopping Knife		i^{s}	vi^{d}
Item 2 Brandirons & Pothook Fire shovell & Tongs) an Iron Mortar & Pestle)		viii^{s}	
Item a Brasse Pot Pestle & Mortar & Chafer		xiiii^{s}	
Item a Ketle a Pot a Skymer & a Warming pan		xxiiii^{s}	
Item 2 dozen of Trenchers a Bole & a Tray			xii^{d}
Item Linnen		xxxv^{s}	
Item 3 Chayres & a litle Table		iiii^{s}	
Item the Loome with thappurtences		xxx^{s}	
Suma totalis	£xiiii	vi^{d}	
Item owing to the decesed one Doubtfull debt upon) Bond by John & Thomas Symons)	£xx		
Suma patet			

51

SKYNNER Robert
W. 21 Dec. 1667 prov. 23 Jan. 1669 PRS/W/15/80

In the name of God Amen I Robert Skynner of the parish of Seavenoke in the County of Kent being well in memory thanks bee to God for it, Doe make and ordaine this my last Will and Testament
Imprimis I bequeath my Sowle to God that gave it hopeing thorough Jesus Christ to have remission of all my Sinnes And my Body to bee buryed by the discretion of my Executrix, Item I give and bequeath unto my Two Sonnes Richard and Robert and to their Heires for ever equaly to be devided that Howse and Land and premisses where my Sonne Richard now dwelleth lying

and being in Penshurst. Item I give unto my Sonne Thomas that Howse and Land which Bartholomew Wood now useth caled the George in Seavenoke to have it for ever to him and his Heires Seaven yeeres after my decease, Item I give unto my Dafters Elizabeth and Mary and Katherin and Dorathy and Frances the Sum of Twelfe pence apeice Item I give unto Sara my Dafter whom I make my sole Executrix That Howse and Land wherein I now live and all the premises thereunto belonging, shee paying my Debts and Legacyes, This my last Will and Testament I sett my Hand and Seale unto it this One and Twentieth day of December 1667 One Thowsand Six Hundred Sixty and Seaven
The marke of Robert Skyner
Witnesseth hereunto John Thornton Henry Swaysland

52

SKINNER Robert
I. 13 Jan. 1669 prov. 28 Jan. 1669 PRS/I/19/50

An Inventory of all and Singuler the Goods & Chattles of Robert Skynner late of the parish of Seavenokes in the County of Kent taken and appraised the thirteenth day of January in the twentieth yeare of the raigne of our Soveraign Lord Charles the Second by the grace of God King of England, Scotland, Fraunce and Ireland, Defender of the faith etc by William Allen of Seavenoke aforesaid Mercer and Thomas Wheeler of the same Tailor as followeth (vizt) Annoque Domini 1668

	£	*s.*	*d.*
Inprimis ready money in his purse and his weareing apparrell	04.	00.	00.
In the Hall			
Item One Table a forme and five Chaires and three Cushions	00.	12.	00.
Item two Spinning Wheeles and three joyned Stooles	00.	05.	06.
Item eighteene peeces of pewter greate and Smale	01.	10.	00.
Item one paire of pewter Candlestickes three pewter potts & Seaventeene Spoones	00.	05.	06.
Item two Iron potts one Iron Kettle two brasse Kettles one brasse and three brasse Skilletts	01.	15.	00.
Item Seaverall small peeces of woodden ware and an old Court Cupboard	00.	08.	00.
Item One warmeing pann one Spitt a Gridiron a Jack fire pann Andirons tongs and bellowes an	01.	10.	00.

Iron backe and pothangers and a frieing pann				
Item two bibles and three other bookes		00.	03.	04.
In the Parlor				
Item One Table		00.	10.	00.
In the Wellhouse				
Item one Buckett one Rope		00.	05.	00.
Item One brewing tubb one Bucking tubb one powdering tubb two Keelers and one other tubb	)	01.	00.	00.
Item two pailes one Sive a Shovell and spade and some other Lumber	)	00.	01.	06.
In the Buttery				
Item five smale tubbs a Stalder a forme and Some Lumber	)	00.	13.	04.
In the Hall Chamber				
Item One Chest one Truncke a halfe bushell a halfe pecke and a Baskett	)	00.	10.	00.
Item five Corne Sackes and five baggs and an Ashcloath	)	01.	00.	00.
In the Parlor Chamber				
Item One Bedstead, curtaines and valance curtaine rodds matt & Cord	)	01.	00.	00.
Item One feather bed one boulster two pillowes two blancketts and a Coverlett	)	03.	03.	04.
Item three Smale Chests and one Smale truncke		00.	08.	06.
Item One Old Buffe Coate		00.	08.	00.
Item Six paire of Sheetes and one odd Sheete		01.	12.	06.
Item One Dozen and a halfe of Napkins eight towells foure table Cloathes and two pillow coates	)	01.	03.	06.
In the farther Chamber				
Item One Trundle Bedstead flockbed one boulster a matt and Cord one blanckett and a Coverlett	)	00.	16.	00.
Item foureteene pound of Lynnen Yarne and a peece of new Cloath	)	00.	16.	06.
Without Doores				
Item two Cord of Wood and foure Hundred of Faggotts	)	03.	05.	00.
Suma totalis		27.	02.	06.

53

THORNTON John Innholder
W. 24 Dec. 1667 prov. 20 Aug. 1668 PRS/W/16/186

In the Name of God Amen, I John Thornton of Seavenoke in the Countie of Kent, Inholder This foure and twentieth day of December in the yeare of our Lord one thousand six hundred sixtie and seaven, Beeing in bodily health and of perfect minde and memory thancks bee to Almighty God for it, yett knowing and well considering the frailtie of this life and the certaintie of death, doe make and ordaine this my last Will and Testament in maner and forme following, First I committ my soull into the hands of God as into the hands of a faithfull Creator And my Body to the earth to bee decently buried, trusting through the alone merrits of my Saviour Jesus Christ to have remission and forgiveness of all my sinns, Item I give to the poore of the parish of Seavenoke twentie shillings to bee distributed according to the discretion of my Executor Item I give and bequeath to my daughter Francis now wife of Samuell Weller, And to her heirs for ever, Those three Tennaments with the Gardens and Backsides thereto belonging where James Walter, Thomas Martin and John West or theire Assignes now dwell, Item I give and bequeath to my daughter Jane now wife of Henery Soan and to her heirs for ever, All that Tennament Backside and Garden thereto belonging where Peeter Durence or his Assignes dwell Item I give and bequeath to my daughter Lucie Thornton And to her heirs for ever, All that Messuage or Tennament with the Garden and Backside thereto belonging where John Small or his Assignes now dwell, And alsoe that Tennament with the Garden and Backside thereto belonging where James Browne or his Assignes now dwell, which I purchased of Elizabeth Allen widdow, Item I give and bequeath to my Sonne John Thornton And to his heirs for ever All those Messuages land and Tennaments which I purchased of Richard Thomas the Hopkelns onlie excepted for ninteen years for the use onlie of my Executor, Item I give and bequeath to my servant Rachell Craft, or to her Assignes dureing her naturall life, if shee continue to live with mee till my death All that Messuage Backside and Garden thereto belonging where John Medherst or his Assignes now dwell, Item I give and bequeath to my Sonne John Thornton And to his heirs forever Those three Tennaments with the Gardens and Backsides thereto belonging which I purchased of William Huchins where John Medherst, Widdow Merrium and William Gyles or theire Assignes now dwell except that where John Medhurst liveth dureing the naturall life of my servant Rachell Craft as before exprest, provided that my Sonne John doe releace my Sonne Robert of and from any Challinge Claime right title or Interest which hee the said John hath or may have to my house att Tunbridge given mee my Ant Richison, Which if hee refuse to doe then my Will and meaning is that those three tennaments which I purchased of the said William Huchins shall bee and remain to my Sonne Robert and to his heirs for ever, Item my Will and meaning is that my Mother shall have eight pounds by the yeare payed her quarterly every quarter dureing her naturall life, the one half to bee Issueing out of the land and Tennaments given to my

Sonne John, And the other half to bee payed by my Sonne Robert, Whom I make sole Executor of this my last Will and Testament, And doe give him all the rest of my Estate reall and personall which is not above mentioned hee paying my debts and legacies in Witness whereof I have hereunto sett my hand and seale.
John Thornton
Witnes hereunto Tho: Chorley   Henry Swaysland

54

THORNTON John   Innholder
I. 24 June 1668   prov. 21 Aug. 1668   PRS/I/20/20

An Inventary of all and singuler the goods chattells & Credits of John Thornton late whilst he lived of the parish of Seavenoke in the County of Kent Inholder decesed Taken and praysed the Fower & Twentieth day of July Annoque Domini 1668 by Richard Cackott and John Berdsworth as followeth vizt.

Inprimis redy Money in his Purse		x^{s}
Item his Wearing Apparell	£iii	
Suma	£iii	x^{s}
In the Kitchen		
Item one Iron Back 1 paire of Pothangers i paire of Iron Racks i Iron to lay before the Fire i Creepe one Fire pan 2 paire of Tongs i Cleaver i Chopping Knife i Jack & that belongs to it 1 tosting Iron 7 spits 2 Iron Dripping pans 1 Leaden Wayte & 1 Grid iron		xl^{s}
Item 3 paire of Pothooks 5 Iron potts 3 Iron Kettles i Frying pan one Smothing Iron & Heaters		xxx^{s}
Item 16 Pewter Flaggons 8 Wine Quart pots 3 halfe pint pots one pottle Wyne pott i Quarter pott 7 Chamberpots		xxxviii^{s}
Item i Nest of Drawers one Settle i Glasse Cage 5 old Chayres 1 old Chest i Chafing dish one Ward Bill one Pitchforke 2 old Gallons		xxii^{s}
Suma	£vi	x^{s}
In the Sellar		
Item 16 Buts & Hogheads 6 Stalders 4er small Trundels 5 Stalders 3 Powdring Tubs 2 great ones 1 little one	£iii	x^{s}
Suma patet		

	£	s	d
In the Litle Parlor			
Item 1 old Setle 1 Table & forme 2 Chayres i Fireback 1 Curten & Rodd		xviii^{s}	
In the Hall			
Item 2 old Cubbers 2 old Chests i Table 1 Leather Chayre 3 Flag bottomed Chayres		x^{s}	
Suma patet			
In the Great Parlor			
Item 3 Iron Cobirons 1 paire of Creepers 1 paire of Bellowes 3 Wodden Chayres 2 Chests 1 old Cubberd 1 Table 2 Formes 1 old Court Cubberd 1 Bedsted Curtens & Vallence 2 Bolsters 1 Coverlet & blancket Mat & Cords		L^{s}	
Suma patet			
In the old parlor			
Item 2 old Tables 1 old Forme 1 old Chest 1 old Cuberd i old Tray 1 Bucking Keeler & parcell of hopbegging yarne and 2 hanging Shelves		xxx^{s}	
Item 1 Fetherbed 1 Flockbed 1 fether & Flockbolster 1 Coverlet & Blankett 2 bolsters 1 Feather & 1 Flock	£iii		
Suma	£iiii.	x.^{s}	
In the Falcon Chamber			
Item 1 Iron Back 1 paire of fireirons 5 Chayres 4er Joyned Stooles 1 side Cubberd i Picture & 1 Table		xxxviii^{s}	
Item one high Bedstedle Matt & Cord Curtens & Vallence Truckle Bedstedle Mat & Cord 1 Featherbed 1 Feather bolster 1 Flockbed 3 Flockbolsters & 1 old Rug 1 old Coverlet & 1 old Blankett	£vi	iii^{s}	iiii^{d}
Suma	£viiii	i^{s}	iiii^{d}
In the Boordes end Chamber			
Item long Table 2 Formes 5 Chayres 1 pair of Andirons		xxx^{s}	ix^{d}
Item 1 high Bedstedle Matt & Cords 1 low Bedstedle Mat & Cords 1 Feather bed & Feather bolster 1 Flock bed 3 Flock bolsters 1 Flock bed 3 Curtens & Vallence 2 old Covelets		xl^{s}	
Item 1 Feather bed 1 Flock bed 1 Curten & 2 Featherbolsters 1 Blanket 1 Coverlet 1 Flockbed 1 Coverlet 1 Cubberd cloth		xxxviii^{s}	
Suma	£v	viii^{s}	ix^{d}
In the Bull Chamber			
Item 1 paire of Iron Creepers 1 paire of Brasse Andirons 1 Fire shovell 1 paire of Tongs 1 Drawing Table 1 plaine Table 3 joyned stooles 3 Lether		xl^{s}	iiii^{d}

	£	s	d
stooles 3 Lether Chayres 2 low Covered Stooles 2 Flat bottomed Chayres 1 joyned Chayre 1 Side Cubberd			
Item 1 Bedstedle Matt & Cords 1 Feather bed 1 Feather bolster 2 Fether pillowes 1 Window Curten & Rod 1 Carpet	£v	x^s	vi^d
In the Crowne Chamber			
Item 1 Iron Back 1 Creeper 2 Tables 4er leather Stooles 1 Joynt Stoole 1 side Cuberd 2 Joint Chayres 1 Joint Chest 2 Flat bottomed Chayres		xxxviiii^s	vi^d
Item 1 high & 1 low Bedstedle Mat & Cord 1 Suite of Curtens & Vallence 1 Fether bed 1 Fetherbolster 2 Fether pillowes 1 old Flockbed 2 Blankets 1 Rug	£vi	xv^s	
Item more in the Crowne Chamber			
1 High bed Matt & Cord Curtens & Vallence 1 Fetherbed 2 Fether pillowes 1 Rug & blanket	£iiii	xviii^s	
Item 11 Silver Spoones 2 small Silver Tasters 1 small Silver Boll 1 larger Silver Boll	£iiii	x^s	
Item 1 paire of holland sheets 6 paires Flaxen Sheets 1 Diaper Tablecloth 1 sidebordcloth 1 dozen of Napkins & i Towell	£vi		
Item 12 fine Tableclothes 4er paire of Pillow beeres 4er dozen of fine Napkins 16 ordinary Napkins & 4er Fine Towells	£iii	x^s	
Item 44 pewter Dishes great & small 2 Pewter Basins 2 paire of pewter Candlesticks 1 pewter Tankard 13 pewter Saucers 15 Plats 6 Pooringers 3 Salts	£v	i^s	vi^d
2 py plats & 1 pewter Ewer			
Item on the Stayres head 1 Bedstedle Matt & Cord 1 old Chest & 1 old Trunke		v^s	
Suma	£xxxii.	xviii^s	
In the Canopy Chamber			
Item 2 Bedstedles Matts & Cords 1 old Table 1 Creeper 1 paire of Tongs 1 old Sidebord & 1 Carpet 1 paire of Curtens & Vallence		xxv^s	
Suma patet			
In the Kitchen Chamber			
Item 1 Brasse pan 6 Brasse Skillets 4er Warmeing pans 2 litle brasse skillets 3 brasse Skymers 2 brasse Ladles 1 brasse Chafing dish 1 Sawcepan 1 brasse Cullinder 1 Iron Forke 1 Apple Roster & 1 Tinne Roster 1 Brasse pan		l^s	

Item 2 high Bedsteds Matts & Cords 2 paire of Curtens & Vallence 2 Fetherbeds 2 Fether bolsters 2 Blankets 2 old Rugs 1 Coverlet & 1 Window Curton	£viii		
Item 1 Presse for Clothes 2 Joyned Chests 2 old Chests 3 Chayres 2 old Stooles & 1 old Wicker Basket		xxx^{s}	vi^{d}
Suma	£xii	vi^{d}	
In the Kitchen Chamber			
Item 26 paire & 1 Sheete 10 Pillowbeeres 12 Towells 1 Corse Tablecloth 11 Course Napkins more 16 course Napkins & 1 Course Towell	£xvii	iii^{s}	
Item 22 Cushins		iiii^{s}	vi^{d}
Item for a Remnant of hops		xxx^{s}	
Item for a small parcel of Flax		xv^{s}	
Item about 4er Akers of Oats upon the Grownd	£iiii		
Item for the Stock of Hopoles upon the Hopgrownd	£xxxiii		
Item for Lumber in the Howse & things unseene & forgotten		xx^{s}	
Suma	£lvii	xii^{s}	vi^{d}
Suma totalis	£cxlvii	xix^{s}	xi^{d}

55

EVEREST William — Tailor
W. 2 Mar. 1668 — prov. 5 Dec. 1668 — PRS/W/5/170

In the name of God Amen; I William Everest of Seavenoke In the County of Kent Taylor; being Weake in body but thankes bee to Allmighty God of Good and perfecte Memory, doe uppon this Second, Day of March Anno domini 1667 make and ordaine this My Last Will and Testamente in Maner, and forme following; First I Commend my Soule to God that Gave It Trusting Thorrough the Merrits of Jesus Christ My Saviour to receive pardon and remition of all my Sinns and to Inherit Eternall life; My Body to the Earth, to bee buried att the discretion of my Executrix heare after named; And for those Worldly Goods God hath Blessed me withall I Bestow as Followeth; Item I give to my Sone William Everest the Sum of Twenty pounds in Money; Dew to Mee one band of John Thornton; to bee payd him after My Decease; together with all the thinges Appertaining to My Trade in My Shope, as My Shopebord and other thinges I also Give to My Sayd Sone William Everest that parcell of Land, Commonly Called Vablands Leying in this parish of Seavenoakes neare Blackhall; being by estimation near one Acer More or Lesse; With the Stocke of Polls thereone; And A parsell of Dunge Leying in the Lane; neare the Same; and also about twenty Boshels of Colls Mor or lesse Lent My Brother John Coulerd; the Sayd Land I Give to him and the heires of his body Lawfully begotten; and for want of Such Ishew; to My Sone Danill Everest; hee the Sayd William or the sayd Danill or the heirs of them; paying of the same; to My sone John Everest the Some of thre pounds in money Within one Month after My Decease; and unto John Everest Sone of My sayd Sone John Everest the Sume of five pounds; at his respective Age of one and twenty years; Paying Also to My Dafter Anne Everest the Sum of fifteen pounds in thre months after My Decease; And unto My Sone Petter Everest the licke Sum of Fifteen pounds Soe soon as he shall attaine the Age of one and twenty years; and to My Sone Frances Everest the Sum of Fifteen pounds att his respective age of one and twenty years; and to My Sone Danill Everest the Sume of fifteen pounds att his respective age of one and twenty years; and He My Sayd Sone William Also to bringe up My Sone Danill; Item all the remaynder of My Goods Houshould stufe Debts bonds Bills Money & My Parte of and In A Parsel of Hops Bettwen Mee and My Brother in Law John Coulerd and all beloing to me or which shall belonge to Me at the time of My Decease and not before Given; together with My Parte in and off the Leasse of Ceirtaine hopp-ground; in Leasse to My Sayd Brother Coulerd; And Mee My Parte of the profitt therof arising or Which Shall arise theron; And also My Parte of the Stocke of Polls thereon; My Debts first payd and funerall ritts Discharged; I Give and Bequeath to My Loving Wife; (Whom I Make the Sole and only Executrix of this My last Will) Shee bringing up and Educating My thre younger Children (to witt) Dorithy Margaret and Percnall, and shee paying to My two Dafters Dorithy Everest and Margaret Everest fifteen pounds apeece att or soe Soon as they Shall Attaine the age of twenty years; and to My Sone Percvall Everest the Some of fifteen pounds att his respective age of one and twenty years; I also Give to My Loving Wife; My Dwelling house in Seavenoaks; Deuring her naturall Life; and after har Decease to My Sone William Everest; and to the heirs of his body Lawfully begotten; and for Want of Such Isheu; to My Younger Sone Percnall Everest; Provided allways and It is My Mind and Will that the Cubbod in the hall and the Jacke; and the plate behind the fire thear and the furnace in the Chichen Shall not bee Aprized to the Executrix but bee and Remayne to the House; Lastly I doe intreate My Loving freind Mr. William Allen, And My Loving Brother John Everest to bee overseers of this My Will; to Assiste my Loving Wife in the performance of the same; and for every Day they shall spend; in and aboute the Same, My Minde and Will is; that besid ther expences borne they shall have two shillinges six pence a pece; for their paines; In Wittnesse Whereof to this My Testement and last Will I the sayd William Everest have Subscribed My Marke and put to My Seale the day and yeare first above Writen; Sealed Published and Declared In the presence of

Richard Cakott — Georg Norize — Isaack Day

The Marke of William Everest

56

EVEREST William　　Tailor
I. 26 Nov. 1668　　prov. 7 Jan. 1669　　PRS/I/5/21

An Inventary of all and singuler the Goods Chattels and Credits of William Everest late whilst he lived of the parish of Seavenoke in the County of Kent Tayler deceased Taken and praysed the xxvith day of November Annoque Domini 1668 By Richard Cockett and William Allen as followeth vizt.

	£	s	d
Inprimis the deceaseds wearing Apparell and redy Money in his Purse		xl^{s}	
Item 16 paire of Sheets with Pillowcoats Napkins and Tableclothes	£x		
Item in the Chamber over the Hall 2 Bedstedles with Curtens and Vallence and Beds with thappurtenences belonging	£viii		
Item one Table 2 Chests 3 old Stooles 2 litle Andirons 2 Cushins		xviii^{s}	
Item in the Chamber over the Shoppe one high Bed one Trucklebed with 2 Beds and Furniture belonging to them with Bolsters Coverlets & Pillowes	£iiii	x^{s}	
Item I Table 4er Chests one Forme 2 Stooles & 2 Cushins		xxvi^{s}	
Item in the Clossett one dozen & a halfe of Pewter with some small peices & spoones & salts & Candlesticks	£iii	xxx^{s}	iiii^{d}
Item in the Garret 2 Flaskets with other Lumber		vi^{s}	viii^{d}
Item in the Hall 2 Tables one Settle 4er Chayres & 2 Stooles		xviii^{s}	
Item in the Washowse 4er Pots 3 Kettles 4er Skillets with 3 Trayes & small Lumber		xxxiii^{s}	
Item in the Buttery 7 small Drinke Tubs & 2 Powdring Tubbes		xxii^{s}	
Item in the Bakehowse a Meale Tubbe with some other small Lumber		vi^{s}	viii^{d}

Item certaine Hoppes with the deceseds part of the Stock of Hoppoles	£xx		
Item Debts owing to the decesed at the time of his death	£xxxii		
Suma Totalis	£lxxxv	xviii^s^	ii^d^

57

STEVENSON Edward — Husbandman
W. 12 April 1668 — prov. 15 June 1668 — PRS/W/15/72

In the name of God Amen I Edward Steevenson of Sevenoaks in the County of Kent husbondman being Aged and infirme in body but of sound and perfect minde and memory thanks be given unto God therefore: And being mindfull of my Last End and desirous to settle that Estate as it hath plesed god in mercy to Lend me doe make and Ordaine this my Last will and Testament in maner and forme following. vizt first I Comitt and Comend my spirit into the hands of God and my body to be buried by the descresion of my Beloved frinds which I ordaine to be my overseeres which I under shall menstion Item I give and bequeth unto Margarett Joy my daughter five shillings of Lawfull mony of England Item I give unto James Winset of Yalding in the said County of Kent husbondman my sone In Law Twelve pence of Lawfull mony of England and All the Rest of my goods and Chatells & Cattell and Redy mony and housold stuff and movabls whatsoever not heare in before given And bequethed my debts Legises funerall Expences being first paid satisfied and discharged: I give and bequeath unto my three grandChildren After my decese: my will and mind is as foloweth (vizt) I give unto them All the Remainder of my Estat Equally to be devided unto theme when they shall Come to aComplish the Age of one and twenty years or other wis at the day of marig which first shall Come and if it shall hapen that any one or mor shall dy before they shall aComplish the time my will and mind is that it shall Returne to be devided to the survivours Remaning of him or them the names of which I doe heare Expres vizt Sarah Bound Steeven bound and mary bound my three grand Children to be sole Executors which I doe apoynt to have my Estate to be Equally devided as above said and further mor I nominat thes my overseer whome I Comit the prosicution of this my will that is to say I apoynt William Fuller of the parish Tunbridge Robert Pelling of Etonbridg and John Jeffery of Sevenoks Overseers of this my Last will and Testament whome I doe Impresure To take Care that this my will be Truly Executed acording to the tru mening of it and farther I doe apoynt and ordayne that After my buriall what my Estate amounteth to after my Funirall Charges & debts & Leges be paid I desire my good frinds my overseers to make the best Improvement to pay unto my three grand Children the Intrest that they shall make of it which is Twelvence pence in the pound if they shall soe obtain for it untill they shall aComplish the time abovesaid which I doe Apoynt thes my three overseer to see that my

Children be not deprived of this my Estat to be desposed as abovesaid In wittnes herof I have set my hand and sealle The twelveth day of Aprill In the yeare of Our Lord on Thousand six hundred sixty and Eight this was enterlined before the Enseling herof
The mark of Edward Seevenson
Signed sealed and published in the presence of Tho Broad
John Wallis

58

GILL Alice Widow
W. 18 Jun. 1668 prov. 23 Oct. 1668 PRS/W/7/60

In the name of God Amen, I Ales Gill of Sen-oks June 18th 1668, being in perfect memorie doe bequeath my soule to God, whoe gave it me, & my body to the grave to be decently buried. Item I will and bequeath to Mary Tomsonne one ringe with a posie gods providence is our inheritance, and a payer of flaxan sheets. Item I bequeath to Ales Thomsonne one payer of flaxen sheetes. Item I will to the other six children of Thomsonne which were by my former husbande one pound or twenty shillings a peice or each of them one yeare after my decease. I give to George Gill five pounds one year after my decease. Item I give to John Gill five pounds one yeare after my decease/ Item I will and give to Cicilie Jenkins five pounds sixe monthes after my death. Item Mary Browne five pounds one month after my death. Item I give to Tamasin Weston one morhair petticote, my best gowne, and forty shillings. Item I give to Mother Ridges 20^s one month after my death. Item I give the widow Merriam 20^s one month after my death. Item I give to the Widow Butterfielde 20^s to be paide one month after my death. I will and bequeath thre pounds to be distributed to my executors discretion. Item I give to Miss Boss senior one small ring. Item I give to Goodwife Murchin my nurse my ordinaire wearing apparell as one westcoate and twoe petticoates, and 20^s in money. Item I give unto Oliver Smith the summe of five pounds to be paide one yeare after my decease. Item I ordaine and constitute Oliver Theobalde of Sen-oks Physitian sole executor of this my last will and testament whereonto I have set my hand and seale the day and yeare above written:-
Alic Gill
Witnes John Theobald Thomas Weston

59

GILL Alice Widow
I. 3 Sep. 1668 prov. 28 Sept. 1668 PRS/I/7/17

An Inventary of all and singuler the goods Chattles and debts of Alice Gill late of Seavenoke in the County of Kent widdowe Deceased taken and appraized the third day of September in the 20th yeare of the Raigne of our Soveraigne Lord King Charles the Second etc Annoque Domini 1668

Inprimis her wearing Apparrel and money in her purse	£xv		
In the Hall			
Item 1 feather bed 3 feather pillowes 3 feather boulsters 1 old flock bedd with a bedsteddle, matt Cord, Curtaines and vallence, 2 blancketts 1 Coverlett one small featherbed & bolster 1 Flock bolster and pillowe one blanckett & 2 coverletts with a trundle, bedstedle, Matt & Cord & Curtaine Rodds	£vii	x^{s}	
Item 1 payre of brasse Andirons 1 payre of Creepers 2 warming panns fire shovell and Tongs 4 pewter dishes 3 pewter pottes 3 pewter Salts five pewter porringers 1 glasse Cupboard 1 smale Trunke with Severall peeces of old Lynen, 15 payre of old Sheetes 4 boxes 1 Trunke & 3 Chests Curtaine Rods bellowes and other lumber	£iiii	i^{s}	vi^{d}
In the old Chamber			
Item 1 old bed 8 small pillowes 4 old Blancketts 2 Coverletts and 1 old Rugg some peeces and other Lumber about the Roome	£v		
In the Hall			
Item one forme 1 table 1 fly Cupboard 1 Neading Trough five Chaires 3 Stooles 1 Jacke 2 Spitts Andirons Fireshovell bellowes Tongs pothangers Shelves Kettle brasse pott 5 Skilletts 1 other small Kettle 2 latten dripping panns and other Lumber	£ii	ix^{s}	
In the Shopp			
Item the Shopp goodes	£vi	x^{s}	
Item Things forgotten vizt one Silver Bowle and one silver spoone	£ii	x^{s}	
Summa totalis huius Inventarii	£XLiii–vi^{d}		

60

JOHNSON George
I. 15 Jul. 1668 prov. 30 Jul. 1668 PRS/I./10/23

A true and perfect Inventory of all & singuler the goods and Chattells of George Johnson late of Seavenoke in the County of Kent deceased taken and appraised the fifteenth Day of July One Thousand six Hundred sixtie & eight by William Allen of Seavenoke in the County of Kent Mercer Richard Cackott of the same Cordwayner & Phillipp Ridges of the same Brasier as followeth:

	£.	*s.*	*d.*
Inprimis ready money in his purse	00.	01.	00.
Item his weareing apparrell	00.	13.	04.
In the Hall:			
Item one greate joyned Cupboard	01.	00.	00.
Item one Drawing Table	01.	00.	00.
Item a pewter still and bottome	00.	10.	00.
Item a brasse greate Kettle	00.	05.	00.
Item a little brasse Kettle	00.	01.	06.
Item a brasse pann	00.	06.	08.
Item a brasse Chaffing dish	00.	01.	00.
Item a brasse pott	00.	02.	00.
Item a brasse morter and Pessle	00.	02.	06.
Item an Iron worme Jacke and twoe Pulles	00.	06.	08.
Item an Iron Kettle	00.	05.	06.
Item two dish plates	00.	00.	08.
Item a tinn Candlesticke	00.	00.	06.
Item two pales	00.	01.	00.
Item a flaskett	00.	01.	02.
Item a tinn Dripping pann	00.	01.	04.
Item eleaven dishes of pewter greate and smale six pewter porringers a pewter Flaggon a pewter candlesticke and foure Sawcers about 30 lb.	01.	10.	00.
Item two low wright Stooles	00.	02.	00.
Item two Spitts	00.	01.	06.
Item one little table two leather chaires a low joynt stoole a high joynt stoole a chaire and an elbow chaire	00.	06.	08.
Item a Keeler	00.	03.	00.
Item a paire of Andirons fire Shoveel tongs and Bellowes	00.	03.	00.
Item an Iron pott and Gridiron	00.	04.	00.
In the Shopp:			
Item foure Dozen & nyne paire of mens woollen Stockins	03.	00.	00.
Item five Dozens of woomens woollen Stockins	03.	02.	06.
Item foure Dozen of Childrens woollen	01.	00.	00.
Item eleaven paire of Boys Gray Stockins	00.	06.	08.
Item eight & thirtie paire of Cotten and Kersy hose	01.	18.	00.
Item three paire of boote hose	00.	05.	00.
Item six paire of Dimity Drawers	00.	12.	00.
Item five Cotton wastecoates and one Kersey wastecoate	00.	15.	00.

Item eleaven Flannell Wastcoates	00.	10.	06.
Item three Shirts	00.	04.	00.
Item nyne frockes	01.	01.	00.
Item Six paire of Trowses and coloured linnings	00.	15.	00.
Item three paire of Sockes	00.	01.	00.
Item three Speckled wastcoates	00.	06.	00.
Item six paire of canvas lynnings	00.	06.	00.
Item severall sorts of eathen ware	01.	10.	00.
Item a smale Truncke	00.	01.	06.
In the best Chamber:			
Item one joyned bedstead and a trundle bedstead	01.	00.	00.
Item one flock bed two flock boulsters and three flock pillowes matt and coard	01.	00.	00.
Item one old rugg one blanckett Curtaine & valance and curtaine roods	00.	10.	06.
Item one old flock bed and boulster an old Coverlett on the trundle bedd matt and cord	00.	05.	00.
Item one other beddstead matt and cord curtaines and valance one feather bedd two boulsters a blanckett and coverlett	03.	00.	00.
Item an old presse	00.	10.	00.
Item an old Court Cupboard	00.	05.	00.
Item one Chest	00.	05.	00.
Item three Chaires & one stoole	00.	03.	00.
Item one Greene Blanckett	00.	04.	06.
In the inner Chamber			
Item a bedstead and cord	00.	02.	06.
Item halfe a cord of wood and some Lumber	00.	06.	08.
In the Closett att the Staireshead			
Item one table & an old Sword	00.	03.	06.
In the Buttery			
Item a powdring Tubb twoe Smale tubbs and some Lumber	00.	06.	06.
Suma totalis	£xxxi	vi^{s}	iiii^{d}

61

WESTON Thomas Mercer
I. 4 Nov. 1668 prov. 6 Nov. 1668 PRS/I/23/43

An Inventary of all and singuler the Goods chattells and Credits of Thomas Weston late whilst he lived of the parish of Seavenoke in the County of Kent Mercer decesed Taken and praysed the Fourth day of November Annoque Domini 1668 By William Allen and William Wall as followeth vizt:

Inprimis the deceaseds Weareing Apparell xxx^{s}

Item Three Hundred and Three Quarters of Tobacco in the Leafe at 10^{d} a Pownd	£xvii	x^{s}	
Item 100 of Tobacco at 5^{d} per Pownd		xlvi^{s}	viii^{d}
Item 2 Grose of Pipes		xxx^{s}	
Item a Reame & a halfe of Paper		v^{s}	
Item severall Boxes and 40 lbs of Tobacco at 9^{d} per pound		xxx^{s}	
Item a Skrew		x^{s}	
Item a Knife Sive & Dryer		iiii^{s}	vi^{d}
Item some old Boxes and a litle more Tobacco		x^{s}	
Item a Counter		x^{s}	
Item Shelves & a Bench		iiii^{s}	
Item one small Featherbed & Bolster & 3 Blankets		lv^{s}	
Item 2 Tables		xii^{s}	
Item a Pott a Kettle a Warming pan a Skillett a Gridiron a Chamber Pott a Chafing Dish a Pint Pot a halfe pint pott a Quarterne Pott and 3 Porringers a Smothing Iron some Earthen Ware and other Lumber		xxx^{s}	
Item 18 dozen of Bottells at 2^{s} 6^{d}		xlii^{s}	
Item 2 Drinke Tubs		v^{s}	
Item an old payre of Sheets and some small old Linnen		viii^{s}	
Summa Totalis	£xxxii	xix^{s}	

62

WICKENDEN Thomas Mercer
I. 16 Nov. 1668 prob. 21 Nov. 1668 PRS/I/23/64

An Inventary of all and singuler the Goods chattells and Creditts of Thomas Wickenden late whilst he lived of the parish of Seavenoke in the County of Kent Mercer deceased Taken and praysed The Sixteenth day of November In the yeere of our Lord 1668 By Nicholas Best William Allen and Thomas Allen as followeth vizt.

Inprimis the deceaseds Weareing Apparell and ready money in his Purse		xl^{s}	
Item in the Shoppe in Drugs Cownters and Grocery Wares and Utensills	£xxx		
Item in the Hall One Table 4er Stooles and One Skreene with some small Chayres		xii^{s}	
Item in the Hall Chamber One Bed & Bedsteadle and Curtens & Vallence with Blankets & Coverletts	£iii		

	£	s	d
& Rugge and Bolster Truckle Bed and Bed and Bolster and Coverlett			
Item a small Table and Sideboard and Shelves		x^{s}	
Item in the Chamber over the Shoppe one Bedstedle and Flockbed & Bolster Coverlett and Blankett with some old Trunks & Lumber in the Chamber		xL^{s}	
Item in the Buttery iii Drink Tubbes and some Potts with 2 Chafers & 5 Pewter Dishes & one Cubberd & one Dripping Pan one Frying Pan one Spitt & other Lumber		xxxiii^{s}	iiii^{d}
Item Bookes fowned valued at		x^{s}	
Item for Linnen 7 pare of Course Sheetes one dozen of Napkins and one dozen of Towells & 5 Tableclothes	£iiii	iii^{s}	iiii^{d}
Suma totalis	£xLiiii	viii^{s}	viii^{d}

63

BURGESS Margery — Widow — Bur. 29 Jan. 1672
W. 25 Feb. 1669 — prov. 20 Apr. 1672 — PRS/W/2/6

In the name of God Amen, The five and Twentieth Day of February in the one & twentieth yeare of the Raigne of our Soveraigne Lord Charles the Second by the grace of God of England, Scotland France and Ireland, Kinge, Defender of the faith etc, Annoque Domini 1668. I Margery Burges of Sevenoake in the County of Kent, Widdowe being sicke and weake in body but of sound & perfect mind and memory (prayse be Given to God for the same) And knoweinge the uncertainety of this life on earth, And beinge desireous to settle things in order, Doe make this my last Will and Testament in manner and forme followeinge, That is to saye, First and principally I Comend my Soule into the hands of allmighty God my Creator, Assuredly believeinge I shall receive full pardon & free remission of all my Sinns, And be saved by the precious death and Meritts of my blessed Saviour and Redeemer, Christ Jesus, And my body to the Earth from whence itt was taken, to be buryed in such decent and Christianlike manner as to my Executor hereafter named shalbe thought meete & Convenient, And as touchinge such worldly estate, As itt hath pleased the lord in his infinite Mercy to lend me, My Will and meaneinge is, The same shall be ymployed and bestowed as hereafter in and by this my Will is expressed, And first I doe Revoake, Renounce, frustrate, and make voyd, All Wills by me formerly made either by word or Writeinge, And doe declare and appoint this my last

Will and Testament, Iem I give devise and bequeath unto the poore people of the towne and parishe of Sevenoake aforesayd the sume of five pounds of Lawfull money of England to be paid to (and distributed amongst) them within Sixe Monethes next after my decease by my Executor hereafter named, In such manner as hee And the Churchwardens of the sayd towne of Sevenoake for the tyme beinge shall thinke meete and Convenient, Item I give devise and bequeath unto my daughter Anne Coney nowe wife of John Coney One Bedsteddle, Matt Coard & Curtayne Rodds, togeather with the Greene Curtaynes, and Valens, thereunto belonginge, and alsoe one greene Rugg beinge made of Worstead and Likewise two greene Cloth Stooles & two Greene Chaires, one great yellowe satten Chaire, And alsoe one paire of gray Curtaynes and Valens, All which nowe are in my owne Lodginge Chamber, Item I give devise and bequeath unto my sayd daughter Anne Coney one Table Carpet, and Cupboard Cloth belonginge to my Parlour, to be delivered to her ymediately after my Interrment, Item I give devise and bequeath unto my sayd daughter Anne Coney Tenn pounds of Lawfull money of England to be paid to her within Sixe Monethes after my decease by my Executor hereafter named, Item I Give devise and bequeath unto my Grand-daughter Sarah Coney my Silver Tankard to be hers ymediately after my decease, And alsoe, Tenn Pounds of Lawfull Money of England to be paid to her, or to her father for her use within Sixe Monethes after my decease, by my said Executor, Item I give devise & bequeath unto my two other Granddaughters Mary and Hannah Coney Tenn pounds a peece of Like Lawfull money, To be paid to them & each of them alsoe within Sixe Monethes next after my decease by my sayd Executor, Item I give devise and bequeath unto my Sonne Edmond Burges All my Messuages Lands tenements hereditaments and reall estate whatsoever, To have and to hould to him the sayd Edmond Burges his heires and Assignes forever, All the rest and residue of my Goods Chattells, debts ready Money and personall estate whatsoever Not herein before devised & bequeathed, my debts, Legacyes, and funerall Charges, beinge first paid, sattisfied and discharged, I give devise & bequeath unto my said Sonne Edmond Burges, Whome I make ordayne & Constitute my Sole and only Executor of this my Last Will and Testament Desireinge him to be Carefull in the due execucion of the same, In wittnes whereof I have (to this my Last Will and Testament Written in two sheets of paper) to the first sheete thereof sett my hand, And to the last sheete my hand and Seale, the daye and yeare first within Written:
Margery Burges her marke

Signed, Sealed, published and declared to be the last Will and Testament of me the sayd Margery Burges in the presence of us whose names are hereunder written

Richard Bosse   Robt. Newman   Thomas Power

64

BURGESS Margery Widow bur. 29 Jan. 1672
I. 8 Oct. 1672 prov. 25 Oct. 1672 PRS/I/2/159

An Inventory of all & singuler the goods & Chattells of Margery Burges late of Seavenoke in the County of Kent widdow deceased taken & apprized the 8th day of October 1672 By us Thomas Allen of Seavenoke aforesaid Sadler & John Beardsworth of the same barbor as followeth (vizt).

	£.	*s.*	*d.*
Inprimis her ready money in her purse	01.	0.	0.
Item her weareing apparell Lynnen & Woollen	10.	0.	0.
Summa totalis	11.	00.	00.

65

CLIFFORD Elizabeth Widow
W. 10 Sep. 1669 prov. 20 Oct. 1669 PRS/W/3/249

In the name of God Amen the 10 day of September 1669 according to the computation of the Church of England I Elebeth Clifat widdow of the parish of 7okes in the County of Kent being of perfect memory and remembrance praised be God to make and ordain this my last Will and testament in manner and form following
Item I give to my datter Ales A Payr of Sheets and A gret Iorn Poote and the gret Coped
Item I give to my datter Francis my buckintoub and A Cheest and A drink vesel and A oIarn Cettell
Item I give to my sonn William a smale toub
Item I give to my sonn after the beger toub
Item I give to my sonn Robard the Poodering toub and Celler
Item I give to my sonn Qumfree my houes and the rest of my goods
Item I make my sonn Qumfree fully Axcaker of all I have and so I rest haveing nothing more to give
Seled the tenneh day of September onn thouthan sex haundred sexty nine 1669
the mark of Elibeth Clifat
witness John Wood

66

CLIFFORD Elizabeth Widow
I. 15 Oct. 1669 prov. 26 Oct. 1669 PRS/I/3/55

An Inventary of the Goods and Chattells of Elizabeth Clifford late of the parish of Seavenoke in the County of Kent Widdow decesed Taken and prized the fifteenth day of October 1669 By Xpofer Thomas Gentleman and Thomas Hawes as followeth vizt

Inprimis a Gridiron, Frying pan Brandirons Spitt Pothangers 2 Iron Pots one Brasse Ketle a brasse Chafer 2 Payles an old Table a Forme 2 old Cubberts 2 Litle Pewter dishes 2 old Chayres with other old Lumber		xx^{s}	
Item one Bucking tubbe 2 Drink vessels & a Powdring Tub with three old Wheeles		x^{s}	
Item hir Wearing Apparell		xx^{s}	
Item 3 old Chests 2 old Bedstedles with the furniture		xx^{s}	
Item 4er pare of course old Sheets		xiii^{s}	iiii^{d}
Summa totalis	£iiii.	iiis	iiiid

67

WOOD George Yeoman
I. 3 Nov. 1669 prov. 10 Dec. 1669 PRS/I/23/82

An Inventary of all and singuler the Goods Chattells and Credits of George Wood late whilst he lived of the parish of Seavenoke in the County of Kent yeoman decesed. Taken and prized the Third day of November Anno Domini 1669 By Richard Evridge William Wall and John Leigh as followeth vizt.

Inprimis the deceseds wearing Apparell and his Purse	xl^{s}	
Item in the Hall One Table with a Frame 8 Joyned Stoles one small Cubberd one Joyned Chaire one Table Chayre 3 other small Chaires one small Settle one paire of Pothangers one paire of Brandirons one Firepan one paire of Tongs one Gridiron one Chopping Knife one dozen of Trenchers & one Spitt	xxxvii^{s}	x^{d}
Item in the Drinkhowse one Firkin 3 Panns one		

Bruing Tub one Linnen Wheele one Churne one Sack 3 old Stalders one Kilderkin & one Tumell		xvi^{s}	
Item in the Kitchen 2 small Brasse Kettells 2 brasse Skillets one Iron Kettle 3 Iron pots 4er payles one Frying pan 4er small pewter Dishes one paire of Pothangers one Wodden Mesure 2 Wodden Dishes		xliii^{s}	ii^{d}
Item in the Milkhowse 6 Milktrayes one Wodden Dish one paire of Skales & 4er Leaden Wayts one old Keeler 6 Crocks		ix^{s}	
Item one Cheese presse 2 Tubs one Keeler one Forme 2 old Ostheares		xx^{s}	
Item in the Chamber over the Kitchen one old Chest one Bushell & a halfe of Wheate one Wollen Wheele one Stone Wayte of Hempe 8 lb of Hops 6 lb of Wooll		xv^{s}	
Item in the Chamber over the Hall one Fetherbed & Bolster one Blankett 2 Coverlets one Flock bed & Bolster 2 Blankets one Rug one Bedsted & one Trundlebedsted 2 Chests one Trunke one Warmeing pan 3 lb of Woll 4er paire of corse Sheets 6 old Tableclothes 4er Napkins 4er Towells certen Cheese	£iiii	xvii^{s}	vi^{d}
Item in the Chamber over the Buttery one Flockbed one old Bedstead		xviii^{s}	
Item at Edward Cripss one Flockbed one Bolster one Pillow one paire of Sheets		xv^{s}	
Item 4er Hogs		£iii	
Item 2 Horses & 2 Mares		£vii	
Item the Stock of Hoppoles on the Land		£xix	
Item 14 Sheepe		£iiii	iiii^{s}
Item 3 Kine & 2 yong Bullocks		£xi	
Item certaine Hay & Corne Swips 4er Sives one Shall one Forke & a Cutler		£xv	iii^{s}
Item one Waggon Plow & Wheeles Harrowes Roll & all the other Husbandry Tacklings		£iii	
Item for one Pitcher one paire of Wagon Ropes & other Lumber & things owt of sight not worth prizing			viii^{s}

Item Debts owing to the decesed	£x	v^{s}	
Item for Lime layd on the Grownd and Seed to Sow)	£iii	xiii^{s}	
Suma totalis	£lxxxxii	vii^{s}	vi^{d}

68

BEST Francis	Innholder	
W. 8 Jan. 1670	prov. 3 Feb. 1670	PRS/W/1/289

In the name of God Amen I Francis Best of Sevenoake in the County of Kent Inholder being sicke and weake in body but of sound and perfect memory praised be God doe make & ordayne this my last Will and Testament in manner followeing First I comend my soule into the hands of Almighty God my Creator hopeing and Assuredly beleiving through the merritts death and passion of my blessed Saviour Jesus Christ to Receive a free pardon for all my sinns and my body I committ to the earth from whence it came to be decently buried att the discretion of my Executors hereafternamed Imprimis I give and bequeath unto my Loveing wife Elizabeth such and soe many of my goods and householdstuffe as shall be worth the full sume of Twenty pounds of lawfull mony of England according as the same shall be Apprized in my Inventory to be made by honest men and she the said Elizabeth to take her choyse of what goods she likes best when they are Apprized to be of the said value of twenty pounds. Also I give more unto my wife One large Joyned Chest marked with E. B. and all the Lynnen therein being And my will is my said wife shall peaceably hold and enjoy my house and outhouses yards and gardens & orchards according to her Joyneture. Also I give and bequeath to my two sons Nicholas Best and William Best my Messuage or Tenement wherein I now dwell and all outhouses yards gardens and orchards thereunto belonging (after my wives decease) And also all my Lands and Tenements whatsoever & wheresoever to have and to hold the said premisses unto my two sonns Nicholas Best and William Best and to their heirs and assignees for ever equally to be divided between them And alsoe I give unto my two sonns Nicholas and William and their heires and assignes all my goods Cattell Chattells Ready money debts and householdstuffe whatsoever (not before bequeathed) equally to be divided betweene them they payeing out of the same all such legacyes as are hereafter mencioned Also I give and bequeath unto Elizabeth Best my daughter the sume of Two hundred pounds of lawfull mony of England to be payd unto her by my Executors att her age of one and twenty years or day of Marriage which shall first happen. Alsoe I give and bequeath unto Mary Best my Daughter the sume of two hundred pounds of lawfull money of England to be paid unto her by my Executors at her age of one and twenty years or day of marriage which shall first happen. And I give unto my daughter Ann the sume of one hundred and fifty pounds of lawfull money of England to be payed unto her by my Executors att her age of one and twenty yeares or day of marriage which shall first happen. And I give

unto my daughter Katherine the like sume of one hundred and fifty pounds of lawfull money of England to be payed unto her by my Executors at her age of one and twenty yeares or day of marriage which shall first happen. And if any of my said Daughters shall happen to dye before her or their porcion shall become due Then my Will is that the same shall be equally divided amongst all my surviving children and I doe hereby make and ordayne my two sonns Nicholas and William full and sole Executors of this my last Will and Testament. And my will is that my Executors shall pay interest unto my four Daughters for their several porcions after the rate of five pounds per cent untill their severall porcions shall become due & payable the same to be payed halfe yearly att my now dwelling house provided always and my will further is that if my Executors shall make defaulte in payment of my said severall Legacyes unto my four daughters or of any parte thereof to them or any of them That then she or they whoe shall not have her or their porcion or Legacy paid togeather with the Interest as aforesaid shall enter into and upon all my lands and tenements beforegiven to and now payed their several Legacyes and sumes of money due to them togeather with such costs & damages as she or they shall susteyne by reason of the non payment thereof the eldest to enter and be payed before the youngest.
In Witnes whereof I the said Francis Best have hereunto sett my hand & Seale the Eighth day of January in the one and twentieth yeare of the Raigne of our Soveraigne Lord Charles the second by the Grace of God Kinge of England Scotland France and Ireland Defendor of the Faith etc. Annoque Domine 1669
Francis Best
Signed sealed published and Declared to be the last Will & Testament of the said Francis Best in the presence of
Henry Streatfield Thomas Streatfield

69

BEST Francis Innkeeper
I. 30 Jan. 1670 prov. 27 Feb. 1670 PRS/I/2/84

An Inventorye of the Goods & Chattells of Mr. Francis Best late Deceased that he Dyed seased of Prized by Richard Cocket and William Allen the thirtyeth Day of January in the yeare of our Lord 1669

	£	*s.*	*d.*
Imprimis his wearing Apparell	05 –	00 –	00
Item mony in his Purse and oweing uppon Bills Bonds booke Debts & otherwise)	200 –	00 –	00
Item two silver bowles and six silver spoones	8 –	0 –	0
In the Chamber called the Forten			
Item One Bedstedle Curten and valance matt & Cord & Curten Rods)	01 –	05 –	00

Item two Feather Beds three Blanketts two Boulsters with three Pillowes	05	02	00
Item one Rugg one Coverlett and one Trundle Bedstedle with one Long Table two Shorte Tables & one Coort Cupboard	03	15	04
Item Fower Carpetts with two windowe Curtens	01	10	00
Item Eight Lether chayres three Greene Stooles with one Dosen of Quishons	01	17	00
Item one payer of Andirons with Creepers with Brases and one Looking Glasse with fire pan and Tongs	00	17	00
In the Crowne Chamber			
One Bedstedle mat and Cord with Curtens and valance & curten Rods	02	01	00
Item two Fether Beds two Ruggs two Boulsters two Pillowes two Blankets with one Trundle Bedstedle mat & Cord	07	15	00
Item one Drawing Table one Coort Cubord two Carpetts one ewer	01	08	00
Eight Chayres Six Cushens	01	04	00
Item one payer of Brasse Andirons with two Payer of Creepers with Fire pan & Tongs with one payer of Bellowes	00	14	04
In the little Hall Chamber			
One Bedstedle with Curten & Valence Curten rods matt & Cord with one Trundell Bedstedell mat and Cord	01	02	00
Item two Feather Beds two Boulsters three Pillowes one rugg three old Blanketts	04	12	06
Item one old Small Table and one old Carpett Fower old Chayres three old Cushens one Glasse	00	12	06
Item one payer of Andirons Fier pan and Tongues	00	02	00
In the Bedchamber			
Two old Bedstedls with old Curtens matts Cords & Curten Rods	00	18	00
Two Feather Beds two Boulsters two Blanketts two ruggs one Table & one Carpet	05	10	00
In the Greene Chamber			
One Bedstedle Curtens and Valence mat and Cord			

and Curten Rods with one Trundle Bedsted mat & Cord)	02 – 00 – 00
Item two Feather Beds two Boulsters two Pillows one Rugg two Blancketts one Coverlett)	06 – 05 – 00
One Table one Carpett one Foorme Fower Chayres one Joyne Stoole one Cushen)	00 – 16 – 00
In the Star	
Item two Bedstedles Curtens and valance Curten rode mat and Cords)	01 – 10 – 00
Two Feather Beds two Feather Boulsters thre Feather Pillowes Fower Blanketts one Flocke Boulster two Coverletts & two Ruggs)	05 – 10 – 00
One Table three Foormes one Carpett one old Chayer	00 – 06 – 08
In the Chamber over the Gatehouse	
Item two Bedstedles with Curtens and valance matts Cords and Curten Rods)	02 – 10 – 00
One Trundle Bedstedle matt & Cord	00 – 04 – 00
Three Fether Beeds Three Boulsters Three Feather Pillowes Fower Blancketts Two Rugs one Coverlett)	08 – 15 – 00
One Longe Table & Carpett Three Quishons Six Stools one payer of Andirons & Creepers and a windowe Curtaine & rod)	02 – 01 – 06
In the yellowe Chamber over the Gatehouse	
One Bedstedle Curtens & valance Matt & Coard with Curten Rods and one Trundle Bedstedle matt & Coard)	00 – 18 – 06
Two Fether Beds Two Fether Boulsters one Fether Pillowe Three Blancketts One Rug one Coverlett)	04 – 17 – 06
One Table Two olde Carpetts Two Chayers Two Joyne Stooles one Coort Cupboard one Quishon One Curten Rod with windowe Curtens)	00 – 14 – 00
In the Garrett over the Gatehouse	
One Bed & Bedstedle with other Lumber	01 – 00 – 00
In the other Garett next	
Two olde Bedstedles Two olde Flock Beds & Two olde Blancketts and Coverletts)	01 – 00 – 06
The Chamber over the Entrye	

One Bedstedle with Curtens & valance Matt & Cord with Curten Rods with one Trundell Bedstedle	02	00	00
One Fether bed one Boulster Two Blancketts One Ruge one Coverlett Two Pillowes	03	02	00
One presse Three Joyne Chayres one Table	02	05	00
Fower payer of Sheets & Nyne Dozen of Napkens Ten Table Clooths one dozen & a halfe of pillowe Coats & one dozen of Towells	36	13	4
In the Two Little Chambers comonly called the Maids Chambers			
Item Two Bedstedells with Curtens and valance Matt and Cord	01	08	00
Item Two Fether Beds one Flocke Bed Three Fether Pillowes Two Fether Boulsters	05	03	04
Two Rugs Three Blancketts	01	02	00
One Joyne Chest	00	03	00
In the Barbers Shop			
One Bedstedle with olde Curtens & valance Matt and Cord & Curten Rods and one Smale Fether Bed & Flock boulster & Pillowe with Two Blancketts one Ruge and a little Round Table	02	10	00
In the Parlor			
One Bedstedle Curtens & valance Matt Cord & Curten Rods one Feather Bed one Boulster of Flocks & one of Feathers Two Blancketts one Ruge	03	15	00
Two Tables Two Carpetts fower chayers one Forme one Quishon one payer of Cast Andirons	01	08	00
In the Hall			
Item Two Tables one Forme Fower Joyned Stools one Jacke one Clocke one peece of hanging and one windowe Curten and Curten Rod one payer of Cast Andirons	02	14	00
The little Roome next the Hall			
One small table	00	04	00
In the Kitchen			
Pewter Ditches weighing two hundred & a halfe	10	8	4
More Nynety Fower Pound Waight of Flagens & Wine Potts & other Potts	02	10	00
Item Brasse Kettells & warmeing Panns	02	16	00
Five Spitts	00	11	00
One Jacke	00	15	00

One Iron Pan & one Firepan & Tongs and Creepers one payer of Andirons with Two payer of pott hangers	)	00 –	14 –	06
Fower Iron potts one Iron Kettle		02 –	00 –	00
One Gridiron one Iron for to lye before the fire one Tosting Iron one Joyned Settle & Cupbord	)	01 –	04 –	00
In the Buttery				
One Bakeing Troffe with the Cover & one kneding Troffe one powdering Tub & one olde Table	)	01 –	00 –	00
Six Trayes Five Kellers Two Tubs		01 –	11 –	00
One Brasse Frieing pann		00 –	02 –	00
In the brewhouse				
One Meash Fatt & one under Vate & one Tun with Two Colers & Two Shoots One Pumpe with Two Smale beareing Tubs and one Lardge Furnance	)	25 –	02 –	06
In the Washe house				
One Smale Furnace and Fower Small Kellers		01 –	10 –	00
In the Garrett				
Fower hundred of Oystery Faggotts		01 –	08 –	00
In the yard				
Item Three Cowes		11 –	15 –	00
Item one Mare Two Cowlts		09 –	00 –	00
Item one Thousand of Faggotts		05 –	00 –	00
Item Six Cord of Wood		02 –	10 –	00
Two Fatt Hoggs		02 –	10 –	00
One Sowe & Six Sheets		04 –	00 –	00
In Hay		15 –	00 –	00
The Oates not Threshed		01 –	10 –	00
For Oates & Beans		07 –	09 –	00
Item Barlye		10 –	00 –	00
One Score of Sheepe		10 –	00 –	00
In the Celler				
Beere and Wyne		10 –	00 –	00
Seaven Hogsheads & Three barells Fower halfe wine hogsheads and Two Runletts	)	01 –	15 –	00
Item poles in the hopgarden		13 –	10 –	00
One olde Cupbord with other lumber not seene		01 –	00 –	00
Sum Total		510 –	13 –	4

Debts oweing by the Testator	
Imprimis due to Edward Thornton	33 – 00 – 00
Item due to Mr Blishe for wyne	20 – 00 – 00
Item due for Servants Wages	04 – 00 – 00
	57 – 00 – 00

70

COPLAND John Wheeler
W. 24 Feb. 1670 prov. 20 Mar. 1670 PRS/W/3/250

In the name of God amen. I John Copland of Sevenoke in the Countie of Kent Wheeler, sick of Bodie but of Good and perfect memorie god be praysed, Doe make and ordaine this my last will and testament in maner and forme followinge, that is to say first I Commend my soule to God my Creator, Hopeing assuredlie through the merits of Jesus Christ my Saviour to be made partaker of everlasting life and I Commend my bodie to the earth wher of it was made Item I will that all such Debts as I owe of right to anie parson or parsons be well and trulie Contented and paid bie mine Executrix hereafter named and after my Debts paid and my funarall expences performed, then I will and give to my Daughter An Copland the sum of fortie poundes that is to say twentie pound thre months after hir day of marrig and the other twentie poundes after the death of my Executrix likewise I give to my said Daughter An Copland one wooden drincking boule. Item I will and give unto my Daughter Elizabeth Copland the sum of fortie poundes that is to say twentie pounds thre months after hir daie of marrage and the other twentie after the Death of my Executrix likewise I give to my said daughter Elizabeth Copland one plaine Chest. Item my will and meaning is that if ether of my Daughters An or Elizabeth hapen to die before they or ether of them be maried that then the said portion of fortie pound be equally devided betwixt the surviving sister & my sonn William Copland Item I give to my sonn William Copland one large Bible in folio after the death of my Executrix Item I Give all the residue of my Goodes & Chatells to my well beloved Wife An Copland, whome I make ordaine Executrix of this my last will and Testament: and I doe intreat my Loving Brother in Law Percivall Smith of the said parish of Sevenokes, Glasier to be overseer of this my last will and testament, in wittness hereunto I set to my hand and seale this foure and twentieth day of februarie one thowsand six hundred sixtie nine
the marke of John Copland
seled & subscribed in the presence of us
Ri Hackeness the marke of William Fenn

71

WALTER John — Tailor
I. 10 Mar. 1670 — prov. 18 Mar. 1670 — PRS/I/23/17

An Inventory of all and singuler the Goods and Chattles of John Walter late whilest he lived of Seavenoke in the County of Kent Tailor, taken and appraized by John Butterfield and Richard Hawkes the tenth day of March in the two and twentieth yeare of the Raigne of our Soveraigne Lord Charles the Second of England Scotland Fraunce and Ireland King Defender of the Faith etc Annoque Domini 1669

Inprimis his weareing apparell and ready money in his purse	xxvi^{s}	viii^{d}	
In the Hall			
Item One Cupboard and one Table	xiii^{s}	iiii^{d}	
Item a forme and Six joyned Stooles	x^{s}	vi^{d}	
Item one Chaire	ii^{s}	iiii^{d}	
Item severall peeces of Pewter and brasse	xxxii^{s}	iiii^{d}	
Item two Smale Spitts	ii^{s}	vi^{d}	
Item fire Shovell tongs Andirons & Bellowes	v^{s}	vi^{d}	
In the Buttery			
Item severall smale beere Tubbs	x^{s}	viii^{d}	
Item a Bucking Tubb	iii^{s}	vi^{d}	
Item a paire of Andirons	iii^{s}	iiii^{d}	
Item two potts and a pann	ii^{s}	vi^{d}	
In the Hall Chamber			
Item one halfe headed bedstead	vi^{s}	viii^{d}	
Item one Trundle Bedstead	iii^{s}	iiii^{d}	
Item one feather bed with two blancketts and a Rugg	L^{s}		
Item one Flockebedd two blancketts and a Coverlett	xiii^{s}	iiii^{d}	
Item one Chest and foure Stooles	vi^{s}	viii^{d}	
In the Chamber over the Shopp			
Item one halfeheaded bedstead	vi^{s}	viii^{d}	
Item one flockbedd with Blancketts anc coverlett	xxv^{s}		
Item two Chests with severall parcells of Lynnen in them)	xxxxviii^{s}	iiii^{d}	
Item in money oweing unto him on his booke some sperate and some desperate)	Liii^{s}	iiii^{d}	
Item some old Lumber about the house	iii^{s}	iiii^{d}	
	£xvi	vii^{s}	x^{d}

72

OVERY John Tanner
W. 13 Apr. 1670 prov. 23 Mar. 1671 PRS/W/12/113

In the name of God Amen. I John Overy of Seavenoke in the County of Kent Tanner being in perfect health and sound memory praised be God Do make and ordaine this my last will and Testament in manner and forme following. First I Will and Bequeath my Soule unto Allmighty God my Creator and Redeemer, And by Body to the Earth from whence it was taken, and to be Buryed in Sundrish Churchyard neere my wife and Children, And as for the disposeing of my Temporall Estate as Followeth. Item I Will and Bequeath unto the poor of the parrish of Sundrish aforesaid the sum of Five pounds to be Distributed unto them by my Executrix hereafter mentioned within one month after my Decease, Item I Will and Bequeath unto my Beloved Daughter Anne Greene One Feather Bed and Boulster three Blanketts, a Greene Rugg and Bedsteadle, a presse one Table with a frame, one Joyne chaire Two Chestes, one greate Bedsheete, seaven paire of fine Sheets four Dozen of Fine Napkins, Four paire of pillow Coates, and Board Cloathes and Cubbard Cloathes, One Hundred pounds of Lawfull mony of England Six Twenty Shillings peces of old gold and one Ten Shillings pece, All which mony and Goods Shall Remaine unto my said Beloved Daughter Dureing her Naturall life, And after her Decease unto Mary Greene my grandchild And God Daughter – Item: all my household linnen and all other goods unbequeathed I Do will and give unto my said Beloved Daughter Anne Greene whom I Do make my whole and Sole Executrix. In Testemony wherof I have hereunto Set my hand and seale this Thirteenth Day of Aprill, In the yeare of our Lord God, one Thousand six Hundred and Seaventy, And in the Two and Twentyeth yeare of the Raigne of Our Soveraigne Lord King Charles the Second.
Sealed and deliverd in the presence of John Overy
Samuel Sharpe George Field

73

HODGE John Labourer
W. 18 Oct. 1670 prov. 7 Jan. 1671 PRS/W/8/124

In the name of god Amen I John Hodge of the parish of Seavenoke in the County of Kent labourer being weake and infirme in body but of perfect memory and understanding doe make and ordaine this my last will and testament first I bequeath my Soule into the hands of God my Creator trusting for eternall Salvacion in the worlde to come through the onely meritts of Jesus Christ my redeemer my body I dispose to the earth to be Decently buried according to the Discrecion of my Executor hereafter named Item I give and bequeath unto my nephew John Hodge all that my bed

boulsters bedsteedle bedcloathes Matt and Cord and other furniture belonging unto the bed wherin I now lye and one paire of Sheets my Truncke and Chest and Table my Ironpott Andirons firepan Tongs Gridiron Pothangers and my Cupboard Item I give unto Sarah Hodge my mother one paire of Sheets Item I give to my sister Sarah Ware one other paire of Sheets Item I give unto young Mrs Jane Blome my three largest pewter dishes two pewter poringers and my brasse Skillett Item I give and bequeath unto my Loveing brother Abraham Hodge all my weareing apparrell and I make him sole Executor of this my will hereby willing and Declareing that he the said Abraham shall ymediately after my Death give unto Mr John Blome of Seavenoke gent such security as he shall approve of for the payment of my said mother of the interest of five pounds dureing her life and of for the payment of the said five pounds unto my said nephew John Hodge after her death which money I appoint shall be then putt out at interest by the advise of Mr Blome for the benefitt of my said Nephew when he shall attain his age of one and twenty yeares And whereas Mary Beardsworth of Seavenoke Spinster is indebted to me tenn pounds on bond my will and meaneing is & I doe hereby Declare that she shall out of the same detayne and pay unto herselfe all such some and somes of money as I shall happen to be indebted to her at the tyme of my death either for Lodging Dyett or otherwise wherein if any difference hapen to arise I appoint my said Executor to be concluded and submit to such order and direccions therein as the said Mr Blome shall thincke fitt And I doe farther Declare that the overplus of my estate if any shall be besides what I have hereby disposed of and what the charge of my buriall and probate of this my will shall amount unto shall be equally Devided amongest my Nephews Francis Hodge Giles Hodge James Hodge and Richard Hodge and secured for theire use in such manner and forme as my said Executor with the advise of Mr Blome shall thincke fitt And I hereby revoke all other and former wills In wittnesse wherof I have hereunto sett my hand and seale this eighteenth day of October in the two & twentieth yeare of the Raigne of our Soveraigne Lord King Charles the second Annoque Domini 1670
The marke of John Hodge
Signed sealed and published by the said John Hodge to be his last will and testament in the presence of us
Wil Allen George Bruere

74

WESTON Thomasin Widow
I. 24 Oct. 1670 prov. 5 Nov. 1670 PRS/I/23/44

An Inventory of the Goods & chattells of Thomasin Weston of Seavenoke in the county of Kent widdow taken & Appraised by John Martin & David Durtnell the 24th of October 1670

	£.	*s.*	*d.*
In the Shopp			
Item 40 glasses & some crackt potts	0.	7.	0.
In the Kitchin			
Item one great brasse Kettle one midle one & one Small all old)	1.	0.	0.
Item 2 more little Kettles	0.	6.	0.
Item one brasse chaffing dish & 2 skilletts	0.	3.	0.
Item a pair of old Andirons a creeper a pair of tongues a pair of pothookes 3 small spitts & a pair of bellowes)	0.	6.	0.
Item an Iron Kettle 2 Iron potts & a Skillett with the 2 pottlids)	0.	14.	0.
Item 3 brasse Skimmers & 2 ladles 2 cleavers a warming pan & a old frying pan & a tinder box & some old lattin a Gridiron)	0.	11.	0.
Item an old bible 2 Sermon bookes & other old bookes 4 dozen trenchers 2 Smothing Irons & 2 heates)	0.	10.	6.
Item an old cupboard	0.	4.	0.
Item 11 old dishes 2 payles & other lumbar 2 old tables & a dresser)	0.	6.	0.
In the Hall			
Item 13 glassills of waters & syrrup	0.	12.	0.
Item 12 glasse more of stilled waters	0.	4.	0.
Item 8 earthen dishes 2 flowre potts 6 earthen dishes)	0.	3.	0.
Item a silver taster	0.	5.	0.
Item 2 cupboards	0.	12.	6.
Item 2 Tables 4 joyned Stooles	1.	0.	0.
Item a little payre of Andirons fire pan tongues pothookes & a fire Iron)	0.	3.	0.
Item some old pictures 4 old chaires a glasse case & an old dresser)	0.	4.	0.
Item 2 curtain rods & an old curtain	0.	2.	0.
In the cellar			
Item an old pewter still	0.	7.	0.
Item 4 Keelers 2 brewing tubs an old bucking tub a powdring tub an old Kettle 4 trayes and other lumber)	2.	15.	0.
In the Hall Chamber			
Item 112^{lbs} of pewter at 9^{d}	4.	4.	0.

Item 12lbs of chamber potts	0.	6.	0.
Item one feather bed & boulster bedsted curtaine & valence an old rug 2 blanckets matt & cord)	6.	0.	0.
Item 4 stooles & 4 chaires	1.	10.	0.
Item a side bord & table and window curtain	0.	10.	0.
Item a payre of Andirons & tongues	0.	8.	0.
Item 3 chests and a trunck	1.	5.	0.
Item 10 payre of sheets	8.	0.	0.
Item 4 payre of old sheets an od sheet & a pair of pillow coats & some other old linnon)	1.	0.	0.
Item 3 diaper table cloathes & an old one	1.	0.	0.
Item 9 other table cloathes 2 duzen of napkins pillow coates & other peices of linnon)	2.	6.	0.
Som feathers in a bagg 3 lin pillowes & a glasse	0.	5.	0.
Item 4 cushions	0.	3.	6.
In the Kitchen chamber			
Item one old feather bed & boulster a old blancket covering stedle curtaines matt cord & truckle bedsted)	3.	10.	0.
Item a box with drawers	0.	3.	0.
In the chamber over the Shopp			
Item 2 little flock beds a chaire a stoole a trunck a chest a hamper all old lumber things & a hall)	1.	10.	0.
	42.	8.	6.

Millicent Colequike John Martin David Durtnell

75

STEVENS Christopher Innholder
W. 19 Nov. 1670 prov. 25 Jan. 1671 PRS/W/15/88

In the Name of God Amen I Christopher Stevens of Seavenoke in the County of Kent Innholder being in Reasonable health and sound memory praised be God, Do make and Ordaine this my last Will and Testament in Manner and Forme following
First I will and Bequeath my Soule unto Almighty God my Creator And Redeemer and my Body unto the Earth from whence it was taken, and for the Disposeing of my worldly Estate as Followeth./ Item I will and Bequeath unto Margarett my Loving wife and her three Daughters the Sum of Fourty pounds according unto the Security I gave her therefore upon our Contract in

Marryage Item I will, Give and Bequeath unto Anne Stevens my Daughter One moitye of my Goods Cattell and Chattells after my Debts and Funerall Expences are Discharged, Item I will and Bequeath unto my Daughter in Law Anne Bayly the sum of Twenty Shillings at the age of Twenty and One yeares, The said Anne Bayly haveing Liberty to take her Bed and Steadle in the Greene Chamber and her Brasse pott, Item I will and bequeath unto Margarett Bayly my Daughter in Law the like Sum of Twenty Shillings at her age of Twenty and One yeares Item I Will and Bequeath unto Mary Bayly the sum of Fourty Shillings to be paid unto her at the age of Twenty and One yeares, Item all the Remainder of my Goods Cattell and Chattells unbequeathed I will give and Bequeath unto the said Margarett Stevens my Loving wife whom I Do make my whole and sole Executrix, Item my will is that my said Daughter Anne Stevens have her part or moity of Goods before Expressed, Devided and Delivered unto her within one mounth after my decease, Item I do Nominate and apoint my Brother in Law Henry Care to be Overseer to this my last will and Testament, in Testemony wherof I the said Christopher Stevens have hereunto sett my hand and Seale this Nineteenth Day of November in the yeare of our Lord God, One Thousand Six Hundred and Seaventy in the Two and Twentyeth yeare of the raigne of our Soveraigne Lord King Charles the Second/
Christopher Stevens
Sealed and delivered in the presence of
Thomas Weller   John Overy

76

BAKER Edward	Innholder	bur. 16 Jan. 1671
W. 13 Jan. 1671	prov. 25 Jan. 1671	PRS/W/1/293

In the Name of God Amen I Edward Baker of Sevenoke alias Sevenokes in the County of Kent Inholder being sicke and weake in body but of sound and perfect mind and memory praised be almighty God therefore revokeing all former wills by me made doe make and ordaine this my last will and testament in maner and forme followinge First I recommend my soul into the hands of Almighty [God] my maker hopeing through the only meritts of Jesus Christ my blessed [Saviour] and redeemer to obtaine remission of all my sins, And my body to the earth from whence it was taken to be decently buried att the Discretion of my Executrix And for my worldly goods my will is that my Executrix shall sell and dispose thereof for the payment of my debts funerall Charges and Expences, And after my Debts soe paid as aforesaid I give and bequeath all the residue of my personall estate whatsoever and wheresoever unto my Loving wife Elizabeth Baker whom I make sole Executrix of this my last will and Testament. And I doe desire my trusty and welbeloved freinds David Durtnall of Sevenoke aforesaid Baker and John Brattle of Sevenokes aforesaid gent to be Overseers of this my last will and Testament desireing them to be aiding and assistyng to my Executrix

In witness wherof I have heerunto sett my hand and Seale the Thirteenth day of January in the Two and Twentieth yeare of the Raigne of our Soveraigne Lord Kinge Charles the Second etc Annoque Domini 1670.
The marke of Edward Baker
Signed Sealed published and Declared to be the last will and testament of the above named Edward Baker in the presence of
John Brattle
the marke of David Durtnall James Beecher

77

BAKER Edward	Victualler	bur. 16 Jan. 1671
I. 18 May 1671	prov. 26 May 1671	PRS/I/2/4

The Inventory of all and singular the goods Chattles and debts of Edward Baker, late of Seavenoke in the County of Kent victualler deceased taken, valued and apprased the Eighteeneth day of May Anno domini 1671 by John Beardsworth and David Durtnall as followeth vizt

Inprimis his wearing Apparell & money in his purse	£ii	x^{s}	
At the Catt in the Gatehouse Chamber			
Item a Shovelboard, Table, 6 stooles, i Court Cubboard and three Chaires)	£i	x^{s}	
In the Round Chamber			
Item i Court Cubboard and 6 Chaires		viii^{s}	
Item i Court Cubboard, i bedsteddle with matts and Cords, i Trundle bedsteddle & strawe bed 1 old bedsteddle & i old Cubboard at the stayer head)	£ii	iii^{s}	vi^{d}
In the Box Roome			
Item i Little Table and i Chayre		ii^{s}	iiii^{d}
In the Little Parlor			
Item i presse Cubboard 1 Curtaine & Rodd & i table 2 formes i flag chaire & i Chaire Table)	£i	v^{s}	
In the new Chamber			
Item 2 bedsteddes Matts & Cords i Table 1 Table Chaire i Chest and i Flag Chaire)	£i	vi^{s}	viii^{d}
In the yellowe bed Chamber			
Item i bedsteddle 2 matts & Cords the backe of a settle and one old Ladder)		vii^{s}	vi^{d}
In the Kitchine			
Item i Table i forme i settle i Chaire i Joyned stoole & one salt box)		viii^{s}	x^{d}
In the Sellers			
Item i Butt 2 hoggsheads i Kilderkin 4 Stalders and 1 bearing Tubb & 3 old stalders)	£i	xviii^{s}	vi^{d}
In the Sinke			

Item i presse i Saveall & 2 old Tressells			v^{s}	
In the Washhouse				
Item i little brasse Furnace 2 barrells 1 Kilderkin i Tunnell i bucking Tubb i bearing tubb 5 Keelers i washing stoole one Buckett and one Fire Shovell and one Chest	)	£i	ix^{s}	
In the Brewhouse				
Item i furnace Meash fat Tunn Cooler shoote i pump one underback 2 old Tubbs & a Stalder	)	£xiiii	xii^{s}	
Item i Acre and a halfe of hopps newe planted the poles thereof	)	£vii		
Suma totalis huius Inventorii	)	£xxxv	vi^{s}	iiii^{d}

78

WOOD Thomas — Victualler — bur. 14 Jul. 1671
NW. 11 Jul. 1671 — prov. 7 Nov 1671 — PRS/W/18/3

Memorandum that upon the Eleaventh day of July 1671 Thomas Wood of the parish of Seavenoke in the County of Kent Vitler being sick in Body but of perfect Mind and Memory with an intent and purpose to make his Will and dispose of his Estate spake theis wordes following vizt: He said he would give his Daughter Joane Halfe a Skore Lambes And to his Sonne John he gave one great Chist which was his Grandfathers and the part of a Tenement and Land lying below Baylies Hill which was his Mothers And to his Sonne Thomas he gave a Cow and a yong Bud or Heyfer which he willed to be Sold and putt owt for his use, And being asked what he would give to his Daughter Anne he said that he would give hir nothing for that shee had allredy more than hir share, All the rest and residue of his Estate he gave to Elizabeth his Wyfe and hir Daughter Susan. Theis wordes or the selfe same in effect he spake in the presence and heareing of Sarah Woodgate Widow and Elizabeth Medhurst Wyfe of James Medhurst And severall other persons.
Signed Sarah Woodgate   Signed Eliz: Medhurst

79

CRONKE John — Tailor — bur. 5 Nov. 1671
W. 23 Oct. 1671 — prov. 1 Jun. 1672 — PRS/W/3/256

In the name of God Amen, The Three and Twentieth day of October in the three and Twentieth yeare of the Reigne of our Soveraigne Lord Charles the

Second By the Grace of God Of England, Scotland France and Ireland King Defendor of the Faith etc Annoque Domini 1671. I John Cronke of Sevenock in the Countie of Kent Taylor being sick and weake in body but of sound and perfect mind and memory Thanks be given to Almighty God therefore, After my peace made with God in a sure and certayne hope of Resurreccon to Eternall life, through the Attonement propiciacon Sacrifice and Sattisfaccon of my Blessed Saviour Christ Jesus, Revoakeinge and (by this my will) adnullinge, All former Wills by me made either in word or writeing Doe make, Constitute ordayne and appoint this my last Will and Testament in manner & forme followeing (That is to say) First and principally I Comit and Comend my Soule into the hands of Almighty God that gave it me, And my body to the earth from whence it was taken, to be buryed in such decent and Christian-like manner as to my Executor hereafter named shall seeme meet & Conveinent And as touchinge such temporall Estate As it hath pleased Almighty God in his infinite mercy to lend me, I dispose thereof as followeth, Inprimis I will That all those debts and dutyes as I owe in right or Conscience to any person or persons whatsoever be well and truely payd (or secured to be paid) within Convenient tyme after my decease, by my Executor hereafter named. And my will & meaneinge is, That hee shall make Sale of my Messuage or tenement, garden and backside with the appurtenences scittuate in Sevenock aforesayd, And nowe in the occupacon of one Samuell Weller or his assignes, And of all other my reall and personall estate whatsoever For and towards the payment & sattisfaccion of the same, And for defrayeinge my funerall Charges, and proveing this my will, Item I give and bequeath unto my youngest sonne Henry Cronke the sume of tenn pounds of lawfull money of England for and towards the mainteyneinge, bringinge upp, and placeinge him out, as an Apprentice, Item I give and bequeath unto my Second sonne William Cronke one full third parte of the Remaynder or overplus of my estate whatsoever, to be paid or delivered to them within one Moneth after my debts and funerall Charges payd, All the rest and residue of my Sayd estate I give and bequeath to my Sayd Sonne John Cronke whome I make and ordayne Sole executor of this my sayd Will In wittnes whereof I have hereunto sett my hand and Seale the day and yeare first above written
John Cronke
Signed Sealed and published to be the last will and testament of the sayd John Cronke in the presence of Richard Cronke
David Woodroofe his marke Robt. Newman

80

CRONKE John	Tailor	bur. 5 Nov. 1671
I. 14 Nov. 1671	prov. 7 Jun. 1672	PRS/I/3/110

An Inventary of all and singuler the goods Chattles and debts of John Cronke late of Seavenoke in the County of Kent Taylor deceased Taken, valued and apprаysed the Fowerteeneth day of November in the yeare of our Lord 1671 by Martine Pike and Robert Norman as followeth vizt.

In the Inner Chamber			
Inprimis one peeced feather bed and boulster 1 bedstedle Matt and Cord one payer of Curtaynes vallens and Curtaine Rodds Two blancketts and one Rugg	£iii		
Item one Joyned Chest & 1 Joyned Box		x^{s}	
Item Two Cushions		ii^{s}	
Item one Joyned Stoole and some other Lumber there			xii^{d}
In the Chamber called the Shopp			
Item i Long Table 1 little Table and one wooden Chaire		x^{s}	
Item one Iron pott one little Iron pott one payre of Brand Irons one payre of old Tongs & Fire Shovell one payre of bellowes 2 old Chaires & one warming pann		xii^{s}	
Item Two old Chests 2 peeces of pewter one brasse basting Ladle, severall wooden dishes Spoones and Trenchers		x^{s}	
Item 9 payre of Sheetes both fine and Course severall other peeces of Lynen and woollen Cloths	£iiii		
Item divers shelves boxes and other Lumber there		xv^{s}	
Summa totalis huius Inventorii	£x		

81

CAKOTT Richard	Cordwainer	bur. 10 Jun. 1672
W. 29 Oct. 1671	prov. 21 June 1672	PRS/W/3/257

In the name of God Amen I Richard Cakott Sinior of Seavenoaks in the County of Kent Cordwiner being of parffict memory thanks be to god For it I doe make And ordaine this my Last will and Testament in maner & Forme Following Inprimis I bequeth my Soule to god that gave it hoping in & through my Lord & Saver Jesus Christ For remission of all my Sinnes And my body to be buryed after the descrestione of my Executrex
Item I give to my Sonne William Cakott his heires & executors the Lease of the Farme wherein now he Liveeth And the Lease of that Farme which I hire

now of Nicholas Trice which belongeth to Dame Margret Bossell my sonne William Cakott paying The rent According to the Leases
Item I give to my Sonne Richard Cakott his heires And executors The Lease of this house & Land where in now I Live he to take all the priveledges of all the other Leases that Are Lett under the grand Lease he paying the rent According to the Lease Further I give to him My sonne Richard Aforesaid all The stoke of hoppoles & Corne & hay or grase whatsoever whether without dores or within And all the mexsons of Dung that Are belonging to this Farme And all the goods that belong to the bruhouse & the seller & all the shelves And things Fixed to the house belonging to the tennant
Item I give to my Sonne Robert Cakott his heires executors twenty pounds of Lawffull mony of Eingland To be paid him A quarter of A yeare After the decease of My Executrex
Item I give to my Dafter Grace Edwards my bead where now I Lyone & All the Furinture belonging to it And one Trunk bound About with Iron standing in the Farther Chamber she to have them after the desese of My executrex
Item I give to my Dafter Rebakco Couldard the sume of tenn Shillings of Lawffull mony of Eingland to be paid A quarter of A yeare after the desece of My Executrex
Item I give to my Grandchild Jane Write the sume of Five pownds of Lawffull mony of England to be paid A quarter of A yeare after the desese of My Executrex
Item I give to my Grandchild Thomas Gorton the sume of tenn pownds of Lawffull mony of Eingland to be paid A quarter of A yeare After the desese of my Executrex
Item I give to my Grandchild & Godsonn Richard Cakott sonn of the Above writen Richard Cakott my sonn The Draw Table in the Lettle paller & the Carpet & 6 Joyn Stoules after the desece of My Executrex.
Item I give to My Dafter Ann Bankin one draw Table & A Carpet In my owne Chamber where now I Lye after the desece of My Executrex Item I give to my Cusen Edward Medhurst The sume of thirty shillings of Lawffull mony of Eingland to be paid by my Executrex this thirty shillings I give because he should be willing to goe out of the house if Occation serve Item I give to Jane Caket my Wife whome I make my Full & sole Executrex three roomes of the said house where now I live which Edw: Medhurst now useth of me For the Terme of the Lease if shee so Long Live For her to Leive in rent Free if she please Further I doe give to my said Wife all the rest of my goods & Chatels whatsoever paying my debts all which I give to her For her Life & after her Deth to goe to my sonns William Cakott & Richard Cakott & my Dafters Grace Edwards & Ann Bankin to them & there heires For Ever to be Equally devided betwixt them & paying the Leageses Above writte giveen betwene them Equally & this my Last will And testament I have here unto sett my hand & seal the ninne And twentyth Day of October in the three & twenteth yeare of the raine of our Soverant Lord Charles the Second by the grace of god King of Eingland Scotland France & Ireland defender of the Faith etc. Anno Domini 1671
Richard Cakott
Witness Henry Swaysland George Morgan

82

CAKOTT Richard bur. 10 Jun. 1672
I. 12 Jun. 1672 prov. 28 Jun. 1672 PRS/I/3/1

An Inventary of all and singuler the goods & Chattles and Debts of Richard Cakott late of Seavenoke in the County of Kent deceased Taken valued and appraysed by Thomas Chorley, William Allen and Nicholas Trice the Twelfth day of June in the yeare of our Lord One Thousand six hundred Seaventy and Two as followeth vizt

Inprimis for his wearing Apparrell and money in his purse	£x		
Item 1 bedstead with Matt and Cord and Curtaines and vallens one Flocke bed, – one Flocke bolster & 4 feather pillowes 1 Rugg and 1 Blanckett	£iii	x^{s}	
Item 2 Joyned presses, one Joyned Chest one old Table	£i	xviii^{s}	
Item 2 Elbowe Chayres and one wicker Chaire and 6 Turkey worke stooles		xii^{s}	
Item one a payre of Andirons One Fire pann and Tongs and a payre of bellowes One old Court Cubboard 2 old Boxes		xiii^{s}	iiii^{d}
In the Inner Chamber			
Item i bedsted with matt and Cord with Curtaines and vallens one feather bed i Flocke bolster i Rugg i blanckett	£ii	xv^{s}	
Item 3 old Trunks 2 old Chestes one old Table one stoole		xii^{s}	
Item 3 payre of flaxen sheetes and 12 payre of hempen and Towen sheetes 3 hempen Table Clothes, 1 dozen of dyaper Napkins i dozen of hempen Napkins 4 payre of pillowe Coates 6 Course Table Cloths & 6 Towells	£vi	xiii^{s}	iiii^{d}
Item i old Carpet		ii^{s}	
In the Topp of the staires			
Item one halfe head bedstead with matt and Cord i Flockebed 1 Flocke bolster i blanckett and one old Rugg	£i	i^{s}	
In the Closet			

Item five stone of woole	£i	iii^{s}	iiii^{d}
Item i box with some woollen yarne		vi^{s}	viii^{d}
In the Kitchine			
Item i Table 1 forme, 6 old Chaires and stooles 2 glass Cases		xi^{s}	
Item one Jacke 3 spitts i Andiron i payre of Creepers with fire pann and Tongs 2 payre of pott hookyers i old Ironbake one Gridiron		xix^{s}	
Item 21 pewter dishes i payre of pewter Candlesticks 4 pewter potts, 2 Flaggons 1 pewter Cullender 2 Saltes Sellers 6 porringers i Aquevite bottle	£ii	viii^{s}	
Item one Still 4 Chamber potts		xi^{s}	
Item 4 brasse Kettles i brasse pann, 2 warming panns, 2 little brassepotts 4 brasse skilletts	£ii	v^{s}	
Item 3 Iron potts one Iron Kettle one Iron Dripping pann		xvi^{s}	vi^{d}
In the Buttery			
Item 2 old Cubboards 2 dozen of Trenchers one Wooden Morter one Iron pastell		xiii^{s}	iiii^{d}
In the Milke House			
Item Two powdering Tubbs 6 Milke Trayes one old Cubboard, one stalder one old Forme		xviii^{s}	
In the Bake House			
Item one Bacon Trough one bunting Hutch 2 sives		vi^{s}	viii^{d}
Item Two Chests		vii^{s}	
In the Stable			
Item 9 horses one Colt	£xxx		
Item 12 Horse harnesse	£iiii		
Item one Rod Sadle and Bridle		v^{s}	
In the Yard			
Item Two Waggons	£x		
Item one plowe and plow Irons		xv^{s}	
Item one harrowe and Roale		v^{s}	
Item 2 Cart & one water Cart	£iii	v^{s}	
Item one Beame and scale and weights belonging to them	£i		
Item a parcell of Coales	£i		
Item Two Sheates		xvii^{s}	
Item Nine & forty sheepe at 6s. 8d. a sheepe	£xvi	vi^{s}	viii^{d}
Item 29 Lambs at 4s. a Lamb	£v	xvi^{s}	
Item three Cowes	£ix	xv^{s}	

Item three hundred of Faggotts and some Cordwood and Loggs about the yard	)	£ii	viii^s	
Item a parcell of Hay in the Barne		£vi		
Item some Lumber in and about the house unseene and forgotten	)		xii^s	
Suma totalis huius Inventarii		£cxxxiiii	iiii^s	x^d

83

GROOMBRIDGE John   Innholder   bur. 17 Jun. 1672
I. 22 Jun. 1672   prov. 15 Jul. 1672   PRS/I/7/60

An Inventory of all and singuler the Goods chattles and debts of John Groombridge late of Seavenoke in the County of Kent deceased taken valued and appraysed by Thomas Greene and John Beardsworth the two and Twentieth day of June Anno Domini 1672 as followeth vizt.

Inprimis his wearing Apparrell and moneys in his purse	vi^l		
In the Kitchin			
Item Brasse pewter Jacks Spitts with diverse other things valued at	viii^l	xv^s	
In the Parlor			
Item 2 Tables with Chaires Stooles and certaine other things valued at	ii^l	i^s	
In the Shopp			
Item an old Table and other things valued at		x^s	
In the Buttery			
Item 6 old Iron potts and other things valued at	i^l		vi^d
In the Mill House and Brewe House			
Item Two Furnashes a Mesh fatt a Tun a Cooler and other things valued at	xxvii^l	xii^s	
In the yard			
Item an horse mare sowe piggs and other things valued at	xxi^l	v^s	
In the Sellar			
Item 13 hogsheads 4 pipes 5 hogsheads of Beers and other things valued at	xvi^l	ii^s	vi^d
In the Chamber over the Shopp			
Item 3 feather bedds bolsters and other things valued at	xii^l	xv^s	x^d
In the Passage Chamber			
Item a feather bed boulster etc valued at	iii^l	v^s	

In other Chambers			
Item Bedsteads Bedds Trunks linen and some plate valued at	xxiii^{l}	xiii^{s}	iiii^{d}
Item a parcell of Malt Wheate Oates and other things valued at	v^{l}	x^{s}	
Item in supposed good debts	v^{l}		
Summa totalis huius inventorii	Cxxxiii^{l}	xi^{s}	ii^{d}

84

RUNDALL Richard — Gardener — bur. 12 Jul. 1672
I. 23 Jul. 1672 — prov. 31 Jul. 1672 — PRS/I/18/60

An Inventory of all & singuler the goods & chattles of Richard Rundall late of Sevenoake in the County of Kent Gardner taken & apprized by William Wall gent & William Allen Mercer the three & twentyeth day of July in the four & twentieth yeare of the raigne of our Soveraign Lord Charles the second of England France and Ireland defender of the faith etc Annoque Domini 1672

	£	*s.*	*d.*
Inprimis his weareing apparell and ready money in his purse	3.	0.	0.
In the Hall			
Item a Table & frame & forme a joynt Cubboard & joyned setle	0.	18.	0.
Item an Iron Jack & weight a birding peece two spitts & a dripping pann	01.	0.	0.
Item a paire of cast brandiron a paire of tongs a fire pann an iron creeper two paire of pothangers & an iron before the fire & a paire of bellowes	0.	11.	0.
Item one other paire of iron brandirons two warmeing panns & a lanthorne	0.	7.	6.
Item four old chaires & one low stoole & six old cushions	0.	3.	4.
Item 60 pound of pewter att 9d per pound	2.	5.	0.
In the parlor			
Item a table & frame & Carpett Court cubboard &			

cubboard cloath & seaven joyned stooles & two chaires	)	0.	18.	0.
Item two pewter stills & a sideboard		1.	2.	0.
Item a paire of small Andirons fire shovell tongs an Iron forke & a paire of Snuffers	)	0.	5.	0.
Item severall potts bottles & earthen ware		0.	5.	0.
Item severall old bookes		0.	5.	0.
In the buttery				
Item 3 small drinke tubbs a Stalder & a powdring tubb	)	0.	6.	8.
Item a brasse frying pann		0.	5.	0.
In the small buttery				
Item one Kilderkin one shall and one Keeler		0.	5.	0.
In the Milkehowse				
Item an old brasse Ketle & an old table		0.	5.	0.
In the Brewhowse				
Item 3 tubbs & two Keelers		0.	13.	4.
Item one furnace		0.	15.	0.
Item two Iron Kettles three iron potts a skillett		1.	2.	0.
Item five brasse Skylletts & other brasse ware		0.	7.	0.
Item an old Cheesepresse & five pailes & some wooden dishes & other small wooden ware & a halfe hundred leaden weight	)	0.	12.	0.
Item severall Gardners Tooles		0.	10.	0.
In the best chamber				
Item four silver cupps & two dozen of spoones		10.	0.	0.
Item one Bedsteadle matt & Cord Curtaine & Valance of Stripstuffe & Curtaine Rodds	)	0.	10.	0.
Item two feather bedds two blanketts & a coverlett one feather boulster & two feather pillows	)	7.	0.	0.
Item twenty paire of sheetes 8 paire of pillow-beares eight tablecloths & two dozen of Napkins & some od old napkins	)	7.	0.	0.
Item seaven old Chaires one stoole two old Deskes & a table & tablecloath	)	0.	17.	0.
Item three old Truncks and a close stoole & pann & a Court Cubboard & cloath	)	0.	11.	0.
Item a window Curtaine & curtainerod		0.	1.	6.
In the Hall Chamber				

Item one old bedstead matt cord old Curtins & valance	0.	10.	0.
Item one other Bedstead matt Cord Curtaines & valance & Curtaine rodds	0.	10.	0.
Item one Feather bedd one feather pillow two feather boulsters two blanketts & a Coverlett	3.	0.	0.
Item one trundle bedd matt & cord a flockbed a feather boulster a blankett & Coverlett	1.	0.	0.
Item one wainscott presse one truncke three chests a joynt stoole & a looking glasse	1.	0.	0.
In the Brewhowse Chamber			
Item one bedsteadle matt & Cord old Curtaines & curtine roods	0.	15.	0.
Item a feather bedd a flock boulster & two feather pillows two blanketts & a rugg	2.	0.	0.
Item an old Chest & a Flaskett a sadle	0.	6.	0.
In the farther chamber			
Item two old Bedsteadles & bedding very old	1.	0.	0.
Item a folding table & an old corne scry & some old lumber	0.	4.	0.
Item for old lumber & things not seen	0.	6.	8.
In the Barne & other outhowses and in the yard			
Item for Hay in the barne	2.	0.	0.
Item for peaseham in the barne	1.	0.	0.
Item a waggon & two old dung Courts and a wheelebarrow	2.	0.	0.
Item an old plow a parcell of Charcoale & three old hoppframes & two hosthares & three hopp bines & a cole shovell	2.	0.	0.
Item for wood & faggotts in severall places	0.	10.	0.
Item 6 piggs att 8^{s} peece	2.	8.	0.
Item 3 Cowes	9.	0.	0.
Item one horse	3.	0.	0.
Item a Colt	1.	10.	0.
Item a mare & Colt	2.	10.	0.
Item for a stock of Hoppoles on an acre & an halfe of ground	5.	0.	0.
Item one acre of Barley	1.	0.	0.

Item one acre and halfe of oates		1.	10.	0.
Item an acre and a quarter of Roots		2.	10.	0.
Item for severall young nurseries in severall	)			
places of the ground	)	10.	0.	0.
Some totall		97.	9.	8.
Item oweing to the deceased on bond & otherwise	)			
severall debts some whereof are separate and others	)			
desperate	)	20.	0.	0.

Will Wall Will Allen

85

EVEREST Robert Yeoman
W. 28 Jul. 1672 prov. 23 Aug. 1672 PRS/10/5/181

In the Name of God Amen I Robert Everest of Seavenock in the County of Kent yeoman this eyght and Twentyth day of July in the yeere of our Lord God One Thousand Sixe Hundred Seaventy and Two being sick in body, but of sound and perfect memory thanks bee therefore given to Almighty God doe make and ordeyne this my last will and testament in maner & forme following. First I recommend my soule & spiritt into the hands of All-mightthy god who give itt, Assuredly trusting through the alone merritts of my onely Saviour Jesus Christ to obteyne remission of all my sinns, And my body I committ to the earth to bee Decently buryed hopinge for a Joyfull resurreccion to life everlastinge. Item I will and bequeath unto Elizabeath my loveing wife all my goods Cattel and Chattels whatsoever and I doe likewise will unto the said Elizabeath my wife the rents of my tenement in the parishe of Leigh in the County of Kent in the which Mychaell Doane liveth Duringe her naturall life, shee the said Elizabeath I will to pay out of it within sixe yeers after my decease to my two sisters Joane the wife of John Budgin & Christian the wife of Robert French the sume of Tenn pounds apeece, but if it happen that either of my said sisters shall decease before the said money be due and payable that the Children of either of them that shall bee deceased shall have the said money equally betwixt them. And as for the disposinge of my land, I will and bequeath unto William Sutton the sonne of my sister Aymie and his heires all that my meassuage or tenement wherein the said Mychaell Doane liveth lieing in the parishe of Leigh in the County of Kent Imediately after the decease of Elizabeath my wife, And I will that hee the said William Sutton shall pay to William Budgin the sonn of my sister Joane

the sum of Twenty pounds within one yeere after the decease of Elizabeth my wife, Item I will and bequeath to Thomas French the sonn of my sister Christian the sume of Twenty pounds to be paid him by the said William Sutton within one whole yeere after the decease of Elizabeath my wife, And I doe ordeyne and make Elizabeath my loveing wife the executrixe of this my will and Teastament, In wittnes whereof I have to this my present Will written in one sheete of paper put my seale and subscribed my name the day and yeere first above written
Robert Everest
Sealed Signed published & declared in the presence of

the marke of John Polhill   Thomas Rodgers

86

EVEREST Robert   Yeoman
I. 12 Aug. 1672   prov. 9 Sept. 1672   PRS/I/5/25

A true Inventary of all and singuler the goods and household-stuffe Corne Cattell and Chattells of Robert Everest late of Seavenock in the county of Kent Yeoman deceased taken valued and aprized the Twelveth day of August in the Fower and Twentieth yeare of the reigne of our Sovereigne Lord Charles the second by the grace of God King of England Scotland France and Ireland defender of the Faith etc Annoque Domini 1672 by John Children and Thomas Rogers as followeth

	£	*s.*	*d.*
Inprimis the said deceaseds purse girdle and ready money	01	4	0
Item his Wearing apparrell of all sorts	03	0	0
In the Hall two Joyned stooles two Chaires six peeces of pewter one pewter Candlestick one brasse Morter a Warming pann a bread grate certaine small bookes and three Quishions	01	9	0
In the Parlour one baskett one Chaire three Quishions and in a little room adjoyning to the parlour Three powdering tubbs and about a dozen of Trenchers	00	18	0
In the Buttery adjoyning to the Parlour Two drinck vessells Two vinegar vessells two keelers one milktray and two basketts	00	6	8
In the Little Parlour certaine Cheeses and six fleeces of wooll	01	15	0
In the Buttery adjoyning to the Hall Three drinck vessells Fower sacks a saddle an a Pillion	00	13	4
In the Wassh-house Fower brasse Kettles two			

brasse potts one Iron Kettle one brasse skillett and Five Pailes	01	7	0
In the Kitchen one dresser board one forme two chaires two brandirons a fire slice a paire of tongs two paire of Pothanders two paire of potthookes one spitt two smoothing Irons a great brasse Kettle and a paire of bellowes	01	0	0
In the Brewhouse a brewing Furnace	03	10	0
Item two brewing tubbs one bucking tubb one renning tubb two Keelers and certaine Cheese bailes	01	5	0
In the bakehouse one tubb two Keelers two formes and three sieves	00	12	0
In the Milkhouse Fower milk-keelers nyne milk trayes two churnes one frying pann certaine butter and cheese and certaine earthenware	01	5	0
In the Chamber over the Hall one Joyned bedsteddle with Curtaines and vallance one flock bedd one Chaffbedd two chaff bolsters Five blancketts and two Coverletts	02	4	6
Item two Joyned Chests and two boarded Chests	01	5	0
Item Twelve paire of Sheets Five table Cloathes Three dozen and a half of napkins Five paire of Pillowcoates and Sixteene towells	06	6	0
Item one peice of new Linnen Cloth	00	4	0
Item one Wicker Chayre and Joyned Stoole	00	1	6
In the Chamber over the Parlour one Joyned bedsteddle with curtaines and vallance one feather bedd one feather bolster one Coverlett and two blancketts	04	15	0
Item one Table with a Joyned frame one Joyned Chest and one boarded Chest	00	15	0
Item certaine Flax, Hemp, tow and Yarne at the Weavers	01	15	0
Item Thirteene Peices of Pewter Eight Porrengers Tenn sacers one Pewter pott two salts and Eight spoones	02	0	0
In the Chamber over the Buttery one bedsteddle a Chaffbed a Chaffbolster an old Chest and about a Quarter of Barley	00	14	0
In the Garretts certaine Wheate and oates one Parchment scry one shall a tovett and a sieve	01	11	0
In the Oast loft about a Quarter of Mault an oasthair, one Wollen Wheele and two Linnen wheeles	00	15	0
Item about Tenn acres of Wheate	11	10	0
Item about Fourteene acres of Oates	10	3	0
Item Eight Milch Cowes	20	0	0

Item Fower workeing Cattell, Fower steers and one Heifer	24	0	0
Item Three Weaning Calves	02	10	0
Item Tenn sheepe	03	6	8
Item Thirteene Swine	06	5	0
Item Two Mares	05	0	0
Item Two Colts	04	0	0
Item one Waggon one Court, one plow three harrowes one Roll three Yoakes two tights two Chapes and all other Husbandry tooles and tackling	09	8	0
Item certaine hay and Clover	4	0	0
Item certaine debts oweing to the said deceased	01	10	0
Item certaine things of small value unseene and forgotten	00	6	8
Summa Totalis	142	10	4

87

EVEREST John Yeoman bur. 13 Aug. 1672
W. 8 Aug. 1672 prov. 7 Sept. 1672 PRS/W/5/182

In the Name of God Amen the Eighth day of August Anno Domini 1672 I John Everest of the parish of Seavenoke in the County of Kent yeoman being Sick in Body but of perfect mind and memory praysed be god therefore doe make this my last Will in maner following First I beqeath my Sowle to Allmighty God who infused the same And my Body to the Earth to be decently interred assuredly trusting by the merits of my Saviour Christ Jesus to be made partaker of life everlasting And as touching the disposeing of that estate wherewith the Lord hath blessed mee my Will is as followeth Inprimis I give my Landes in Pemberee in Kent now in occupacon of Edward Turner to my loveing wyfe Anne during hir natuall life and after hir decease to my brother Peter Everest during his natural life and after his decease to his daughter Mildred now wife of Thomas Morley Junior and hir heires for ever Item I give to my Sister Margaret wyfe of Lionell Sutton Fifty Shillings of lawfull English Money to be payed to hir by my Kinsman Peter Everest Sonne of my Brother William Everest within Six Moneths after my Wives decease. Item to my Sister Jane wyfe of Robert Pickett Fifty Shillings of like money payable by the said Peter within Six Moneths after my said Wives decease Item to my Sister Elizabeth and hir Sonne Thomas Mathewes Twenty Five Shillings apeice to be payed unto them by the said Peter at the time aforesaid And yf my said Sister Elizabeth dye before payment thereof then I give the whole Fifty Shillings to the said Thomas Item to James Weller my Kinsman Forty Shillings to be payed by the said Peter Everest my Kinsman within Six Moneths after my Wives decease Item to Thomas Smith

Sonne of my Sister Mildred Twenty Shillings to be payed by the said Peter as aforesaid Item to Francis Sonne of my Brother William deceased Forty Shillings to be paid also by the said Peter as aforesaid Item to my Brother Daniel Everest Forty Shillings to be payed by the said Peter my Kinsman as aforesaid. Item to my Brother Francis Everest Forty Shillings to be payed by the said Peter as abovesaid. Item to John Sutton Sonne of Lionell Sutton Twenty Shillings to be payed by the said Peter as abovesaid. To Margaret Sutton xx^{s} to be payed by the said Peter. Item to Anne wyfe of my Cozen John Everest Forty Shillings to be payed by my Executrix within One Moneth after my decease Item to the poor people of the Almes Row of Seavenoke Ten Shillings to be payed them by my Executrix within One Moneth after my decease. Item I nominate Anne my said loveing wyfe Executrix of this my Will And my will is that shee shall have the use of my farme wherein I live caled Elses and all my Stock thereon together with all my Howshold goods during hir naturall life shee paying the Rent for the said farme and makeing noe wilfull wast or destruction thereof And after hir decease I give the said Lease Stock and howshold goods to my said Kinsman Peter Everest his Executors and Assignes upon the Condicon that he pay my Legacies aforesaid And I nominate my loveing freinds William Wall and Richard Children Overseers of this my Will In Witnes whereof I have hereunto sett my hand and Seale the day and yeare above written revokeing all former Wills.

his marke John Everest

Sealed and delivered and declared for his Last Will in presence of Chris Thomas William Wall Richard Children

88

EVEREST John	Yeoman	bur. 13 Aug. 1672
I. 26 Aug. 1672	prov. 9 Sep. 1672	PRS/I/5/24

An Inventary of all and singuler the Goodes Chattells and Credits of John Everest late whilst he lived of the parish of Seavenoke in the County of Kent yeoman deceased Taken and praysed the Six and Twentieth day of August Anno Domini 1672 By Christopher Thomas Gent William Wall yeoman and Richard Children yeoman as followeth vizt.//

Inprimis the deceaseds Wearing Apparell and ready Money in his Purse		xl^{s}
In the Hall		
Item one Table with a Frame a Forme, Two Joyned Stooles 3 Chayres a Settle a Warmeing pan an old Cubberd, Three Spits 2 Iron Dripping pans one Lattin pan 2 paire of Potthookes one Gridiron, Two paire of Potthangers a paire of Brandirons	£iii	

one great Bible with some other small Books	)			
Seaven Cushins a Chafing Dish and a Brasse	)			
Skymer a paire of old Tongs a Fire pan and a	)			
Lether Meale sack	)			
Item Seaven Pewter Dishes 2 Pewter Candlesticks	)			
a Flower pott a small Beaker one Saltseller one	)			
Porrenger Two Chamberpots one pint pott one	)		xv^{s}	
pewter Quart-pott and three Sawcers	)			
Item one Browne Boule				vi^{d}
Item one great Brasse pan one litle Brasse pan	)			
one Brasse Ketle one postnett a paire of Brasse	)		xvi^{s}.	
Candlesticks and a brasse pestle and Mortar	)			
Item Three Basketts and an old Red Sadole			ii^{s}.	vi^{d}.
Suma		£iiii	xiiii^{s}.	
In the Drinke Buttery				
Item Two Kilderkins Two Pins a Powdering Tub an	)		xii^{s}.	
old hutch with certaine Lumber an Iron Beame an	)			
Iron half hundred Wayte with Skales and Five	)			
small Leaden Waytes	)			
Suma patet				
In the Milkhowse				
Item one Iron Ketle 3 Payles a Bole dish with	)			
certen small Dishes and Trenchers an old Tun	)			
Tubbe Two Leather Bottells a Churne 2 old	)			
Kilderkins and a Lanthorne. Two litle Milkeelers	)		xx^{s}.	
Three Milke Trayes a Butter platter with a	)			
Mustard Bole and a Frying pan	)			
Suma patet				
In the Kitchen				
Item a Brasse Furnace Fower Tubbes a Long Keeler	)			
a Kneading Trough a Bacon Trough Two Cheese	)		xxvi^{s}.	viii^{s}.
presses and an old Tun Tub	)			
Suma patet				
In the Hall Chamber				
Item one Bedstedle with Curtens and Vallence, one	)			
Fether bed 2 Fether bolsters 2 Fether pillowes	)			
a Coverlett a Blankett, a Truckle bed a Flock	)	£iiii	x^{s}.	
bed a Bolster and a Coverlett	)			
Item one Cubbert Fower Chists an old Table	)			
Cubbert a litle forme a Chaire, Two Joyned	)	£iii	x^{s}.	
Stooles and about Five Stone of Wooll	)			
Item old Bedstedle				xii^{d}.
Item ten paire of Sheets one paire of Pillowcoats	)			

Eleaven Napkins 9 Towells Five course Tableclothes and 6 old course Napkins	)	£iiii	x^{s}.
Suma		£xii	xi^{s}.

In the Parlor Chamber

Item a Bedstedle a Feather bed a Feather Bolster an old Table a Forme a Table Chaire a Joyned Stoole and an old Chest	)		xxx^{s}.
Suma patet			

In the mens Chamber

Item one old Bedstedle Fower Quarters of Wheate in the Garrett and Five Quarters of Oats	)	£vi	i^{s}.
Item Fifty Cops of Oates in the Barne		£vii	x^{s}.
Item 33 Cops of Wheate		£iiii	x^{s}.
Item Ten loads of Hay		£x	
Item Barley on the Grownd			x^{s}.
Item one old Waggon one old Court an old Plow with all other Implements of Husbandry and Husbandry Tacklings and old Iron	)	£iiii	
Item Two Shawles with Sives Sacks Measures and Swippes	)		xv^{s}.
Item Two great Hogges and Eight Sheats		£v	
Item 12 Sheepe		£iiii	
Item Fower Oxen and Nine Cowes		£xliii	
Item Two Steeres, a Bull Three Heyfars and Three weaning Calves Two Mares and Two Colts	)	£xxxiii	
Item the Lease of the Farme and Amendment of Land	)	£xx	
Item owing to the deceased at the time of his death in Sperat Debts	)	£xv	
Item left by the deceased in redy Money at the time of his death	)	£xxviii	
Suma		£clxxxi	
Suma) totalis		£cciiii	xix^{s}. viii^{d}.

89

EVERIDGE Richard Yeoman bur. 4 Feb. 1673
W. 11 Jan. 1673 prov. 8 Oct. 1673 PRS/W/5/185

In the Name of God Amen. The Eleaventh day of January In the yeare of our Lord One thousand six hundred Seaventy and Two I Richard Everidge of

Seavenoke in the County of Kent yeoman being sick and weake in body but of perfect minde and memory thankes be given to Almightie God doe make and ordeyne this my last Will and Testament (revokeing all former Wills by me made) in manner & forme following vizt. First and principally I will and resigne my Soule into the hands of him that gave it trusting assuredly for salvation through the alsufficient merritts of Jesus Christ my blessed Saviour and Redeemer, and for my body I committ the same to the earth decently to be buryed at the discretion of my Executor hereafter named Item I give and bequeath to the poor of the Weild of Seavenoake Ten shillings to be paid within six months next after my decease by my Executor hereafter named to the Overseers for the poor of the aforesaid Weild and by them to be distributed according to their discretions. Item I give and bequeath unto Elizabeth Everidge the wife of Richard Everidge the younger lately deceased one shilling to be paid unto her upon demand Item I give unto her daughter Elizabeth one shilling to be also paid upon demand Item I give and bequeath unto Ann Everidge one other of the daughters of the said Elizabeth the sum of five pounds of lawfull English money to be paid unto her by my Executors hereafter named when she shall attaine the age of one and twenty yeares Item I give and bequeath unto Thomas Everidge one of the sonns of the said Elizabeth Everidge the sum of Twenty pounds to be also paid him at his age and one and Twenty years. Item I give and bequeath unto Richard Everidge one other of the Sonns of the said Elizabeth the sume of Tenn pounds to be also paid him when he shall come to the age of one and Twenty yeares. Item I give and bequeath to my man Servant Thomas Keeble the sum of Twenty shillings of lawfull English money to be paid unto him within one yeare next after my decease. Item I give and bequeath unto my Granddaughter Mary Everidge the sume of Thirty pounds of lawfull English money to be paid unto her by my Executors hereafter named when shee shall come to the age of one and Twenty years or day of marriage which shall first happen Item I give and bequeath to the said Mary Everidge two needle worke wrought square stooles now standing in the Hall Chamber Item I give and bequeath unto my loving wife Susann Everidge – the Feather bedd in the Chamber where shee now lyeth with the bedstead Curtaines vallens and furniture thereto belonging also I give unto her two paire of the best hempen sheetes one Joyned Chest as she shall elect & chuse and two chaires Item I give and devise unto Susann my said wife in lieu and recompence of all such Dower and title of Dower as she shall may or might have or claime out, of, in, or to all or any of my lands or Tenements whatsoever One Annuitye or yearly rent charge of Eight pounds of lawful money of England (freed and discharged of and from all payments of Taxes and deductions whatsoever) to be yearly issueing goeing forth and received out of and in all and singuler the Messuage or Tenements Lands and premises thereto belonging wherein I now dwell Scituate lying and being in the severall parrishes of Seavenoke aforesaid and Cheevening in the said County of Kent and now in my tenure or occupacion To be paid unto my said Wife or her Assignes dureing her natural life Quarterly That is to say at Feasts of the birth of our Lord Christ the Annunciacion of the blessed Virgine Mary St. John the Baptist and St. Michaell Tharchangell by even and equall porcens the first of the said payments to be made at the next of the said Feasts or dayes of payment which shall happen after my decease And if it shall happen that the said Annuity or yearly rent of eight pounds shall be behinde and unpaid in part or in the whole by the space of one and twenty dayes next after any of the said Feasts or dayes of payment upon which the same ought to be paid as aforesaid (being lawfully demanded) Then and soe often I will that it shall and maybe lawfull to and for my said wife or her Assignes into all or any part of the said Messuage lands and premisses out of which the same Annuitye is issueing & payable to enter and distreyne and the distresse and distresses then & there found to take lead drive and carry away and the same to deteyne and keep untill the said Annuitye or yearly rent of eight pounds with all arrearages thereof (if any be) and all charges and expences occationed by reason of the takeing of such distresse or distresses and non payment after said Annuitye be fully satisfied contented and paid But if my said Wife shall at any time after my decease goe about by suite either in Law or Equitie to recover any Dower or other Interest or estate whatsoever Then and from thenceforth I will that the said Annuitye of Eight pounds shall cease and determine to all intents and purposes whatsoever And that the Messuage and premisses aforesaid out of which the same is issueing and payable shall be thereof altogeather acquitted and discharged And as for touching and concerning all that my Messuage or Tenement wherein I now dwell togeather with all and singuler Barnes Stables stawles outhowses edifices buildings yards Gardens orchards and all those severall peices or parcells of land Arrable meadow pasture and Woodground to the same belonging with the appurtenances commonly called or knowne by the severall names of Hatchlands Pightlakes Courtmeads and the bush or by what other name or names soever the samelands are comonly called or knowne being part or parcell of the Mannor of Bowsell and is Scituate lying and being in Seavenoke and Cheevening aforesaid I give and bequeath to my three Grandsonns Richard Everidge John Everidge and Charles Everidge being the sonns of my late deceased Sonn Richard Everidge and which were borne to him by his first wife To have and to hold to my said three Grandsonns last mencioned and their heires and Assigned for ever by an equall division share and share alike chargeable with and liable to the said Annuitye as aforesaid Item my will and minde is that all my Stock upon my Farme and all my goods & Chattells whatsoever not herein before bequeathed be sold by my Executors hereafter named with what convenient speed maybe after my decease And the money thereof ariseing to be paid to discharge such debts as are owing upon my Land or otherwise soe farr as the same will extend reserving out of the same so much as shall discharge the Legacyes before bequeathed as the same shall become due & payable Also my will & minde is that my said Executors shall cutt downe soe many trees now growing in Hatchlands wood where the underwood is now felling as to them shall seeme meet & convenient and the money thereof ariseing to be imployed towards the payment of my debts. And lastly I doe constitute and appoint my Grandson Richard Everidge my Executor and my Loving Freind James Harborough to be Executor with my said Grandson dureing his minority and to have the disposicon of my goods and payment & receit of my Debts untill he come of age And I doe constitute and

appoint my loving Freinds Mr George Petty of Ottford and Thomas Greene of Seavenoake my Overseers desireing their care & assistance to see this my Last Will performed In witnes whereof to this my last will & Testament written in fower Sheetes of paper to every one of which I have set my hand and to the last have set my seale the day & yeare above written./.
Richard Everidge
Signed Sealed published and declared in the presence of George Petty
The mark of Thomas Keeble
The mark of Richard King

90

EVERIDGE Richard	Yeoman	bur. 4 Feb. 1673
I. 21 Feb. 1673	prov. 4 Jul. 1674	PRS/I/5/37

An Inventary of all and singuler the goods and Chattles of Richard Everidge late of Seavenoke in the County of Kent Yeoman deceased made taken valued and apprized this 21 Day of February in the yeare of our Lord 1672 by Mr. William Wall and Tho: Rogers as followeth (vizt)

Inprimis Money in his purse & weareing apparrell of all sorts	£iiii		
In the Kitchin			
Item one Settle one Iron Jack three spitts firepan & tongs one Iron Back a payre of Cast Brandirons one payre of Iron Racks one Tinn Dripping pan one paire of pot hangers	£i	xii^{s}	viii^{d}
In the Parlour			
Item one Drawing table one folding table one Cupbord of Drawers 4 leather Chaires 5 Joynt Stools 3 old Cushions 2 payre of small Andirons of brass	£ii	xi^{s}	
In the Parlour Chamber			
Item one feather Bed 2 blanketts one bolster 3 pillowes one Rugg 1 Bedstead Curtaines and Valence with curtain rods matt and cord 1 Joynt press 1 side board 4 short Carpetts 3 Chaires 1 old folding table and one table Baskett one payre of Bellowes	£vi	vi^{s}	vi^{d}
Item 10 paire of old sheets fower old Towells	£i	x^{s}	
The Milke House Chamber			

Item one flock Bed 2 feather Bolsters one Coverlett one blankett with Bedstead curtain & Valence Matt & Coard	£ii		
Item one trunk & one old Deske		iii^{s}	
In the Kitchin Chamber			
Item one flock bed 3 blanketts one old coverled one Chest one Side board and one Payre of Iron Andirons	£i	viii^{s}	vi^{d}
Item thirty pounds of Wooll		xv^{s}	
The mans Chamber			
Item one Bedstead one Trundle Bedstead 2 Chaff beds one feather Bolster one flock bolster one Chaff bolster one Chaffe Bolster one Blankett and Coverlid		xv^{s}	
In the Garratts			
Item 14 Bushells of Oates one Corne skry one Bushell one Corne shovell one pitch pong one Cutting box and one pitch marke	£i	xv^{s}	
In the Milkhouse			
Item 12 Milke trayes one lead one Churne one podering tub		xviii^{s}	
In the Bakehouse			
Item one old powdring trough one meale sack one frying pann one Keeler one halfe Bushell one Cup-bard 2 sives one Lanthorne one flower Tubb and one Little table		x^{s}	
In the Brewhouse			
Item one meash Tubb one Tunn Tubb 3 Keelers one Cheese Tubb 3 pailes one Cheese press one Gallon & one stalder	£i	vi^{s}	
In the Beare Buttery			
Item 6 Drink Tubbs two Brakes 2 grate leather bottles one Iron pitcher one pitcher and spoone two Bowles one Tunnell with other lumber	£i	x^{s}	
Item 40 peeces of pewter wheighing sixty pounds	£ii	v^{s}	
Item one silver bowle	£i	x^{s}	
Item two Brasse Kettles and three skelletts		xx^{s}	
Item one Beames scales and weights		xiii^{s}	iiii^{d}
Out Dore goods			
Item Corne in the Barne 20 Bushells of Wheat at 2s. 6d.	£ii	x^{s}	
Item Oates threshed and unthreshed	£i	xii^{s}	

Item 12 loads of Hay and Clover	£xii		
Item two horses and one mare	£xi		
Item fower working oxen	£xix		
Item fower steares	£xiii		
Item fower Cowes	£x		
Item one two yeareling heifer and 3 twelve Monthings	£v		
Item 40 Sheepe & 15 lambs	£xv		
Item foure sheathes and a Sow	£ii		
Item one Waggon one Cart three ploughs with other husbandry Tackling	£vii	x^s	
Item fower Acrees of wheat on the ground	£vi	xiii	iiii^d
Item for ploughing of 8 Acres of ground	£ii	viii^s	
Item for faggers hoppoles and hoopes in Hatchlands Wood to Cutt and Cutt	£xl		
Item things out of sight and unprized		v^s	
Item 6 loads of Ash	£vi		
Item one lease from the Lady Boswell wherein there is ten yeares to come at Michaelmas 72	£v		
Suma totalis hujus Inventarii	£cxc	xvii^s	v^d

91

TAYLOR Walter

I. prov. 9 May 1673 PRS/I/23/38

An Inventary of all and singuler the goods Chattles and debts of Walter Taylor of Seavenoaks in the County of Kent Taken valued and appraysed as followeth vizt

Inprimis his wearing Apparrell Goods and household stuffe and Lynen	£v	
Item due to the deceased in Debts		x^s
Item a Legacy given to the deceased in the will of Lydia Taylor deceased and not received by the Administrix which when she doth she will charge herselfe therewith	£xxx	
Suma totalis hujus Inventarii	£xxxv	x^s

the mark of Mary Jones alias Taylor

92

LAMPARD Edward Yeoman
W. 8 Jul. 1673 prov. 2 Dec. 1673 Prob. 11. 343. F. 162

In the name of God Amen I Edward Lampard of the parish of Seavenoke in the County of Kent yeoman being at this present God by praysed therefore in reasonable health and perfect mind and memory but considering the incerteinty of Mans life doe make this my last Will and Testament in manner following First I bequeath my Soule into the hands of my mercifull Creator hoping through the meritts of my blessed Saviour Christ Jesus to be made partaker of eternal life My Body I Committ to the Earth to be decently interred in the Parish Church of Sundrish in the said County by my Executors hereafter named Item I give to the Poore of the said Parish Twenty shillings of lawful money of England to be distributed amongst them at the tyme of my Buriall More I give to the Poore of Sundrish Nine Pownds of like money to be distributed amongst them by my Executors at the fower feasts of our Lord God next after my decease by equall portions Item I give to the Poore of the Parish of Seavenoke Eight pownds of like money to be distributed amongst them within Three moneths after my decease whereof forty shillings to be dealt amongst the Poore of Seavenoke Weild Item I give to the Poore of the Parish of Leigh in the said County Twenty shillings of like money Item I give to Elizabeth Wall daughter of William Wall of Seavenoke aforesaid yeoman Threescore pounds of lawful money To be paid unto her by my Executors at her day of marriage or within Twelve monethes after my decease Item I give to my Kinswoman Elizabeth Rogers daughter of John Rogers of Kemsing in the said County yeoman One Hundred pownds of lawful money to be paid unto her by my Executors at her age of One and Twenty yeares or day of Marriage which shall first happen And I will that my Executors shall reteine the said Hundred Pownds in theire hands until it be so payable paying unto her yearely therefore fower pounds of like money towards her better education Item to Mary Rogers one other daughter of the said John Rogers One Hundred Pownds of like money to be paid to her at her day of marriage or age of One and Twenty yeares which shall first happen by my Executors They to retaine the same untill it be so payable paying unto her likewise fower pounds a yeare towards her better education And my will is that my Executors shall give security to my Overseers hereafter named to pay the said Two former Legacyes of One Hundred Pownds a peece accordingly Item I give unto Susan Lampard daughter of Richard Lampard late of the parish of Westerham in Kent Taylor deceased Forty Pownds of like money to be paid to her within one yeare after my decease giving sufficient security to my Executors to discharge them thereof Item I give unto Roger Wall of Tunbridge in the County of Kent yeoman Tenn Pownds of Lawfull money payable by my Executors within one yeare after my decease Item I give unto Craft Widdow lyving in Seavenoke Alms Rowe Twenty Pownds of lawfull money if she by lyving at the tyme of my death But if she dye before mee then I will the said sume of Twenty Pownds to such of her children as shall be lyving to be equally devided betweene them to be paid by my Executors within one yeare after my decease I give unto David Durtnall of Seavenoke Baker Five pounds one yeare after my decease Item I give to Elizabeth Brooker Spinster heretofore my servant Five pounds within one yeare after my decease Item to my Aunt the widdow Smith Tenn shillings Item I give to Sarah Brad now wife of Nicholas Stevens of Chepstedd Tenn pownds to be paid to her owne hands within one yeare after my decease Item I give unto William Humphrey senior of Seavenoke shovellmaker Five Pownds one yeare after my decease Item I give unto Anne Stubberfield now wife of George Canfield Tenn Pownds one yeare after my decease Item I give to Margaret Giles of Chepsted Widdow Fower pounds of lawful money and to her Two sonnes Frances and John Twenty shillings a peece one yeare after my decease I give to William sonn of Robert Lampard deceased Sixe Pownds within one yeare after my decease Item to Thomas Lampard of Sundrish Shomaker Forty shilling one yeare after my decease Item to William Lampard Glover Forty shillings one yeare after my decease Item to Jane Plummer heretofore my servant Twenty shillings Item to Christopher Wells of Seavenoke Laborer Five Pownds one yeare after my decease Item to Baker Widdow late wife of John Baker deceased Forty shillings one yeare after my decease Item to Jane Lampard now wife of -- Waler Three pownds one yeare after my decease Item to John Hall of Seavenoke Weild senior Five pownds one yeare after my decease Item to the Two sonnes of Henry Stubberfield late of Chepstedd Rippier deceased Five pownds a peece one yeare after my decease Item to Thomas Hall my Tennant Twenty shillings Item to Richard Bennett my Tennant Twenty shillings Item to the three Children of Hester Lampard deceased late wife of - - Miller deceased Twenty shillings a peece Item to -- Lampard the sonne of Robert Lampard deceased late of Seavenoke Tenn pownds one yeare after my decease Item to loving brother in Law William Wall and his fower sonnes and to his Two daughters Mary and Dorothy to each of them Twenty shillings a peece Item to Christopher Thomas of Chevening Gent Twenty shillings Item I give to my loving wife Elizabeth All such moveable goods as I had with her all such faggotts or Cord wood as I shall leave at the tyme of my death Item I give unto my kinsman John Harmon my great Joyned Chest with Drawers All the rest and residue of my Goods Chattells Debts Cattell utensells ready money and personal estate whatsoever after my Debts Legacys and Funerall Expences satisfyed and defrayed I give and bequeath unto my loving wife Elizabeth and my said kinsman John Harman of Seale Shoemaker to be equally devided betweene them And I make the said Elizabeth my wife and John Harmon Executors of this my last will and I nominate and appoint my loving freinds William Wall of Seavenoke Weild yeoman Roger Wall of Tunbridge yeoman and David Durtnall of Seavenoke Baker overseers of this my will to see this my will performed This is also the last will of me the said Edward Lampard touching the disposicion of my Lands Tenements and hereditaments whatsoever Item I give to my loving wife Elizabeth all that my Messuage of Tenement wherein I now lyve situat at Riverhill in the parish of Seavenoke with all the lands thereto apperteyning conteyning by estimacion Eleaven acres more or lesse with thappurtenences for and during the term of her naturall life she committing no Waste And after her decease I bequeath the same to Edward Lampard son of Richard Lampard late of Westerham Taylor deceased my kinsman for and during his naturall life and after his decease to the right heires of him the said Edward forever Item I give to the said Edward Lampard all that my little parcel of meadowland lying in Westreete in Sundrish aforesaid against the highway leading from Sundrish to Brasted conteyning One Acre more of lesse called Debenys or Mordcoxe to him and his heires forever upon condicion nevertheles that he the said Edward or his heires due within one moneth after he shall attaine to his age of One and Twenty yeares make signe seale and delyver unto my said kinsman John Harmon and his heires forever a Release thereby discharging them of the Rent or summe of Eighteene Pence a yeare payable to him and his heires out of my lands in Sundrish And whereas I have by way of a Jointure graunted unto Elizabeth my wife One Annuity of Eighteene Pownds a yeare out of my lands for terme of her life my will is that my said kinsman John Harmon shall in liew thereof pay unto her yearely dureing her life out of my Farme called Essex herein to him given Twenty Pownds of Lawful money of England But if she marry againe then onely Eighteene Pownds a yeare so formerly granted to her Item I give unto the said John Harmon my kinsman all that my Farm called Essex which my brother John Lampard gave mee situat in Sundrish aforesaid now in occupacion of Christopher Waymarke yeoman by Lease to have to him during his life and after his decease to the heires of his body lawfuly to be begotten And for defalt of such issue to the right heires of mee the said Edward Lampard forever Item I give to Edward Rogers the sonne of John Rogers of Kemsing in the said County yeoman and Mary his wife my kinswoman All that my messuage or tenement with all the lands therewithall letten and thereunto apperteyning with thappurtenences situat at Hollenden in the parish of Leigh next Tunbridge in Kent now in the occupacion of Richard Bennett yeoman or his assignes To have and to hold unto him for the terme of his naturall life and after his decease to heires of his body lawfully to be begotten and for defalt of such issue to his next heires and for defalt of such heiresto the right heires of mee the said Edward forever he the said Edward paying unto my said wife Three pownds a yeare during her life half yearely by equall payments to be paid her More I give unto the said Edward Rogers one messuage or tenement with thappurtenences commonly called Deepgate with all the land there withall used now in the occupacion of Thomas Hall conteyning Twenty acres more or lesse Together also with fower parcells of land part and parcell of the said Deepgate Lands conteyning about Fowerteene Acres now in the occupacion of Christopher Weymarke aforesaid All which Messuage and premises I purchased of Mr Thomas Hollenden and my brother Henry Lampard deceased And my will is that the said Christopher Weymarke shall during the term of his lease pay for the said fower parcels of land to the said Edward Rogers and his heires out of his rent Sixe pownds a yeare Vizt Three pownds half yearely To have and to hold all the said Messuage or Tenement and lands unto the said Edward Rogers during his naturall life and after his decease unto the heires of his body lawfully to be begotten And for defalt of such issue unto his next heires and for defalt of heires unto the right heires of mee the said Edward Lampard forever And my will is that if my said kinswomen Mary now the wife of John

Rogers shall happen to overlyve her now husband John Rogers Then I give unto her during her life my said Farme at Hollenden she paying the said Three pownds to my wife yearely And after her decease unto her said sonne Edward in manner aforesaid And my will is that my loving brother in law William Wall one of the overseers of this my will shall receive the rents of my said lands herein formerly given to the said Edward Rogers until he shall accomplish his age of Eighteene yeares And if his Parents will put him forth as soone as he shall be capable to board and scholing That my said overseers shall out of the profitts of the said Lands pay for the same And if the said William Wall shall dye before he shall atteine the age of Eighteene yeares Then my desire is that his sonn William Wall shall after his death receive the profitts in like manner And I give unto him so receiving the same out of the said profitts Forty shillings a yeare for his paynes and care herein Together with all his necessary Expences and Charges about the same In Witness whereof I the said Edward Lampard have hereunto set my hand and seale to this my last Will conteyned in five sheets of paper Vizt to fower therof my hand and to this last my hand and seale Revoking and disannulling all former wills by mee made this Eighteday of July in the yeare of our LordChrist One Thousand Six Hundred Seaventy and Three
Edward Lampard
Sealed and delyvered and declared for his last will and testament in the presence of Christopher Thomas Notary Publique Ellen Thomas
John Smith his marke

93

KIPPS Gilbert Innholder bur. 21 May 1673
I. 15 Jul. 1673 prov. 5 Aug. 1673 PRS/I/11/21

An Inventory of all and singuler the goods and Chattles of Gilbert Kipps late of Seavenoke in the County of Kent Inholder taken and appraized the fifteenth day of July in the five and twentyeth yeare of the Reigne of our Soveraign Lord Charles the Second of England Scotland France and Ireland King defendor of the faith etc. By William Allen and Isaac Day of Seavenoke aforesaid Mercers as followeth

	£.	*s.*	*d.*
In the Chamber over the Hall			
Inprimis his weareing apparell and money in his purse	2:	0:	0:
Item one featherbedd bolster and pillow a red rugg blankett & bedstead Curtaines and Vallance curtaine rodds	2:	13:	4:
Item one Wicker chaire & two other chaires	0:	4:	0:
Item one table one forme and one chest	0:	5:	0:
Item one paire of Andirons fireshovell & tongs	0:	3:	0:
In the Chamber over the Entry			
Item one featherbedd Bedstedle one boulster			

coverlett and Blankett	)	1:	0:	0:
Item three chests & one box		0:	5:	0:
Item nyne paire of sheetes two tableCloathes	)			
twelve napkins two pillowcoates & twelve towells	)	3:	0:	0:
In the Chamber over the Shopp				
Item one featherbedd two boulsters one old Rugg	)			
and blankett Bedstead Curtaines and Valance	)	2:	5:	0:
Item one Canvas bedd and Bedstead		0:	6:	6:
In the Chamber over the Brewhowse				
Item one old Bedstead and table		0:	10:	0:
Item one old chafe Bedd two old Blancketts an old	)			
forme	)	0:	3:	4:
In the other Brewhowse chamber				
Item an old Bedstead and chaire		0:	2:	6:
In the Garrett				
Item one bedstead a table and a Chest		0:	5:	0:
In the Hall				
Item 28 lbs of pewter		1:	1:	0:
Item twelve Flagons two Chamber potts two	)			
porringers and three little salts	)	1:	9:	0:
Item one Jack and line & four spitts		1:	0:	0:
Item one Cubboard and one setle		0:	10:	0:
Item one Table one forme three stooles		0:	6:	8:
Item two paire of Andirons two paire of tongs	)			
two paire of pothangers one Gridiron one chaire	)	0:	5:	0:
and forme	)			
Item one frying pann and one dripping pan		0:	1:	6:
In the Brewhowse				
Item three Iron potts three Skilletts		0:	10:	0:
Item the Brewing Vessells and other Lumber		2:	10:	0:
In the Stable				
Item two horses		4:	0:	0:
Item sadles and bridles pillion and pillion cloath		0:	10:	0:
In the yard				
Item five hoggs and tenn piggs		3:	10:	0:
In the Seller				
Item beere five hogsheads		4:	10:	0:
Item eighteene Hogsheads		2:	14:	0:
Item six stalders a tunn Tubb Calers and four	)			
dozen of bottles	)	1:	15:	0:
Item one Quern and Spouts		1:	10:	0:
In the old Shop				

Item one forme one old Cubboard one Chaire and three pailes	)	0:	3:	4:
Item Lumber in and about the howse		0:	13:	4:
		39:	2:	0:

94

BERRY Edward — Tobacconist — bur. 16 Dec. 1673
W. 2 Dec. 1673 — prov. 27 Jan. 1674 — Prob. 11. 344 f. 6.

In the name of God Amen I Edward Berry of Seavenoakes in the County of Kent Tobacconist beinge weake of body but of sound and perfect memory and understanding (Praysed be God for the same) Doe make publish and ordaine this my last will and Testament in manner and forme following (That is to say) Inprimis I Commend my Soule into the hands of Almighty God my Creator and Redeemer hopeing and assuredly believing through the merritts death and passion of my blessed Saviour Jesus Christ to receave a full and free pardon for all my sinns and a joyfull resurrection in the Kingdom of Heaven And my Body I committ to the Earth from whence it came to be decently buried at the discretion of my Executrix hereafter named and as for that worldly Esate with which it hath pleased God to blesse me I dispose thereof as followeth Item I give and bequeath unto my Loveing and Tender Mother Mary Berry the sume of Five pounds to be paid her within one year next after my decease by my Executrix hereafter named Item I give and bequeath unto the two Children of my brother in law Adrian Woodards John and Elizabeth the sume of Fifty shillings a peece to be put out to use for them by my said Executrix hereafter named within one moneth next after my decease And to be paid to them with the interest which shall grow due when they shall attaine to the age of one and twenty yeares each of them And if shall happen that either of them shall depart this life before he or she shall attaine to the age of one and twenty yeares Then his or her part soe dyeing shall fall to the other which shall survive or if both of them shall dye Then the said Five pounds shall fall with the interest of it to their now Mother Margaret Woodards or if she be dead to the next of kinne Item all the rest of my goods Cattel Chattells Stock in my Shopp and Elsewhere Credits and debts oweing and all other my goods and chattells whatsoever I give and bequeath unto my deare and loveing wife Elizabeth Berry whom I do make nominate and appoint full and sole Executrix of this my last Will and Testament And I doe hereby revoke disannull and make void all former wills and testaments by me heretofore made In Witnes whereof I the said Edward Berry to this my last Will and Testament being conteyned in half a sheete of paper have sett to my hand and seale this second day of December in the Twenty fifth yeare of the Reigne of our Sovereigne lord Charles the second

by the Grace of God King of England Scotland France and Ireland Defendor of the Faith etc Annoque Domine 1673
Edw. Berry
Signed and sealed in the presence of Edm. Weston William Smith

95

BERRY Edward bur. 16 Dec. 1673
I. 15 Jan. 1674 prov. 27 Jan. 1674 Prob. 4.10020

A true and perfect Inventory of all and singuler the goods and Chattells of Edward Berry late of Seavenoke in the County of Kent taken and appraised by us Edmund Weston and Isaac Day of Seavenoke aforesaid Mercers the fifteenth day of January in the five and twentyeth yeare of the Reigne of our Sovereigne Lord Charles the second of England Scotland France and Ireland King Defender of the faith etc.

	£	*s.*	*d.*
Inprimis his weareing apparell and money in his purse	40	13	4
In the Hall			
Item one table and three leather chaires and five other chaires a little table and a joyne stoole	1	1	6
Item one Iron Jack three spitts tripping Andirons fire shovell and tongs and tosting Iron	0	16	8
Item four pewter dishes seaven porringers three sticks and some small peeces of pewter	1	5	0
Item a Chafin dish frying pann and some other small lumber	0	5	0
Item two brasse potts two Iron potts and two brasse skilletts	1	14	0
In the Entry			
Item three Tubbs and two Keelers	0	13	4
In the Shopp			
Item one great screw	1	10	0
Item eight reames of paper	1	4	0
Item a cutting Knife and two Tubbs			
Item fourteene boxes and a counter and a neast of boxes	0	16	6
Item weights and scales and fourteene grosse of pipes	1	10	0

Item six small runletts with some strong water in them	1	4	0
Item one hundred weight of cutt and dryed Tobacco	3	0	0
Item three joyned stooles	0	1	6
In the passage roome			
Item one great screw	1	5	0
Item five Tubbs and some boxes	0	10	0
Item Tobacco there one hundred weight	2	16	0
Item four scives and a tryer a table and forme and other lumber	0	10	6
In the Seller			
Item four hundred and a halfe of Tobacco	14	0	0
Item eight drink Tubbs a poudring Tubb and a stalder	0	16	0
In the forechamber			
Item one feather bedd and boulster one Blankett and a Coverlett Bedsteadle curtaines and valance matt and Cord	5	10	0
Item one other feather bedd and boulster one Blankett and one Rugg Bedsteadle curtaines and valance matt and Cord	4	13	4
Item one Trundle Bedstead a feather bedd and blankett and coverlett	1	5	0
Item seaven leather chaires	1	4	0
Item one table one Chest of Drawers one chest and two trunks	1	18	0
Item one looking glasse Andirons bellows fire shovell and tongs	0	9	2
In the Hall Chamber			
Item one feather bedd and boulster and blankett and a rugg bedstaedle curtaines and valanse matt and Cord	4	0	0
Item two chaires two chests a stoole and a paire of Andirons	0	6	6
Item twelve pair of sheetes and six pillowberes	4	1	0
Item tenn table Cloathes four dozen of Napkins and four and twenty towells	2	15	0
In the Closett			
Item Glasses and potts and some Lumber	0	10	0
In the Garrett			

Item one cord of wood		0	10	0
Item one hundred and a halfe of faggott		0	13	0
Att the Stayerhead				
Item one half headed bedsteadle one flockbed	)			
blankett and Coverlett and three chaires	)	1	7	6
In the Stable				
Item one load of Hay		1	4	0
Item in debts sperate		28	0	0
Item in debts desperate		5	10	4
		139	17	2

Edm. Weston
Isaac Day

96

WESTON Edmund bur. 9 May 1675
W. 19 Nov. 1673 prov. 5 Jun. 1675 PRS/W/18/12

In the name of God Amen I Edmond Westone of Seavenocke in the County of Kent being in Good health and of Sound & perfect memory & understanding praised bee God for the same doe make publishe & ordaine this my last will & testament in maner & forme followeing (that is to say) Inprimis I comend my Soule into the hands of allmighty God my creator & Redeemer hopeing & Assuredly beleiveing through the merritts death & passion of my blessed Saviour Jesus Christ to receive a full & Free pardon for all my sinnes and a Joyfull resurection in the Kingdome of heaven and my body I comitt to the Earth from whence it came to bee decently buryed att the discretion of my Executor hereafter named and as for that wordly estate which it hath pleased God to blesse me with all I dispose thereof as Followeth Item I give & bequeath unto my Loveing wife Mary the sume of Five pounds of lawfull mony of England for to buy her a Ringe the same to be payed unto her by my Executor hereafter named within Two Months after my decease Item I will & bequeath & my will & meaneing is that my Executor hereafter named shall pay out of my Goods Chattells stocke creditts & debts oweing the sume of Tenn pounds of lawfull money of England for the putting out and bringing upp of my youngest sonn Thomas untill he shall bee in capacitye to bee putt out to prentice Item all the rest & residue of my Goods Cattell Chattells Stocke in my Shopp & elsewhere Creditts & debts owing and all other my Goods & Chattells whatsoever I give & bequeath unto my Executor hereafter named for the paying of debts & legacyes & for the use & benifitt of my Seaven Children (that is to say) Edmund Richard William Elizabeth Ralph Thomas and Mary Westerne and my will & meaneing is that All my Goods Cattell Chattell Stocke & other Goods & Chattells whatsoever bee Apprized & sold for the most they can within a shorte tyme after my decease & the monys thereof or otherwise raised of my estate to be equally devided betweene my aforesaid Seaven children namly Edmund Richard William Elizabeth Ralphe Thomas & Mary Westerne and if either or any of my said

Children shall happen to departe this life before hee her or they shall receive their severall shares & portions hereunto them given then he she or them soe dyeing his her or there portions soe dyeing to bee equally devided betweene the survivour or survivours of them And Alsoe my will & minde Farther is that my daughter Mary after my Goods & chattells are aprized shall have the libertye to take and chuse her proportionable share out of my aforesaid Goods & Chattells where and of what she pleaseth, And I doe hereby nominate ordaine and Appoynte my trustye and very Loveing Freind Robert Rentmore of Seavenokes aforesaid Gent sole Executor of this my last will & testament uppon trust and confidence in him Reposed for to dispose of All my Aforesaid personall estate according as is in this my last will mencioned And to give a true Account of the disposeing thereof unto my Eldest sonn Edmund when he shall Attaine his Age of Three and Thirty years And after All my aforesaid Children that shall be then liveing shall have Attained his, her or there Ages of One & twenty years or day of Marriage, And my will & meaneing Further is & I desyer my said Executor For to putt out & place att Intereste as secure as he can my aforesaid severall Childrens portions and the Interests of soemuch as shall bee made thereof for to goe towards bringing them upp & puting them out, and my will & meaneing is and I desyer my Executor for to take care & place out my aforesaid Children to such trades & ymployments as my said Executor shall thinke fitt & best for them out of & with there owne mony which shall bee due & arise for his her or there share & portion and the overplus if Any bee for to pay unto them when he shee or they shall Attaine there severall & respective Ages of One & twenty years or Day of Marriage of my said daughters. Item I give & bequeath & desyer my said Executor for to Accept of Forty shillings for to buy him a Ringe for his paines & care herein. In Witnes whereof I the said Edmund Westerne have to this my last will & testament Revokeing All former wills by mee made conteyneing allmost Two sheets of paper I have to Each Sheete of paper sett my hand and Seale the Nyneteenth Day of November in the Five and Twentyeth yeare of the Raigne of our Soveraigne Lord Charles the second by the Grace of God, Kinge of England Scotland France and Ireland Defender of the Faith & etc Annoque Domine 1673
Edm Weston
Signed sealed published & declared to bee the last will & Testament of the said Edmund Westerne in the presence of Tho Streatfeild
Will Lines

97

WELLS Christopher Labourer
I. 14 Sep. 1674 prov. 15 Sep. 1674 PRS/I/23/38

An Inventary of the Goods and chattells of Christopher Wells late of Seavenoke in the County of Kent Labourer decesed Taken the Foureteenth day of September 1674 By Christopher Thomas Gent and John Coggar yeoman as followeth vizt:

Inprimis one old Cubbert i brasse pot one Iron pott 2 little Skillets 3 old Chaires & other old Lumber in the Lower Roome		x[s]
Item one Flock bed with the furniture 2 old Chists a Box and other Lumber		xx[s]
Item one Legacy Given by Edward Lampard yeoman to the decesed.	£v	
Sume Totalis	£vi	x[s]

98

NICCOLL Joane　　Widow　　bur. 25 Sep. 1674
I. 21 Oct. 1674　　prov. 30 Oct. 1674　　PRS/I/14/15

A true and perfect inventory of all and singuler the goods household stuff corne cattell and Chattells of Joane Niccoll late of Seavenoke in the county of Kent Widdow deceased taken valued and aprized the One and Twentieth day of October in the yeare of our Lord God one Thousand Sixe Hundred Seaventy and Fower by William Turner and William Spilstedd as followeth:

	Li	s	d
Inprimis the said deceaseds purse girdle and ready money	06	5	0
Item her Wearing apparrell of all sorts	01	10	0
In the Hall one Fire slice a paire of Tongs one paire of pothangers three spitts an Iron to lay before the Fire one Iron morter and pestle and two smoothing Irons	00	6	6
Item Two chaires and sixe Quisshions	00	4	0
Item one Bible and two other small bookes	00	5	0
Item one linnen wheele	00	1	6
In the Kitchen Two Brasse Kettles one brasse pann and Three Brasse Skilletts	00	12	6
Item two pailes and some dishes and spoones	00	2	0
In the Milkhouse and Buttery Twelve milk trayes	00	12	0
Item Fower drinck vessells three Keelers two tubbs and one half busshell measure	00	12	8

In the Chamber over the Hall one Joyned bedsteddle one half headed bedsteddle one Trundle bedsteddle two Flockbedds Fower flock bolsters Fower feather pillows Three blancketts and Three Coverletts	04	1	4
Item Three Joyned Chests one boarded chest & one box	01	8	0
In Linnen Three Paire of Fine sheets and one odd sheet one Cubboard cloth two table cloths Three Pillow coates six napkinns and Three long towells	04	4	0
Item Sixteene paire of Course sheetes Five course table clothes and two course towells	04	8	0
Item Five Yards of Linsey woolsey	00	7	6
Item Tenn pewter dishes three porrengers two salts one Candle stick one Pewter Pott one Cupp one pewter bottle one old bason and one Chamber pott	00	19	6
Item two Leather baggs and one baskett	00	2	0
Item two Cowes	06	0	0
Item two Swine	01	5	0
In the Barn about Tenn Copps of Oates	01	5	0
Item about Three Loads of Hay	02	5	0
Item certaine Wood and other things of small value unseene and forgotten	00	8	4
Summa totalis huius inventarii	37	4	10

99

FLECHER Edward bur. 8 May 1675
W. 5 May 1675 prov. 28 Aug. 1675 PRS/W/6/74

In the Name of god amen I Edward Flecher of the parish of Seavenoks in the Countie of Kent being sick of bodie but of parfict memorie praised be god doe make and ordaine this my Last Will and Testament in maner and Form Following First of all I bequeave my Soule into the hands of god my Creator trusting through the mercie and merits of Jesus Christ my redemer to be made an inheritor of his heavenly Kingdom and I bequeave my bodie to the earth From whence it came to be decently buried by my executor hoping for a Joyfull resurriction at the Last day and as For the worly goods which it hath pleased god to bless me withall I give and bequeave as followeth inprimis I give unto my Loveing Wife Martha the summe of Five pounds to be paid hir by my executor at or before Michelmus next insuing Item I give to my

youngest sonne Thomas the summe of Five pounds and my will is that the said five pounds shall be paid to my wife at or before Michelmus nixt and shee to bring up my sonne Thomas and to put him out at hir discrestion Item I give to my sone Charls the summe of Five pounds to be paid to him by my executor one yeare and a halfe after my decease Item I give unto my sonne Georg the summe of Five pounds to be paid to him by my executor one year and a halfe after my decease Item I give unto my dafter Margrit the summe of Five pounds to be paid to hir by my executor within on year after my decease Item I give unto my dafter Elizabeth the summe of Five pounds to be paid hir by my executor within one yeare after my decease Item I give unto my dafter Ane the summe of tenn pounds to be paid hir by my excutor one yeare after my decease. Item I give unto my dafter Dorothi the summe of five shillings to be paid to hir one yeare after my decease Item I give unto my sonne Edward all my goods deptes Readie money bonds Catell Chatels and whatsoever els I have whome I make and ordaine my executor of this my will he discharging my Funerall Charges and paying my deptes and leggeceis and I doe renounce all formmer wills and make this my Last will in witnes wheareof I have hereunto set my hand and seale this Fift day of May in the yeare of our Lord one thousand six hundered seaventie and Five 1675–
The mark of Edward Flecher
Received signed sealed and declared the Last will of Edward Flecher
in presenc of us William Wall Edward Page

100

FLETCHER Edward — bur. 8 May 1675
I. 14 May 1675 — prov. 3 Sept. 1675 — PRS/I/6/29

An Inventary of all and Singuler the Goods Chattells and Credits of Edward Fletcher late whilst he lived of the parish of Seavenoke in the County of Kent deceased Taken and praysed the Fourteenth day of May Anno Domini 1675 by William Wall Arthur Children and Richard Children as followeth vizt.

Inprimis the deceaseds Weareinge apparell and ready Money	£vii		
Item in the Hall One old Table and forme one old Cubbert 3 old Chayres one paire of Tongs 2 paire of Potthangers one Andiron one Creeper 2 Spitts & one Dresser		xi^{s}	x^{d}
Item 11 Pewter Dishes one Pewter Cup & one old Pewter Bottle		xi^{s}	v^{d}

Item in the Washowse one Bucking Tub one high Kooler 2 small Koolers 3 old Tubbs 4er Iron pots 2 brasse Kettles 3 Skillets 2 Payles one Flasket 3 Wodden Dishes 2 Woden Platters)		xvii^{s}	x^{d}
Item one Warmeing pan one Iron Pestle & Mortar		ii^{s}	vi^{d}
Item in the Parlor one old Table & Frame 2 Shelves one old Chayre)		iiii^{s}	
Item in the Milkhowse one Churne 4er small Drinke Tubs one Tunnell one Brasse Ketle 7 Milke Bowles one litle Koolar one Frying pan)		xv^{s}	
Item in the Chamber over the Hall one Bedstedle with an old flockbed one Blanket one old Rug 2 old Chists one Flock bolster & 2 Feather pillows)		xx^{s}	
Item in the other Chamber one old Bedstedle 2 old Bolsters one Pillow one Sidebord 2 Chists)		vii^{s}	viii^{d}
Item 4er pair of old Sheets & a litle other old Linnen		v^{s}	
Item in the Garret 2 old Wheeles one payre of Stockards & things forgotten)		iii^{s}	
Item in the Millhowse one Otmeale mill & things belonging to it and five Sacks)	£iii	iii^{s}	iiii^{d}
Item one old Wagon one old Court one old plow & a litle other old Husbandry Tacklings)		xl^{s}	
Item Corne on the Grownd Wheat 2 Akers & a halfe & Oats 5 Akers & a halfe)	£viii	vi^{s}	iiii^{d}
Item one old Cow one old Horse one old Mare & Colt 2 Hogs & 5 litle Pigs)	£ix		
Summa Totalis	£xxxiiii	vii^{s}	ix^{d}

101

EVEREST Anne — bur. 28 Dec. 1677

W. 11 May 1675 — prov. 22 Feb. 1678 — PRS/W/5/191

In the name of God Amen the eleaventh day of May in the year of our Lord one thousand six hundred seaventy & five. I Anne Everest of the Parish of Seavenoakes in the County of Kent being aged and weak in body, but of perfect minde and memory (praised be God therefore) doe make this my last Will in manner following First I bequeath my soule to Allmighty God who infused the Same and my Body to the earth to be decently interred in the Churchyard of Seavenoake aforesayd trusting by the meritts of my mercifull Saviour Jesus Xt. to be made partaker of life everlasting. And as touching such worldly estate wherewith God hath blessed me my Will is as followeth Imprimis I bequeath my house and land in the Parish of Pemberee in the County of Kent now in the occupation of Edward Turner to my loving Kinsman Richard Walter the son of William Walter during his naturall life and after his decease to the Heires of his Body lawfully to be begotten for ever and for want of such yssue to his two sisters Sarah Champian and Anne Reed and to their Heires for ever Item I give unto the poor of the parish of Seavenoakes the summe of forty shillings to be distributed by my Executors either in money or else in bread at my funerall. Item I give to my loving Cousin Mary Mandy twenty shillings peeces of Gold and to have within monethes unto each of her four children Mathew Phelip Thomas and Oliver Mandy I bequeath a twenty shilling piece of Gold to be payd them by my Executors within three months after my decease. Item I Give & bequeath unto Sarah the Wife of Philip Champian a small ring and the summe of tenne pounds to be payd within three monethes after my decease. Item unto her sister Anne Reed I bequeath the Summe of tenne pounds to be payd at the time aforesayd. Item I give unto the daughter of Sarah Champian a Brasse Kettle without a bayl and a Trevett. Item I give unto James Weller twenty shillings to be payd within three monethes after my decease. Item I give unto my Cousin Anne the Wife of John Everest the sum of twenty shillings to be payd within two monethes after my decease for the reciept whereof her aquittance shall be a sufficient discharge notwithstanding she be female covert. Item to Anne the Wife of Richard Jarrett I bequeath the summe of twenty shillings to be payd at the time aforsayd. Item to my two cousins Jane Piggott and Thomas Mathews I give the summe of ten shillings apiece. Item I give unto my Cousin Mildred the wife of Thomas Morely junior the summe of thirty shillings to be payd within two moneths after my decease. Item to Margaret the wife of Lyonel Sutton the summe of thirty shillings to be payd at the time aforsayd. Item I give unto John Blanks the Son of Sylvanus Blanks the summe of fifty shillings to be payd within three months after my decease. Item to his two sisters Mary & Elizabeth Blanks the summe of fifty shillings apiece to be paid within the time aforesayd. Item I give unto his younger Brother Sylvanus Blanks the summe of fifty shillings to be payd unto him at the age of one & twenty years and (if he should die before) my will is that the sayd fifty shillings should be divided amongst his sisters and Brother aforesayd. Item I give unto my Sister in Law Anne the Relict of Will Everest the summe of twenty shillings to be payd within two monethes after my decease. Item I give unto her Eldest son William Everest the summe of eleavon pounds to be payd by my Executors at the time aforesayd and as a token of my love to his little child Margaret Everest I bequeath a twenty shilling piece of old gold to be payd by my Executors unto her Father for her use Item I give unto my Cousin Peter Everest the summe of forty Shillings to be payd within two monethes after my decease. Item unto my Cousin Francis

Everest his Brother the summe of twenty shillings to be payd at the time aforesayd. Item to my Cousin Anne Neale the Wife of John Neale the summe of twenty shillings to be payd at the time aforesayd. Item to her sister Dorothy Everest the summe of twenty shillings to be payd at the time aforesayd. Item to my Cousin Margaret Everest the summe of twenty shillings to be payd unto her Mother for her use at the time aforesayd. Item I bequeath unto my Executors the summe of tenn pounds for the defraying of all funerall charges And I doe nominate and appoint my two Loving Freinds Mr Richard Bosse and Mr William Wall to be my Executors to whom paying my debts & Legacies I doe will give and bequeath all my money bills bonds debts goods chattells and household stuffe whatsoever In wittnesse whereof I have hearunto sett my hand and seale the day & year above written revoking all former wills
The marke of Anne Everest
Sealed Delivered & declared to be my last Will and Testament in the presence of Peter Trice John French

102

EVEREST Anne	Widow	bur. 28 Dec. 1677
I. 11 Feb. 1678	prov. 22 Feb. 1678	PRS/I/5/26

An Inventary of all & singuler the Goods chattells & Credits of Anne Everest late of Seavenoke in the county of Kent widow deceased Taken and prized the Eleaventh day of February Anno Domini Stilo Anglie 1677 By Peter Trise & William Everest as followeth vizt

Inprimis the deceseds wearing Apparell	£ii		
Item one old Bedsteadle one old Trundlebed stedle one old flockbed 5 small peics of Pewter one pewter Chamber pot one small brasse Ketle one small Iron Trevet		xix^s	viii^d
Item two pare of Sheets and Tablecloth one Towell all Old		xii^s	
Item one old Trunke		i^s	vi^d
Item one small Iron pot and other Lumber and things not seene		ii^s	iiii^d
Item in ready Money	£vi		
Item owing to the deceased upon Bonds	£Lxx		
Item owing to the deceased in sperat Debts		Lv^s	
Summa totalis	£Lxxxii.	x^s.	vi^d.
Item owing to the deceased in desperat Debts	£iii.	v^s.	
Suma patet.			

103

BUCKMINSTER Thomas Tanner bur. 24 Dec. 1677
W. 17 Aug. 1675 prov. 12 Feb. 1677 PRS/W/2/31

August the 17th 1675

In the name of god Amen I Thomas Buckminster of New Slleeford Tanner in the countey of Lincolne though in good & perfecte health: & Blesed be god in good & perfecte memorey: hath: For Divers good Causes & Considerations me therunto moving: made this to be my Laste will & Testement: In manour & Forme As Follouth:
Item I give unto Elizabeth Sall my Daughter in lawe my house in New Slleefford with All the Appurtanances there unto belongging In A certaine place ther Caled the hen Laine: Not only to her but To hir & hir Hayres For ever with this provisor that If I Do not live to pay hir fouerscore & ten poundes which is hir sertain portion: which If I doe or Anney by my Apointment: that then the Aforesaid house with All the Apportanances shall be to me & mine As before. . .
Item I give unto Elizebeth Sall my daughter in lawe halfe my houssall: goodes that I Am At my death posest of: If she Receve not hir Fouerscore & ten pounde: which if she do I give hir none.
Item I give unto marey Buckminster daughter of John Buckminster If she be then Alive twenty shillinges: for to be paid to hir with in sixe monthes After my decease if she so longe live.
Item I give to An oslin daughter of Richard oslin my sisters Childe the sume of Twenty shillings to be paid within sixe monthes After my Decease if she so longe live
Item All the Rest & residue of my goodes & Chateles I give unto marey Buckminster my Deare & Loving wife: home I do Apointe And ordaine for to be my soley & hole Execetor & Furder more I doe Renounce Revocke & disAnull All former wills & testements made by me what so ever & doth ordaine & Consstitute this to be my last will & none other in witnes wher of I have here unto set my hand & seale the Day Above wrighten in the yeare of our Lord god 1675 etc
Thomas Buckminster
sealed in the presence of John Buckminster John Beardsworth
The Mark of Robert Hockinn

104

BUCKMINSTER Thomas Gentleman bur. 24 Dec. 1677
I. 7 Jan. 1678 prov. 12 Feb. 1678 PRS/I/2/140

An Inventary of all & Singuler Goods chattells & Credits of Thomas Buckminster late of Seavenoke in the County of Kent Gent deceased Taken and praysed the 7th. day of January Anno Domini Stilo Anglie 1677 by John Beardsworth and Robert Hockham as followeth vizt

Inprimis in the Parlor Chamber the deceseds wearing Apparell & ready Money in his Purse	£v		
Item 2 Bedstedles & Mats & Cords one paire of Curtens one Rug one Counterpary 2 paire of Blankets & 2 Featherbeds 2 Feather bolsters One Flock bolster & 5 Feather pillowes	£vi		
Item one Table 5 Chaires & a Lookinglasse		xx^s^.	
Item 6 paire of Sheets one dozen of Napkins & 3 Tableclothes & 6 Towels		xxxv^s^.	
Item 4er pewter dishes & 3 kettells & one Skillet of Brasse		xv^s^.	vi^d^.
Item for other things about the Roome		v^s^.	
Summa totalis	£xiiii	xv^s^.	vi^d^.

105

WILSON William — Seafaringman
W. 13 Sept. 1675. — prov. 18 Feb. 1676 — Prob. 11. 350 f. 27

In the name of God Amen I William Wilson of Seavenokes in the County of Kent Seafaringman now belonging unto the Olive Branch Pinok under the command of Captain Norman and I knowing the great and many dangers of the Seas and desireing to put things in order have thereupon made and ordained this my last will and testament denying and revokeing all other will and wills and testaments but this and that this and none other shall be taken for my last will and testament Inprimis First and principally I commend my soule unto Almighty God my Creator and Redeemer trusting in the infinite mercies and blood of our Lord and Saviour Jesus Christ to be saved And my body to the Grave there to remain in Christian Buriall till the Resurrection of all Flesh which I beleeve and expect And as touching the disposition of my temporall things First I give and bequeath unto my Father John Wilson the sum of five shillings Item I give unto my Mother five shillings Item I give and bequeath unto my sister Lucie the sum of twelve pence Item I give and bequeath unto my sister Dorothy the sum of twelve pence the residue of all and singular my Goods Chattells Debts Leases Plate Householdstuffe (after all my legacies and portions given) the residue I hereby give and bequeath unto my Executor hereafter named desireing him to pay my said legacies and I do by these presents make and ordaine my well beloved Friend John Baker of Deptford in the aforesaid county victualler to be my Executor of this my present last will and testament And that when he hath received all my Wages and Goods as aforesaid to pay my legacies And if I dye at Home to see me fairly buried and to discharge and pay for my funerall charges In witness whereof I put my hand and seale the thirteenth day of September in the seventh and twentieth year of the Reign of our Sovereign Lord King Charles the Second of England etc. Annoque Domini one thousand six hundred seventy five

William Wilson Signed sealed and delivered and published in the presence of Henry Daldarne
Richard Perkins Le. Walter

106

BANISTER John bur. 19 Nov. 1675
NW. 13 Nov. 1675 prov. 14 Jan. 1676 PRS/W/2/24

Memorandum that John Banister late of Seavenoke in the County of Kent – deceased haveing and intent and purpose to make his will and to settle and dispose of his estate, did on or about the Thirteenth day of November 1675 being of perfect mind and memory make and declare his last will and Testament Nuncupative or by word of mouth in these or like words following Vizt. I doe give unto John Bannister my Sonne Ten pounds to put him out to bee an Apprentice & Three pairs of sheets vizt. Two paire of Towen sheetes and one paire of Fine sheets. I give to Ann Bannister my Daughter, one Box of Lynnen as it is now put up. The rest of my goods and personall estate I leave to Katherine Bannister my wife and I make her my Executrix or hee used Words to the same effect in the presence of credible Witnesses.
The mke of Thomas Rowett The mke of Ann Wells

107

BEECHER Thomas Yeoman bur. 15 Dec 1675
W. 10 Dec 1675 prov. 29 Jan. 1676 PRS/W/2/25

In the Name of God Amen The tenth day of December in the yeare of our Lord one thousand six hundred seaventy & five I Thomas Beecher of Seavenoake in the County of Kent yeoman being aged & weak in body & therby putt in mind of my departure out of this world but of perfect minde and memory (Thanks be given to Allmighty God) doe make and ordaine this to be my last Will and Testament in manner & forme following. First & principally I commend my soule in to the hands of Jeses Christ my mercifull Saviour and my body to the Earth in a good hope of a joyfull resurrection unto eternall life. And for that temporall estate wherewith it hath pleased God to blesse me I thus will and devise thereof. To my Loving Wife Margaret Beecher I give and bequeath my house wherin I now live together with that part of it which is inhabited by my Kinsman James Beecher and the garden &

ground thereunto belonging during her naturall life and after her decease I give the same House and Messuage and ground thereunto belonging unto my Loving Kinswoman Elizabeth Beecher daughter of my Brother James Beecher deceased now living in Maidstone in the County aforesaid during her naturall life and after her decease I will and bequeath the same unto Thomas Wicken the son of Richard Wicken the younger during his naturall life and after his decease to the Heirs of his Body lawfully to be begotten and for want of such yssue to my right heirs forever: Item I give unto my Kinswoman the Wife of Nicholas Welch of Chidingstone the summe of forty shillings to be payd within two moneths after my decease: Item I give unto my Loving Sistar in Law Dorothy Randall the summe of forty shillings to be payd within two moneths after my decease: Item I give unto my Loving Kinsman James Beecher the Son of my Brother James Beecher deceased the summe of five pounds to be payd likewise within two moneths after my decease: Item I give unto my Loving Freind Mr. Richard Bosse the summe of forty shillings to be payd at the time aforesayd: Item I give unto the poor of the Parish of Seavenoak the summe of tenn shillings to be layd out in bread for them at my funerall; and my will is that my Executrices hereafter named shall lay out the summe of five pounds which I have left for the defraying of my funerall charges. The residue of my money goods & householdstuffe whatsoever I wholly Will and Bequeath unto my Loving Wife Margaret Beecher and my Loving Kinswoman Elizabeth Beecher of Maidstone in the County aforesayd to be equally shared and divided between them whom alsoe I make constitute and ordaine to be the ioynt Executrices of this my last Will and Testament; onely my minde is that what firewood is left in my house shall belong wholly to my wife and what timber is left behind me shall be reserved by both my aforesayd Executrices for the repairing of my house from time to time: And I do entreat my Loving Freind Mr. Richard Bosse to be the overseer of this my last Will and Testament wishing my Executrices to be ruled and advised by him in all things relating to this my Will: And in wittnesse that this is indeed my last Will and Testament and all things therein contained according to my minde and meaning revoking all former Wills and Testaments I have hereunto sett my hand and seale the day and year first above written:

The marke of Thomas Beecher

Sealed Delivered and declared to be my last Will & Testament with those words during his naturall life interlined in the presence of

The marke of William Spilsted The marke of George Wood

James Beecher

108

BEECHER Thomas	Yeoman	bur. 15 Dec. 1675
I. 17 Dec. 1675	prov. 29 Jan. 1676	PRS/I/2/72

A true and perfect Inventary of all and singular the goods Chattells and debts of Thomas Beecher late of Seavenoake in the County of Kent Yeoman deceased taken vallued & apprized the 17th of December 1675 by us Richard Childry and John Beardsworth as followeth vizt.

Inprimis his hatt and weareing apparrell and mony in his pockett		xviii^{s}
Item 3 paire of Tow Sheetes one paire of hempen sheetes ii bands 3 handkercheifes 1 capp 14 Ells and an halfe of newe lynnen cloath 2 tablecloaths 4 shirts 2 paire of pillowbeeres 2 lynnen baggs and 9 napkins	£ii	v^{s}
Item 3 cushions 3 old chests 7 yards of Lynsey-woollsy 2 yards of coarse towe cloth one Pitch-forke i musket i paire of bandeleeres one Sword one box of old bookes a fire shovell and tongs a paire of scales and five brasse weights & 3 leaden weights	£i	v^{s}
In the Chamber over the Kitchen		
Item i feather bed 3 pillowes i blanckett a table without a frame 2 Chests & a Pyke	£i	x^{s}
In the Chamber next the Staires		
Item i Auger 3 Sawes a gun a tape loome a long sawe and severall other od tooles		x^{s}
In the Kitchen		
Item a paire of tongs 2 tables a Joyned Stooles an Iron Morter a Spitt a toasting Iron a chopping Knife a paire of pothangers an Iron Kettle an Iron pott, a Trevet a tyn dripping pann 3 Skilletts a paire of Scales a greate Iron beame 2 fourteene pound weights and other small weights a brush a paire of bellowes a paire of sheares a dogg of Iron an old cuppord 3 cushens and a Trowell	£i	
In the Shopp		
Item an old Jack a warding bill i0 small peeces of pewter a warming (sic) 3 old chaires 2 locks a Smiths Vice 3 sickles a forme a Joyned Stoole a weaven and old tackling	£i	xv^{s}
In the Entry		
Item 4 Ladders 3 Spades 7 wedges and other old Tooles		x^{s}
Item In ready mony	£Lx	
Item Lumber & things forgotten		vii^{s}
Summa Totalis huius Inventory	£Lxxiv	

109

MORLEY Thomas | Yeoman | bur. 15 Jan. 1677
I. 30 Jan. 1677 | prov. 5 Feb. 1677 | PRS/I/13/72

An Inventary of all and singuler the Goods Chattells and Credits of Thomas Morley Senior late of the parish of Seavenoke in the County of Kent yeoman deceased Taken and praysed the Thirtieth day of January Anno Domini 1676 By William Walls William Morley and John Everest as followeth vizt.

Inprimis the deceaseds weareing Apparell and ready Money in his Purse		xl^{s}	
Item in the Hall one Table and Frame, one Forme one Wicker Chayre 4er other old Chayres one old Cubberd Three Iron Pots 2 Iron Kettells 2 brasse Kettles one Skillet 2 Skumers one Warmeing pan 2 Spits one Dripping pan one Gridiron one paire of Brandirons Firepan and Tongs Two paire of Potthangers Pewter of all sorts weying 26 pownds and two Brasse Kettles		Lvii^{s}	x^{d}
Item in the Parlor One Table and Frame 7 Joyned Stooles one Sidebord one Gunne		xxix	vi^{d}
Item in the Chamber over the Parlor One Featherbed one Bedsteadle one Blanket one Coverlet with Curtens and Valance one Chaire Table one Chest one paire of A[illegible]rons one old Bedstedle one Chaffe bed Three Feather bolsters and Fower Pillowes	£iiii	vi^{s}	viii^{d}
Item in the Buttery 5 small Drinke Tubs 4er small Colers one Churne and 4er Milke Trayes		xviii^{s}	
Item in the Kitchen one Brewing Tub 3 other old Tubs 3 Payles		x^{s}	
Item in the Chamber over the Hall One Bed & Bedstedle one Coverlet 2 Blankets 3 Chests 8 paire of Sheets 4er Tableclothes 15 Napkins 4er towells foure Pillowcoats	£vi.	v^{s}.	
Item in the Barne Wheate Thressed & unthressed Fower Quarters & a halfe Oats Thirty Cops Sacks Sacks & Measures 2 Shawles & 2 Sives	£viii.	xi^{s}.	viii^{d}.

Item one old Waggon 2 Plowes 2 old Courts one Harrow & other Husbandry Tacklings	£vi		
Item Fower Oxen one Cow 5 yong Cattle	£xxxiiii	iii^{s}	iiii^{d}
Item 3 Horse 14 Sheepe & 3 Hogs & Wheate on the Grownd 7 Akers	£xv.	v^{s}.	
Item old Lumber & things unseene and forgotten		iii^{s}	iiii^{d}
Summa Totalis	£Lxxxii.	x^{s}.	iiii^{d}
Item in Desperat Debts		L^{s}.	

110

FLOATE William — Cordwainer — bur. 24 Nov. 1677
W. 12 May 1677 — prov. 9 Jan. 1678 — PRS/W/6/77

In the name of God Amen I William Float of sevenoke in the County of Kent Cordwinder being sick and weake in body, but of good understanding and memory God be praised for it ordaine this to be my last will and testament as hereafter followeth: I doe in the first place humbly commend my soule at the houre of death into the hands of God my maker, trusting through his free grace alone, and by the allsufficient merits of Jesus to be eternally saved. And after my decease I commit my body to the earth out of which it was taken, therein to be decently buried at the discretion of my executor. And as to that worldly estate which the Lord hath given me, I dispose of it as is hereafter mentioned. Inprimis I give that house where William Wright now lives, and the stable adjoyning to it, and that part of the garden from the raddels southward, adjoyning to a little field now in the occupation of James Smith to my nephew John French, sonne of my sister Jane French Widow. Item I give that house where Widow Collier now dwells and that where I now dwell, with the other part of the garden northwards, to a narrow way from the well westward; to my Niece Dorothy French, daughter of my sister Jane French widow aforesaid, and my will and pleasure is that both my Nephew John French, and his sister my Niece Dorothy French shall each of them have free liberty to come and draw of the water in the well for their use upon all occasions, I give also unto my Niece Dorothy French all my moveables in the house and elsewhere: Item I give unto my Sister Mary Mercer five pounds, and to her daughter the wife of Edward Hills five pounds: Item I give unto my Cosen Edward Hills aforesaid forty seven shillings which he now owes me, being money lent him out of my purse: Item I give unto the three children of my Nephew William Wells deceased, to each of them ten shillings: Item I give unto the three children of my Nephew John Wells to each of them five shillings: Item the residue of my ready money, and debts

owing me, my funerall expences first deducted, and all my debts and legacies before given fully satisfyed and paid according to the true intent and meaning of this my will, I give unto my Nephew John French aforesaid, whom I appoint and constitute sole executor of this my last will and testament: And I doe hereby revoke and make void all former, and other wills by me heretofore made: In witnesse wherof to this my last will and testament conteyned in one sheet of paper I have set my hand and seale this twelfth day of May in the 29th yeare of the reign of our soveraign Lord Charles the second by the grace of God of England, Scotland, France and Ireland King etc: And in the yeare of our Lord 1677:
William Flot
In the presence of us
John Stone

111

FLOATE William | Cordwainer | bur. 24 Nov. 1677
I. 20 Dec. 1677 | prov. 9 Jan. 1678 | PRS/I/6/34

An Inventary of all and singuler the Goods Chattells and Credits of William Floate late whilst he lived of the parish of Seavenoke in the County of Kent Cordwayner deceased Taken and praysed the 20th day of December Anno Domini 1677 By John Beardsworth and Thomas Broad as followeth vizt.

		s.	*d.*
Inprimis the deceaseds weareing Apparell and ready money in his Purse		xxx	
Item in the Chamber backward One Table one Chest		xvi	
Item 3 small Pewter Dishes one Brasse Chafingdish		v	
Item in the Chamber over the Shop one Bedstead Matt and Cord one Flock bed and Bolster, 2 Blankets and one old Coverlett one pare of Tow Sheets.		xxxii	vi
Item one Cubert with Presse in it		xii	vi
Item an old Wicker Chayre & one Joyned Stoole		iii	
Item in the Shop for his workeing Geere and a small parcell of leather		xxx	
Item for Lumber not seene		ii	vi
Suma Totalis	£vi	xi s.	vi d.

112

BEECHER Margarett Widow bur. 17 Oct. 1677
W. 3 Aug. 1677 prov. 11 Dec. 1677 PRS/W/2/30

In the Name of God Amen I Margarett Beecher of Sevenoke in the County of Kent widdow beinge sickly in body but of sound & perfect minde & memory praysed be Almighty God therefor revokeinge all former wills by me hertofore made doe make & ordaine this my last will & testament in manner & forme followinge (Vizt.) First I recomend my soule into the hands of Almighty God my Creator who first gave it me hopeinge through the only merritts of Jesus Christ my blessed Saviour & Redeemer to obtaine remission of all my sinns hopeinge for a Joyfull resurreccion to life everlastinge And my body I comitt to the Earth to be decently buried att the discretion of my Executor herafter named And for those worldly Goods which it hath pleased Almighty God to lend me I give and dispose thereof as followeth (vizt) First I give and bequeath unto the Poore of the Parish of Sevenoke aforesaid the sume of Tenn Shillings of lawfull money of England to be distributed unto them att the discretion of my Executor Within one Moneth next after my Decease Item I give and bequeath unto my Kinswoman Martha Boghurst my Brother Richards Daughter the sume of Five pounds of lawfull English money to be paid her by my Executor within one Moneth next after my Decease Allsoe I give unto her two paire of my best hempen Sheets Item I make and ordaine Richard Childrens of Pantherst within the Parish of Sevenoke aforesaid yeoman Sole Executor of this my last will & testament unto whom I bequeath all the rest of my personall estate
In witnes whereof I have herunto sett my hand & Seale the Third day of August in the Nyne & Twentieth yeare of the Raigne of our Soveraigne Lord Kinge Charles the Second etc Annoque Domini 1677
The Marke of Margarett Beecher
Signed sealed published & Declared to be the last will & Testament of the said Margarett Beecher in the presence of
the marke of George Wood
John Brattle

113

BEECHER Margaret Widow bur. 17 Oct. 1677
I. 19 Oct. 1677 prov. 11 Dec. 1677 PRS/I/2/73

A true and perfect Inventory of all and singuler the goods and Chattells of Margarett Beecher late of Sevenoke in the County of Kent Widdow Deceased taken & Apprasyed the Nynteenth Day of October Anno Domini 1677 By John Beardsworth and Henry Swaysland vizt

Inprimis her wearinge Apparrell & money in her purse	£ii	0^{s}	0^{d}

Item Nyne paire of flaxe & hempen sheets Tenn paire of Course towen sheets Three dozen of Napkins & three old napkins Seaven paire of Pillow coats three Table Cloathes & one Cupbord cloath	£x	v^{s}	0^{d}
Item Two Feather bedds one feather bolster two feather pillowes with a steddle Matt & cord coverlett and blanketts	£iiii	x^{s}	0^{d}
Item three old chests & five old boxes	£0	xi^{s}	vi^{d}
Item one old Table & frame & three old chests	£0	vii^{s}	vi^{d}
Item three brasse skillets & three brasse Kettles	£i	i^{s}	0^{d}
Item one Little Iron Pottage Pott & one Iron Kettle one Table and frame one Spitt one old cupboard one paire of Andirons fireshovell & tongs one paire of Pothangers one Iron Pott one Cupboard Twelve pewter dishes one pewter pott and other small pewter	£i	x^{s}	0^{d}
Item old Lumber & things forgotten	£0	xv^{s}	0^{d}
Item money Due by bond & otherwise	£xxvi	0^{s}	0^{d}
Summa Totalis	£xlvii	0^{s}	0^{d}

114

BROOKSTEAD Alice Widow bur. 28 Aug. 1677
I. 29 Aug. 1677 prov. 4 Sep. 1677 PRS/I/2/138

A true and perfect Inventary of all and singular the goods chattles and debts of Alice Brookstead alias Brookside late of Seavenoakes in County of Kent widdow deceased taken vallued and appraized the 29th day of August Anno Domini 1677 by us William Spencer Thomas Young and Thomas Wibourne as followeth viz

	£	*s.*	*d.*
Inprimis her weareing Apparell	iii	x	
Item in ready money and booke debts	£ii		
Item in the greate Chamber 2 feather bedstedles 2 trundle bedstedles 2 feather beds 2 flock bedds 3 feather boulsters 4 feather pillowes one flock boulster two setts of curtaines and vallences one rug 2 Coverledds & 3 blanketts	£x		

Item one Court Cubbord one little Table 2 little Carpetts 3 joyned chests one plaine Chest one old trunke 2 little boxes and one Chest of Drawers	£i.	xvi^{s}
Item 4 leather chaires one old chair one paire of Andirons 2 fire panns one paire of tongs one paire of Creepers one paire of bellowes and one glass case		xv^{s}
Item 6 paire of sheetes and other small Lynnen one window Curtaine and Curtaine rodd	£i.	xv^{s}
Item certaine pewter dishes and Tinn ware	£ii	
Item a dozen of Small Iron potts one old Iron pott and one brass kettle	£i.	x^{s}
Item certaine potters ware		x^{s}
Item 2 paire of pothangers one paire of Andirons one fire Iron 2 paire of tongs 2 spitts one hand Jack 5 chaires one Court Cubbord one table and frame and carpet one forme one Joyned stoole 2 little tables one window curtaine and rodd	£i.	x^{s}
Item in the Buttery 2 Iron potts one Iron kettle one frying pann two basting Ladles 3 woodden bowles one tubb one keeler one gridgeiron and certaine trenchers and an Iron slice		xv^{s}
Item in the Shopp certaine pewter and Iron potts and other Iron wares and tynn wares and potters wares and certaine other things and brass wares	£xxx	
Item certaine plate	£ii	
Item in the Yard a house of Ease and certaine Faggotts		xv^{s}
Item certaine other Lumber not seen nor thought upon		x^{s}
Suma totalis huius Inventorii	£ lix	s vi

115

HOPE James bur. 17 Jun. 1672
I. 22 Jun. 1672 prov. 15 Jul. 1672 PRS/I/7/60

An Inventory of the Goods of James Hope late of Seavenoke in the County of Kent deceased. Taken the xxth day of October 1677 by John Bloome gentl. and Christopher Thomas gent. as followeth vizt.

Inprimis his Apparell		xiii^s	iiii^d
Item due to the deceased out of a Settlement of Lands	£x		
Suma Totalis	£x	xiiis	iiiid.

116

SMITH John Gentleman
W. 22 Nov. 1677 prov. 7 Feb. 1678 Prob. 11. 356 f. 18.

In the name of God Amen I John Smith of Seavenoks in the County of Kent Gent being weak in body but of perfect memory praised be God for it revoking all other and former wills do make and ordaine this my last Will and Testament in manner and form following Inprimis I bequeath my soule to Almighty God that gave it hoping in and through the merritts of my Lord and Saviour Jesus Christ for the remission and forgiveness of all my sins And my body to be buried decently after the discretion of my Executrix Item I bequeath unto my nephew Richard Smith eldest son of my brother Richard Smith which he had by his first wife All my lands lying in the parish of Sundridg and Chevening now in the occupation of Richard Skinner To have and to hold to my said Cosen Richard Smith after the decease of my wife Elizabeth Smith to him and his heires forever Item I give to my brother Richard Smith the sum of ten pounds of good and lawful money of England to be paid him by my Executrix within twelve moneths after my decease Item I give to my Cosen Mary Smith daughter to my brother - - - Smith which he had by his first wife the sume of five pounds of good and lawful money of England to be paid her by my Executrix within twelve months after my decease Item I give to my sister Coxe and to her heires the sum of five pounds of good and lawful money of England Item I give to my Cosens Oliver Godfrey and Elizabeth Wood and Mary Godfrey and Susanna Godfrey the sums of four pounds a piece of good and lawful money of England All which money to be paid within a twelve month after my decease by my Executrix Item I give to my sister Tooth the sum of five pounds of good and lawful money of England to be paid to her by my Executrix within twelve months after my decease Item I give to my Cosen William Tooth the sum of three pounds of good and lawful money of England to be paid to him by my Executrix within twelve months after my decease Item I give to my Cosen

John Tooth the sum of three pounds of good and lawful money of England to be paid to him by my Executrix within twelve months after my decease Item I give to my Cosen Edward Tooth the sum of three pounds of like money to be paid to him by my Executrix within twelve months after my decease Item I give to Anne Hale my Cosen the sum of three pounds of good and lawful money of England to be paid to her by my Executrix within twelve months after my decease Item I give to my Cosen Ellen Haies the sum of three pounds of good and lawful money of England to be paid her by Executrix within twelve months after my decease Item I give to my Cosen Dorothy Tooth the sum of three pounds of good and lawful money of England to be paid to her by my Executrix within twelve months after my decease Item I give to my Sister Atwater of Croydon in Surrey five pounds of good and lawful money of England to be paid to her by my Executrix within twelve months after my decease Item I give to my Sister Styles of Lambeth five pounds of good and lawful money of England to be paid her by my Executrix within twelve months after my decease Item I give to my Cosen John Jesson and to his wife and to their heires the sum of twenty pounds of good and lawful money of England to be paid by my Executrix within twelve months after decease Item I give to my wife Elizabeth Smith all the rest of my goods and chattells whom I make my full and sole Executrix she paying my debts and legacies above mentioned and this is my last will and testament whereunto I have set my hand and seal the Two and Twentieth day of November in the Nine and Twentieth year of his Majesties Raine Annoque Domini 1677
John Smith
Witness Nicholas Best   The mark of Audrey Gesby
Henry Swaysland
Item I give to my within written wife Elizabeth Smith all my Bonds and Bills and book debts which is due to me whatsoever and Leases and all other debts whatsoever

117

BOSS Richard	Vicar	bur. 4 Feb. 1678
W. 1 Feb. 1678	prov. 22 Mar. 1678	PRS/W/2/32

In the name of God Amen The first day of February Anno Domini 1677 I Richard Boss viccar of the parish Church of Seavenoke in the Countie of Kent being Sick in body but of perfect memory God be praised Doe make & ordaine my last will and testament in manner following that is to say first I bequeath my soule into the hands of my Creator in full assurance & hope of resurrection to eternall life and my body to bee interred in the Churchyard of the said parish Church by the discretion of my Executor or else in Mrs. Malories vault if shee please to condiscend thereto And as for my personall estate I doe thus dispose of First I bequeath to the poore of the said parish Church thirtie shillings in bread Item I give the Full third parte of all my goods Chattells Debts Creditts and personall estate except my library in whose hands or custodie soever they are unto my lovinge wife And the other two thirds of my said estate personall I give and bequeath amongst my Children except Richard & Thomas equally to be Devided amongst them att their respective ages of one & twenty yeares or days of marriage which shall first happen And I give to my eldest son my Death head Ring & to my youngest son Thomas the other ring and I give to my two eldest sons my library equally to bee devided betweene them And all my notebooks & sermon notes And I give to my eldest sonn my silver tanker & 2 silver spoones of his godfather gave him I give alsoe to my said two eldest Sons if they take their degrees & be fitted or else to such of them as shall be fitted for the ministrie and such of them to be qualified to have my whole library but if neither of them take upon them the ministry then I will the same be sould by my Executrix & the mony raised thereby bee divided amongst all my children as an addicon to their porcions And I hereby nominate and appoint my loving wife to be the sole Executrix of this my last will And to take care as she by law and nature is bound of all my Children And to take care with the proffitts of my said personall and also of my reall estate hereafter alsoe to bee mencioned for their education And I doe appoint & will that shee shall take & receive the proffitts of my personall estate for that purpose As alsoe the rents & proffitts of my reall estate for & towards her and their respective mayntenance & education And as to my reall estate That is to say all my lands and tenements whatsoever either in possessions or revercion lying & beinge in the Parishes of Seale & Sheborne in the said Countie of Kent and in the occupacion John Martin of Ligh next Tonbridg All lands conteyne by estimacion about fourtie acres I give and devise unto my eldest son Richard Boss and to his heires for ever when hee shall attaine his full age of five & twentie yeares & not before And in the meanetyme I doe appoint my said loving wife as aforesaid to receive the rents & proffitts thereof for her & my childrens mayntenance And my will is that if my said son Richard happen to departe this life before he shall attaine his said age of 25 yeares then I give & devise the same my lands to my three younger sons & their heirs equally to be devided betweene them at their respective full ages of one & twentie yeares & in the meanetime my said wife to receive the rents & proffitts thereof for the use & purposes aforesaid And I doe hereby nominate & earnestly request my wourthy friends Dr. Edward Clark of Cheeveninge & William Lambert Esquire to be the supervisors of this my last will And to direct my Executrix in the ordering of all things in order to the execucion of this my said will In witness whereof I have hereto sett my hand & seale the day and yeare first above written

Richard Boss

Sealed Signed Published and Declared in the presence of

Oliver Theobalds Andrew Weston

Geo. Courthope Peter Trice

118

BOSS Richard	Vicar	bur. 4 Feb. 1678
I. 6 Mar. 1678	prov. 22 Mar. 1678	PRS/I/2/112

An Inventory of all and singuler the goods and Chattels rights and Credits of Richard Boss late of the parish of Seavenoke in the County of Kent Clerk Deceased taken and appraised this sixt day of March 1677 by us Robert Hockham of Seavenoke aforesaid Inholder and Peter Trice of the same yeoman as followeth vizt:

	£.	*s.*	*d.*
Inprimis his wareing apparell and money in his purse	10.	0.	0.
In the Parlor			
Item six leather Chaires and six Turky worke Chaires	02.	8.	0.
Item two Tables two Carpitts the hanging in the Roome and a looking glasse	04.	0.	0.
Item a paire of Andirons fireshovell Tonges & Ironback	00.	4.	6.
Item a Silver Tankard eleaven silver Spoones and two silver porringers	14.	3.	4.
In the Kitchen			
Item twelve pewter dishes two flaggons two paire of Candlesticks and severall other peeces of pewter	04.	13.	4.
Item three brasse Skilletts two brasse kettles and a brasse pott	01.	12.	6.
Item one Birding Gunn	00.	10.	0.
Item one Iron Jacke three Spitts two dripping panns Andirons fireshovell Tonges Bellowes and Ironback	01.	8.	6.
Item two Iron potts one Iron Kettle three Tables two joyned stooles and six old Chaires	01.	7.	0.
In the Brewhouse			
Item one old Copper Furnace foure Tubbs and three Keelers	02.	5.	0.

In the Buttery			
Item foure drincke Tubbs and a Staldard	00.	5.	0.
In the out Buttery			
Item a Chest of Drawers a powdring Tubb two Dozen of Glasse Bottles and some old Lumber	02.	0.	0.
In the Yard			
Item about halfe a Cord of wood	00.	5.	0.
In the Best chamber			
Item one Downe bed and boulster a Rugg and Blanckett Bedstead Curtaines and Vallance matt and Cord	6.	0.	0.
Item one Couch and a Dozen of old Sarge Chaires	02.	10.	0.
Item a Chest of Drawers a Looking glasse and hanging shelfe and two window Curtaines	03.	0.	0.
Item two paire of Andirons with brasse heads	00.	10.	0.
In the Chamber over the Kitchin			
Item one Bedsteed a table two Chaires two stooles and a pillow	01.	10.	0.
In the Parlor Chamber			
Item two Bedsteads and a Trundle Bed	00.	13.	4.
Item two sett of Curtaines and Valance one Coverlett one old Rugg two paire of old Blancketts matts and Cords	04.	0.	0.
Item two feather beds three feather boulsters one feather pillow and one flockbed & boulster	08.	3.	4.
Item a Chest of Drawers a plaine Chest a Chaire and a Stoole	01.	10.	0.
In the midle Roome			
Item one Bedstead one Blanckett one Rugg Curtaines and Valance of greene Sarge a Featherbed and boulster	05.	6.	8.
In the Studdy			
Item two old presses two Deskes a Spainish Table	01.	3.	4.
Item the Library of Bookes	73.	13.	4.
Lynnen in severall Roomes			
Item twenty paires of sheets of severall sorts five dozen of Napkins a dozen of Towells a dozen of Table Cloathes and a dozen of pillow Coates	20.	05.	0.
Without Doores			
Item eight hundred weight of Hopps	16.	00.	00.

Item foure thousand of hoppoles	10.	13.	6.
Item a Load of Hay	00.	15.	0.
Item a Cow and a heifer	05.	0.	0.
Item a horse	07.	0.	0.
Item money out upon severall Securatyes	300.	0.	0.
Some totall is =	£512.	15.	8.

119

EVERIDGE Richard	Innholder	bur. 27 Sep. 1678
I. 8 Oct. 1678	prov. 15 Nov. 1678	PRS/I/5/38

An Inventory of all & singuler the goods and Chattells of Richard Everidge late of the parish of Seavenoke in the Countie of Kent Inholder deceased taken and appraized this eighth day of October in the thirtieth yeare of the Raigne of our Soveraigne Lord King Charles the second Annoque Domini 1678 By us Henry Swasland John Beardsworth and Thomas Levett as followeth:

In the Hall Chamber

	£.	*s.*	*d.*
Inprimis his weareing apparrell and money in his purse	03.	00.	00
Item one paire of Brasse Andirons one paire of Iron Andirons two firepanns Tongs and Bellowes	01.	01.	00
Item one feildbedsteadle matt and Cord and Curtine rods one paire of greene Sarge Curtaines and valance and fringe one featherbed and boulster one greene Rug one Blanckett and two pillowes	07.	18.	06
Item one Joyned Table foure stooles Six Cushions two green Chaires two Leather Chaires one Chest of Drawers and a Sideboard cloath	03.	06.	06
In the Chamber over the Shopp			
Item one feild Bedstead matt and Cord & Curtine rods Curtaines & Valance and a Bed filled with Coney flex two old Boulsters two old pillowes and Blanckett and one old Coverlett two Tables and two formes and one old Chest	03.	01.	06
In the chamber over the Brewhowse			
Item one old Joyned Bedstead matt and Cord one Trundell Bedstead with a Cord one Bed filled with			

Coney flix one feather Boulster and Two feather pillowes one smale Flockbed and Boulster one old Blanckett and one Coverlett	02.	10.	6
Item one large Joyned Chest two joyned stooles one Chest one Truncke and an old box	00.	18.	00
In the Garrett			
Item Two old halfe headed bedsteads one Flockbed and Boulster and two old Blancketts & two old Coverletts	01.	00.	06
Lynnen			
Item two Hempen Tablecloathes foure Tow tableclothes three short Tableclothes eleaven flaxen Napkins nyne Hempen napkins eleaven Tow napkins and six old Towells	02.	02.	04
Item five paire of Hempen sheets one paire of Flaxen sheets Seaven paire of Tow sheets and one od one and three paire of Hempen pillowcoates and one od one and six Thinn Towells	05.	08.	06
In the Shopp			
Item two old Tabells four old formes four old Chaires and one old Cupboard	00.	09.	00
In the Hall			
Item one paire of Crepers firepann Tongs and fireslice and two paire of potthangers	00.	07.	00
Item one old Iron Jack three Spitts two dripping panns and one gridiron with some smale thinges	01.	00.	06
Item thirteene pewter Dishes greate and smale one pewter Bason foure Chamberpotts thirteene pewter flagons one greate pewter flaggon one pewter quartpott one pint pott six pewter porringers and severall other smale peeces of pewter	03.	03.	00
Item two Iron potts one Brasse pott two Brasse Skillets and a warming pann	00.	13.	04
Item one cupboard one old glasse Cage one old Table and forme and Setle foure old Chaires one jointstoole and some old Lumber	01.	00.	06
In the Seller			
Item four Stalders thirteene Hogsheads one Barrell and firkin and one Kilderkin three keelers			

two powdring Tubbs and a Tunnell and six Dozen and a halfe of Bottells stone and glasse	03.	05.	06
Item five Hogsheads of Beere three of which are Decayed Beere	05.	00.	00
In the Brewhowse			
Item one Copper Furnace one Mashfate one Tunn one Cooler one keeler one furkin a Hoy Tubb and foure pailes a Jett a Stirrer a Taphose a Tapstaffe and a smale Stalder	04.	07.	00
In the Yard			
Item one Bucking Tubb one Soape keeler and three other old Tubbs	00.	09.	06
Item three Cord of wood and eight hundred of faggotts	05.	19.	00
In the Barne			
Item eight load of hay	08.	00.	00
Item a parcell of Oates unthrashed	04.	00.	00
Item a parcell of Hempe	00.	14.	09
Item three Baggs of Hopps	07.	10.	00
Item five Hoggs	04.	10.	00
Item one Mare	03.	00.	00
Item two Cowes	06.	10.	00
Item a Silver Bowle and two Silver Spoones	03.	05.	00
Item for Lumber and thinges forgott	00.	10.	00
Item for a stock of Hoppoles being about three and twentie hundred	05.	12.	06
Summa totalis	99.	13.	11

120

FREMLING Joane Widow
NW. 9 Dec. 1678 prov. 2 Jan. 1679 PRS/W/6/78

Memorandum That Joane Fremling late of Sevenoke in the County of Kent widdow beinge in perfect mind and memory and haveinge an intent and purpose to make her will and to settle and dispose of her estate Did on or about the Nynth day of December 1678 make and Declare her last will and Testament Nuncupative or by word of mouth in these or the like words following (vizt) I give to my eldest Daughter Mary Fremlinge my house and land in Nockholl in Kent And all the rest of my lands goods and Chattells whatever else I have I give to the said Mary Fremling and Ann my youngest Daughter to be equally Divided between them And I doe nominate and appoint William Wall and Thomas Tayler both of Sevenoke to be my Executors to doe their best for the good of my said Children or used words to the like effect in the presence of Nicholas Best John Vine and Margarett Suton whom she desired to take notice that this was her will.

121

FREMLING Joane Widow
I. 6 Feb. 1679 prov. 13 Feb. 1679 PRS/I/6/44

A True and perfect Inventary of all and singuler the goods Cattell and chattles of Joane Fremling late of 7oake in the County of Kent widdow deceased Taken & appraized the 6th day of February in the 31 yeare of the raigne of our Soveraigne Lord King Charles the Second etc. Annoque Domini 1678 by Richard Goodhugh & Richard Children as followeth vizt.

Inprimis her wearing apparrell & money in her purse	v^{l}		
Item in the Hall an old table & frame a cupboard 2 pair of pothangers a gridiron a toasting iron 3 latten dripping panns a latten pudding pan 5 flaggd bottomed chairs a fire slice a pair of tongues a rack to lay before the fire a smothing iron an old chaire 2 spitts & 10 cushins	i^{l}	ix^{s}	
Item in the Parlor a saddle and wicker chaire a morter & pestle & a forme		xi^{s}	
Item in the Kitchin a brasse furnace several old tubbs & an iron Packe & a leather sack & an old trevett	i^{l}	x^{s}	
Item in the milkehouse 20 milke bowles a Churne 2 bricks of butter & an old pair of butter scales		xvii^{s}	
Item in the buttery 10 drincke tubbs a flower chest a bunting hutch & an old woollen wheele & some lumber	i^{l}	ii^{s}	vi^{d}
Item 4 brasse kettles a warming panne 2 brasse pottage potts 2 brass skilletts a basting ladle two candle sticks 2 brasse scummers & 2 graters	i^{l}	iiii^{s}	
Item 17 quarters of oats & 6 sacks	viii^{l}	xvi^{s}	
Item in the servants Chamber a flockbed and bolsters & old blanket & chest		v^{s}	
Item in the Hall Chamber 1 bedstedle with Curtains vallence matt & cord curtaine rodds 1 feather bed a feather bolster flock bolster 1 flock bed 2 blanketts 2 old blanketts a truckle bedstedle bed and coverlett & blanketts 4 chests & a Cupboard	iii^{l}	xv^{s}	

Item in the Entry Chamber a feather bed & straw bed & a coverlett Curtains and vallence feather bolster & 6 chests and a truncke	ii^{l}		
Item 15 pounds of hempe and flaxe		xi^{s}	
Item 10 pounds of tow		i^{s}	
Item 4 pair of sheets	i^{l}	xvi^{s}	
Item 1 other paire of fine sheets		ix^{s}	
Item 2 dozen of Napkins		xii^{s}	
Item 3 tableclothes 2 towells 3 pillowberes		xiiii^{s}	
Item 7 course sheets 2 course Napkins 4 pillowcoats 1 course tablecloth 3 blades of cloth & 1 other blade of new course cloth		xix^{s}	vi^{d}
Item in the Garrett 2 pillowes a blankett & 2 old chests		iiii^{s}	vi^{d}
Item Clover seed	ii^{l}	ii^{s}	
Item 2 pair of sheets		iii^{s}	
Item 15 pewter dishes & other pewter in all 72 pounds weight	ii^{l}	viii^{s}	
Item more old pewter		iiii^{s}	
Item 2 iron pottage potts		v^{s}	
Item 3 steers and 2 heifers	xv^{l}		
Item the bull	ii^{l}	x^{s}	
Item 31 sheepe of all sorts	x^{l}	x^{s}	
Item 1 horse and a mare	ii^{l}		
Item 4 oxen	xix^{l}		
Item 8 ceeine	xxvii^{l}		
Item 1 cow and a calfe	iii^{l}	v^{s}	
Item 1 other cow & 3 bulls	vi^{l}		
Item 1 hog		x^{s}	
Item 5 sheats	ii^{l}	x^{s}	
Item Oats in the barne	iiii^{l}		
Item Pease		x^{s}	
Item wheat	ii^{l}		
Item the husbandry Tackling	vii^{l}	x^{s}	
Item hay 12 loads	v^{l}		
Item the Corne in the ground	ii^{l}	xix^{s}	
Item ready money	xxvi^{l}		
Item sperate debts	v^{l}		
Item debts desperate	ii^{l}		
Summa	Clxxvii^{l}	ii^{s}	vi^{d}

122

JEFFERY John	Clothworker	bur. 8 Dec. 1679
W. 17 Apr. 1679	prov. 3 Feb. 1680	prob. 11. 362 f. 23

April the 17th day 1679
In the name of God Amen I John Jeffery of Gritnes in the parish of Seavenokes in the County of Kent Cloathworker being sick in body and knoweing my dayes being uncertaine but in perfect memory praise be unto God for it I doe heare make and ordaine my last will and testament in manner and form following First I committ my spiritt into the hands of the Allmighty God my Creator hopeing that through the passion and blood of Jesus Christ my saviour I shall receive remission of my sinns and a glorious resurrection to life eternal after this is ended and I do desire my Executor hereafter named to bury my body in such a decent manner as she shall think fitt And as to my worldly goods that it hath pleased God to bless me with my mind is to dispose as followeth Imprimis I give unto my six children that it hath pleased God to give me that is to say John Bridgett Anne William Thomas and Elizabeth unto each of them after my decease when they shall accomplish the age of one and twenty years each of them Twenty pounds a peece to be paid out of my personall and yearly estate by my Executor and if it shall happen that either of them shall dye before they shall accomplish the age of one and twenty years my will is that the survivors of them shall have such monyes soe falen to be equally devided amongst them that are liveing of my other children Item I give unto my son John my best Table standing in the Parlor Item I give unto my son William my best bedstead standing in the Parlor Chamber Item I give unto my son Thomas my bedstead standing in the little chamber Item I give unto my daughter Bridgett my Cage Cupboard standing in the Kitchen chamber Item I give unto my daughter Anne my best joined chest standing in the kitchen chamber Item I give unto my daughter Elizabeth my Table with drawers standing in the kitchen chamber my will is that it shall be delivered unto each of them at the day of marriage or at the age of one and twenty years which shall first happen Item I give unto my Mother Dorothy Jeffery Twenty shillings Item I give unto my sister Gunter wife of Thomas Gunter Twenty shillings Item I give unto Anne Marshall my wifes Mother Twenty shillings Item I give unto Anne Stonham wife of John Stonham Twenty shillings Item I give unto my servant John Smith Twenty shillings which five Legacies I appoint shall be paid within three years after my decease Item I give unto my cosen Samuel Serls five shillings Item I give unto my brother William Jeffery five pounds to be paid within four years after my decease by my Executor alsoe after these Legacies and goods my will given I give my whole estate personal and real unto my loveing wife Bridget whome I make sole Executor of my estate and doe give my Lands goods and chattells unto her and her heires forever to execute my will and pay my debts and legacies above mentioned and to bring up my children out of the rents and profitts And my will is she shall sell my Cornmill and that land unto any which will give the most And as to my dwelling house and mill and the premises thereto belonging in my owne occupation with my land

called or knowne by Goodens Land in my occupation my will is that shall be for the bringing upp of my children until my youngest child shall be Tenn years of Age or at the end of nine years from this time and not before and my will is that at the end of nine years if my Executor shall sell my house and fuling mill and the premises thereto belonging with the land called Godens Land my will is my trusty friends my overseers shall at the sale require security for my childrens legacies as they shall come of age I do request my brother William Jeffery of Frittenden and my friend Richard Uridge of Hunton and Frances Corwell of Marden to oversee this my will executed and to be my overseers [to] which I have sett my hand and seale the day and year above written and delivered in the presence of
John Jeffery Thomas Broad Joseph Brown
Frances Broad

123

JEFFERY John	Clothworker	bur. 8 Dec. 1679
I. 20 Dec. 1679	prov. 3 Feb. 1680	Prob. 4. 10969

A True and perfect inventary of all and singuler the Goods Cattells Chattells ready money household stuffe plate and which did belong with John Jeffery late whilst he lived of the parish of Seavenocke in the County of Kent clothworker deceased seene taken vallued and appraised 20 of December in the year of our Lord God 1679 and in the 31 yeare of the Reigne of our most gracious Soveraigne Lord Charles 2nd by the grace of god of England Scotland France and Ireland King defender of the faith etc. (by us) Giles Browne John Chris Waymarke and John Stonam the particulars whereof ensue as followeth

Inprimis the deceased wearing apparrell both Lynnen and woollen and mony in his purse amounting to the sume	£iii	
Item good and bad debts due and oweing to the deceased at the time of his death by Bookes amounting to the summe of	£xx	
Item 4 Cowes valued and appraised at	£xii	
Item for 2 Horses and 1 Mare	£vii	
Item 4 Sheats	£i	xii^s
Item one waggon	£iiii	
Item 1 cart	£i	x^s
Item 1 plow and irons	£i	
Item 1 harrow		v^s
Item all the rest of the Husbandry Tackling and Irons and harness		x^s
Item in the Shop Tooles belonging to the Trade and a Copper	£iiii	

Item 1 presse and 1 Iron to it	£iiii		
Item 2 Tainters	£iiii		
Item 6 paire of sheares with all other implments belonging to the Trade and fulling Earth	£iii		
Item wheate in the Barne with Barly and pease	£vii		
Item 2 Acres of wheate on the ground for plowing harrowing and seed	£i	x^s	
Item 2 loads of Hay	£ii		
Item Faggotts	£ii		
Item Hopp poles	£ix		
Item Dung	£i		
In the Parlor			
Bookes of all sorts	£i		
Item 1 Table 1 forme 1 little square Table stooles 2 Chaires	£i	xiiii^s	
Item 1 paire of Andirons Tongs and fire pan		vi^s	
In the Hall			
Item 1 Chaire Table 1 form		vi^s	vi^d
In the Kitchin			
Item 1 Cuppboard		xiii^s	iiii^d
Item 1 Jack and stone weight belonging to it		x^s	
Item 2 dripping panns and 2 spitts		vi^s	viii^d
Item 12 peeces of pewter and 4 porringers		vi^s	
Item 3 Brasse Kettles 1 Iron Kettle	£i		
Item 2 Iron potts and 3 brasse skilletts		xiiii^s	
Item 5 Chaires and 1 Table Chaire		iii^s	viii^d
Item 2 fowling peeces		x^s	
Item 1 paire of Brandirons fire pann and Tongs		v^s	
Item 1 warmeing panne and 1 paire of Bellowes		iiii^s	
Item 2 paire of potthangers		ii^s	vi^d
In the Kitchen Chamber			
Item 1 Bedd and all the furniture thereunto belonging as it now stands	£iiii		
Item 1 Trundle Bedd and all the things thereunto belonging	£i	v^s	
Item 1 joyned Chest 1 Cage Cuppboard		xii^s	
Item 1 Trunk one Box		v^s	
Item 2 small stooles and 1 old Chaire		iii^s	
Item 1 pair of Brandirons		iii^s	
In the Chamber over the Kitchen			
Item 3 Bedsteadles	£i		
Item 1 small Bedd and Boulster and Three Blanketts		xii^s	
Item Hemp and flax	£i	x^s	
Item 2 Chests		iiii^s	
In the Hall Chamber			
Item 2 small steadles and 2 old Bedds with blanketts thereunto belonging	£i	xv^s	

In the Parlor chamber			
Item 1 Bedd and things belonging to it	£iii		
Item 1 little chest		iii^{s}	
In the Little Chamber			
Item 1 Bedd and Bedstiddle and all the things thereunto belonging	£iiii		
Item 1 joyned chest		vi^{s}	
Item 1 little Table and fower stooles		vi^{s}	
Item in Lynnen 6 paire of sheets of hemp and flax and 4 paire of pilecotts	£iii	xii^{s}	
Item 3 pair of Towen sheets	£i		
Item 3 fine table cloathes and 1 dozen of Napkins	£i		
Item other small Lynnen as course Table cloathes and course Towells and course napkins		xv^{s}	
In the Milke House			
Item Two leads and 12 milke Bowles	£i	ii^{s}	
Item 2 Churnes		vii^{s}	
Item 1 dresser and stolder		iii^{s}	
Item Provision in the House of all sorts	£iii		
In the Cellar			
Item 9 drink Tubbs	£i		
In the Brewhouse			
Item 1 Cheese presse		x^{s}	
8 Wash Tubbs and brew Tubbs	£i	v^{s}	
Item 16 stone of Flax	£ii		
In the Hopp Howse			
Item One Oast hare 1 skreene 1 Ladder some Coales and 2 braks	£i		
Item Malt		v^{s}	
For things forgotten and out of sight with all Lumber as well within dores as without	£i	v^{s}	
Suma totalis huius inventarii	£cxxxv.	viii^{s}	viii^{d}

124

EVERIDGE Dorothy	Widow	bur. 6 Oct. 1679
W. 2 Sept. 1679	prov. 6 Nov. 1679	PRS/W/5/194

In the name of god Amen I Dorothy Everidge of Seavenoke in the County of Kent widow being sicke and weake in body but of perfect mynd and understanding Doe make and ordayne this my Last will and testament in manner and forme following Inprimis I give my Soule into the hands of God my Creator trusting for the Salvacon thereof onely through the meritts of Jesus Christ my body I committ to the Earth Decently to be buryed at the

descrecon of my Executor Item I give and bequeath unto my Daughter in Law Mary Everidge my Silver Bowle two paire of my best Hempen sheetes and a Dozen of my best Flaxen napkins
Item I give and bequeath to my Daughter in Law Elizabeth Everidge my wedding Ring and two paire of good Hempen sheetes Item I give and bequeath unto Ann Jessup Daughter of Joseph Jessup of Seavenoke aforesaid my wedding Gowne and petticoate Item I give unto Mary Jessup one other of the Daughters of the said Joseph Jessup my biggest peece of Gold and I give unto the said Joseph Jessup his wife all other my wearing apparell, both Lynnen and woollen. Item I give and bequeath unto my Loving mother Dorothy Taunton the some of foure pounds which I appoint to be paid within two moneths after my Decease and to be paid in the first place after my Debts and my funerall Expences and the probate of this my will is satisfied And revokeing all former and other wills I Doe of this my Last will make the said Joseph Jessup my full and sole Executor and to him I give the overplus of all my estate after my just Debts Legacyes afore said my funerall charges and the probate of this my will is satisfied In wittnesse whereof I have here unto sett my hand and seale this second Day of September in the one and thirtieth yeare of the Raigne of our Soveraigne Lord King Charles the second Annoque Domini 1679
The marke of Dorothy Everidge
This will was read unto the said Dorothy Everidge and by her signed sealed and published to be her last will in the presence of us
John Blome   Wm Allen   William Heath

125

EVERIDGE Dorothy   Widow   bur. 6 Oct. 1679
I. 14 Oct. 1679   prov. 6 Nov. 1679   PRS/I/5/39

A true and perfect Inventory of all the goods and Chattells of Dorothy Evridge late of Seavenoke in the County of Kent widdow taken and appraized this foureteenth day of October in the one and thirtieth yeare of the Raigne of our Soveraigne Lord King Charles the second Annoque Domini one thousand six hundred seaventy nyne by us Thomas Greene of Seavenoke aforesaid Mercer and David Durtnall of the same Baker as followeth vizt

	£.	*s.*	*d.*
Inprimis her weareing apparell and money in her purse	0.	6.	8.
Item six Cushions	0.	9.	0.
Item Eight pewter Dishes	0.	14.	0.
Item six Flaggons three Chamberpotts with three other small peeces of pewter)	0.	10.	0.

Item three brasse skilletts and a Chaffing dish	0.	4.	0.
Item one Iron pott and brasse Kettle warming pann and Gridiron)	0.	14.	0.
Item one spitt and one dripping pan	0.	3.	0.
Item two Chares	0.	1.	6.
Item two tables and two formes	0.	2.	6.
Item one old Chest and a glasse case	0.	1.	0.
Item nyne sheets tenn napkins and three tablecloathes	1.	2.	6.
Item one Featherbed two feather pillowes one blancket and one old Coverlett)	0.	10.	0.
Item one flockbed boulster and Coverlett and a trundlebed steadle)	0.	8.	0.
Item one feather bed boulster Rugg and blancket Curtaines and valance beadsteadle matt and cord)	1.	10.	0.
Item foure paire of sheets and twelve napkins	2.	10.	0.
Item one Silver boule and a gold ring	3.	10.	0.
Item three pillocoates and an old paire of sheetes	0.	2.	6.
Item an Iron Jack	0.	5.	0.
Item a parcell of Hempe	0.	5.	0.
Item one Table	0.	5.	6.
Item one old bedsteadle	0.	2.	0.
Item a dresserboard and forme	0.	3.	0.
In the Hoppgarden			
Item the stock of poles there standing	5.	0.	0.
Summe totall	18.	19.	2.

126

FULLER Thomas — Husbandman
I. 4 Sep. 1679 — prov. 15 Jan. 1680 — PRS/I/6/67

A true & perfect Inventory of all & singuler the goods chattells & Debts of Thomas Fuller late of Seavenoake in the County of Kent husbandman deceased made taken & appraised the 4th day of September Anno Domini 1679 by John Brattle & William Jarrett as followeth vizt.

	£	*s.*	*d.*
Inprimis his best suite of Apparrell	i	xii	vi
Item an old suite of Apparrell		xiii^{s}	
Item one other old suite		vi^{s}	
Item a pare of bootes & spurrs and shashoons		vii^{s}	

Item a rideing coate & old breeches and stockings		x^{s}	
Item 4 old Hatts		vi^{s}	
Item a pare of shoes and buckles		vi^{s}	
Item Sword & belt old chain and old shoes		iii^{s}	vi^{d}
Item 7 shirts and 3 pare of drawers a white wascoate)		xviii^{s}	
Item a box and old Linnen		i^{s}	
Item bands handkerchiefes and cravates		v^{s}	
Item a box & key and locke		i^{s}	
Item a razor and capp		i^{s}	
Item due for Wages	£v		
Item debts due uppon bonds	£viii		
Suma totalis	£xviii	xi^{s}	

127

MORGAN Richard Yeoman bur. 12 Sept. 1679
I. 21 Sept. 1679 prov. 2 Dec. 1679 PRS/I/13/68

A True & perfect Inventary of all & singuler the goods & chattells of Richard Morgan late of Seavenoke in the County of Kent Yeoman deceased taken & appraized the i twentieth day of September Anno Domini 1679 by Frances French Wm Wall & Wm Morgan as followeth vizt.

	£.	s.	d.
Inprimis his wearing apparell & money in his purse	£ii		
In the Hall			
Item i cupboard i settle i table & frame a sideboard one paire of Andirons 2 pairs of pothangers & fire shovell & tongs 2 spitts 2 panns)	ii.	iii	vi
some old chairs an old porridge pott & 3 payles			
In the Parlor			
Item 1 featherbed & bolster steddle curtains & vallens i table & frame i forme 4 joined stools a cupboard 2 old chests 2 chaires & 1 pair of Andirons)	iiii	xi	iiii
In the Buttery			
Item 2 Trestles 2 boards seaven drinke tubbs 1 powdring tubb & a keeler)		xviii^{s}	
In the Milkehouse			
Item 12 Milke bowles an old table a kneading trough a bacon trough & a Churne)		xiii	vi
In the Brewhouse			

		£.	s.	d.
Item a tun tub a meash tub 2 hog tubs i old tub 2 keelers a cheese presse 2 drinke tubbs & a Washing Keeler	)	i	0	x
In the Kitchen				
Item 2 old tubbs & some old Lumber			$x^{s.}$	
In the Milkhouse Chamber				
Item 1 bedsteddle & feather bed curtaines vallens boulster two blanketts i coverlett i table & frame i forme 4 old chests i old presse an old flock bed & steddle i trundle bed with the Coverletts and blanketts thereto belonging & a joyned stoole	)	£. iii	s. xiiii	
In the Parlor Chamber				
Item 1 scry 1 bushell an old table & an old flock bed	)		xs.	
Item the Corne in the Barne & the Hay		£xxi		
Item the husbandry Tackling		£x		
Item 4 Oxen & 4 steeres		£xxxxi		
Item 18 hoggs & piggs		£v		
Item 6 milch kine		£xvi	xs.	
Item 3 horses		£ix		
Item 3: two yearing 6 weaning calves & 5 12 monethings		£xx		
Item 2 acres of hoppoles		£vi		
Item 50 lbs Weight of pewter at 7^{d} per pd.		£i	ix^{s}	ii^{d}
Item severall peeces of brasse		£ii	x^{s}	
Item Linnen of all sorts		£v	x^{s}	
Item old lumber & things forgott			v^{s}	vi^{d}
Suma		£cxlix	v^{s}	x^{d}
desperate debts owing to the intestate at the time of his decease		£x		

128

DAVIS Daniel — Cheesemonger — bur. 15 Jan. 1680
I. 16 Jan. 1680 — prov. 10 Feb. 1680 — PRS/I/4/16

A true and perfect Inventory of the Goods cattell chattells & personall Estate of Daniell Davis late of Sevenoacke in the County of Kent Cheesmonger deceased taken & Apprized the Sixteenth Day of January Annoque Domini 1679 by us whose names are hereunder written as followeth (that is to say)

	£	*s.*	*d.*
Imprimis the deceaseds wearing Apparell	0	10	0
Item Ready money & debts due to the Testator	3	0	0
Item one Flock bedd two boulsters bedstedle Matt and Cord	–	14	6
Item one Court Cubbert & Cloath one other Court Cubbert one small table & seaven Chayer & Fower Joyned Stooles	–	9	6
Item one warmeing pann one small kettle and two Skilletts	–	4	0
Item one looking glass and a small parcell of Dishes & Trenchers	–	1	6
Item one payer of Andirons Tongs Fyer Shovell and a payer of Bellowes	–	6	0
Item 3 beere tubbs & 3 old chests	–	8	0
Item Butter & Cheese	6	0	0
Item Skailes and waites	–	6	0
Item one old Mare bridle & Saddle	1	15	0
Item a verry small parcell of hay & straw	0	4	0
Item Fagotts & Wood	0	16	0
Item old Lumber things seene unseene & Forgotten	0	4	0
Sume totalis	14	18	6

John Willson)
Thomas Wheeler) Apprizers
Thomas Young)

129

PAYNETER Alington Widower
NW. 29 Jan. 1680 prov. 18 Feb. 1680 Prob. 11. 362 f. 27

Memorandum that Alington Payneter late of Sennock in the County of Kent widower being sick of the last sickness whereof he died at the house of

William Lambard of Sennock aforesaid Esqr where he the said Alington Payneter for some years before had lived but of perfect mind and memory did on the twenty-ninth day of January in the year of our Lord God One thousand six hundred seventy and nine (English style) in the presence of Francis Farnaby of Sennock aforesaid Esqr. George Roberts of the same Clerk John Theobalds of the same Phisitian Mrs Mary Lambard and Mrs Elizabeth Humphreys (being desired to declare his mind and will that the above named persons might take notice thereof) declare and utter his last will and testament nuncupative or by word of mouth in these words or the very like in effect vizt. It is my mind and will that my brother in lawe (meaning and speaking of William Lambard Esqr. his Brother in Lawe aforesaid) shall have the bringing up of my children and manage my estate for them And I make him my Executor all which words or the same effect the said Alington Payneter being of sound and perfect memory did utter on the said twenty-ninth day of January in the year of our Lord 1679 (English style) in the presence and hearing of Thomas Lambard Esqr. Francis Farnaby Esqr. George Roberts clerk John Theobalds Mrs Mary Lambard Mrs Elizabeth Humphreys

130

DALE Anne | Widow | bur. 4 May 1682
W. 9 Feb. 1680 | | Prob. 11. 370 f. 55

In the name of God Amen Know all men by these presents That I Anne Dale of the parish of Sevenokes in the county of Kent Widdow beinge weake in body but of perfect memory Doe make and ordaine this my last will and Testament in manner and forme following Imprimis I resign my soule to God that gave it in hope of eternall Salvacion through the alone merritts of my blessed Saviour Jesus Christ and my body to the ground to be decently buried according to the discretion of my Executrix hereafter named in hope of a blessed Resurrection unto eternall life through my blessed Redeemer And as for those worldly goods that God hath entrusted me withall I give and bequeath them in manner and forme following First I give unto my sonne Edward Dale (if he be yet alive) A Guiney to buy him a Ring I give and bequeath unto my sonne Henry Dale a Guiney to buy him a Ring Also to my Daughter Dickson to Carrilina Bowle to my daughter Cod and to Widgeing Cod to each and every of them I give and bequeath a Guiney The rest of my goods and Chattells money plate bonds or debts whatsoever is due to me my funerall expences being discharged I give and bequeath unto my Grand-daughter Elizabeth Tyre Widdow during her naturall life and after her decease to bee disposed of amongst the Children of the said Elizabeth Tyre as she shall think fitt whom I make my only Executrix of this my last Will and Testament In Witnes to this my last will and testament I sett my hands and Seale this Nineth day of February One Thousand Six Hundred Seventy Nine
Anne Dale
Signed sealed and delivered before us witnesses Sa. French
Isaac Day The mark if Grace Crowhurst

131

EVEREST William	Tailor	bur. 15 May 1683
W. 17 Jul. 1680	prov. 30 May 1683	PRS/W/5/199

In the name of God Amen the Seaventeenth day of July in the yeare of our Lord one Thousand Six hundred and Eighty I William Everest of Seavenock in the County of Kent Taylor being att this time weake in body but of good and perfect memory (God be praised) Doe make and ordaine my last will and testament in maner and forme following First I comend my Soule into the hands of my Creator hopeing through the merrits and mediacon of my Redeemer Jesus Christ to inherite Eternall happyness in the world to come, and my Body I committ to the Earth to be enterred att the discretion of my Executrix hereafter named And as touching my personall Estate which it hath pleased God to bestow upon mee I give and bequeath as followeth First I give and bequeath to my only Daughter Margarett Everest a Silver Cupp and Three Silver Spoones – All the rest of my Goods chattells and personall Estate whatsoever (after my Debts paid and my funerall expences discharged) I give and bequeath to my Loveing wife Elizabeth whom I make sole Executrix of this my last will and Testament, And I doe nominate and Appoint my loveing Brothers Peter Everest and Peter Trice to be the overseers of this my last will and Testament. And I doe revoke all former wills by mee att any time heretofore made In witnes whereof I the said William Everest have hereunto sett my hand and Seale the day and yeare First above written
William Everest
Sealed Signed published and declared in the presence of
Thos Streatfeild John Harrison Gilles Durtnall

132

EVEREST William	Tailor	bur. 15 May 1683
I. 24 May 1683	prov. 30 May 1683	PRS/I/5/28

An Inventory of all & Singular the goods & Chattells of William Everest late of the Parish of Seavenoke in the County of Kent Taylor deceased taken & appraized the 24.th day of May 1683 by us, Thomas Greene of Seavenoke aforesaid Mercer, And Peter Trice of the Same Yeoman as followeth Vizt

	£	s	d
Inprimis his wearing apparell and money in his purse	02	00	00
In the Shop Chamber			
Item One Bedstead flockbed & bolster	00	10	00
Item three Chests one Trunk one box and Two stooles	01	00	00
Item Two Cupboards & one Table	00	04	00
Item Six paire of Sheets, one dozen Napkins	01	00	00
Item fower pillowCoats with old Lynnen	00	04	00

In the Chamber over the Hall			
Item One bedstead, Curtains & Valance a featherbed with old covering)	02	00	00
Item a Chest of drawers & foure Chaires	01	00	00
Item one feather bolster & three pillows	00	12	00
Item a paire of bellows one paire of Andirons & a Jack	00	05	00
Item Lumber in the Closett	00	03	00
In the Hall			
Item Three Tables one forme Three chaires, three joyntstooles Three Spitts, a frying pan, one warming pan one gridiron one paire of Tongs and fierpan)	01	00	00
In the Kitchin			
Item fifteene pewter dishes with other small pewter	01	00	00
Item Two kettles & Five skilletts	00	08	00
Item Two Iron kettles & Two Iron potts	00	10	00
Item six Tubs & Six brewing Vessells	01	01	00
In the Shop			
Item one Shopboard one Chest Two smoothing Irons one paire of Sheares and one forme)	00	10	00
In the Buttery			
Item one Cupboard	00	02	06
Item one hundred & halfe of Faggotts	00	15	00
Item a flaskett & other little things	00	05	06
Summae totalis	14	10	00

Thomas Greene   Peter Trice

133

THORNTON Edward   Husbandman   bur. 6 Sep. 1680
W. 2 Sept. 1680   prov. 24 Nov. 1680   PRS/W/16/210

In the name of God Amen I Edward Thornton of Seavenock in the County of Kent husbandman this second day of September in the Two and Thirtyeth year of the raigne of our Soveraigne Lord Charles the second by the grace of God King of England Scotland France & Ireland defender of the Faith etc. Anno Domini 1680 Being weake in body but of Sound and disposing minde and memory praised be God therefore doe make and ordaine this my last will and Testament in maner and forme following First I bequeath my Soule into the hands of Allmighty God my Creator and his Sonn Jesus Christ my Redeemer in whom through his death I trust to be saved and my body I comitt to the Earth from whence it was taken to be decently buryed att the discretion of my Executor hereafter named And as concerning that Estate which God hath lent mee here on Earth I give and dispose thereof as followeth Item I give and bequeath unto my Sister Julian Lippword the sume of Twenty pounds of lawfull mony of England to be paid unto her by my Executor hereafter named within Three Moneths after my decease Item I give and bequeath unto Jane and Elizabeth Thornton the Two Eldest daughters of my brother William Thornton the sume of Twenty pounds a peice of lawfull mony of England to be paid unto them by my Executor hereafter named within Three Moneths after my decease Item I give and bequeath unto Mary and Sarah Cox the Two Eldest daughters of my brother in Law George Cox the sume of Tenn pounds a peice of lawfull mony of England to be paid unto them by my Executor hereafter named within Three Moneths after my decease Item I give and bequeath unto John Mary and Anne Thornton the Three next Eldest Children of my brother William Thornton the sume of Twenty pounds a peice of lawfull mony of England to be paid unto them Att their severall Ages of one and Twenty years a peice by my Executor hereafter named which last Three Twenty pounds I will and desire my Executor to putt out att Interest for the use of the aforesaid John Mary and Anne Thornton till they attaine to their said severall Ages of One and Twenty years a peice Item I give and bequeath unto John Lippword Sonn of my aforesaid Sister Julian Lippword the sume of Twenty pounds of lawfull mony of England to be paid unto him by my Executor hereafter named when hee shall attaine his age of one and Twenty years And I desire my Executor to putt out the said Twenty pounds att Interest for the use of the said John Lippword untill he shall Attaine his Age of One and Twenty years Item I give and bequeath unto Elizabeth and George Cox the Two next Eldest Children of the aforesaid George Cox by my Sister deceased the sume of Tenn pounds a peice of lawfull mony of England to be paid to them att their severall Ages of one and Twenty years by my Executor And I will and desyre my Executor to putt out the said Two Tenn pounds att Interest for the use of the aforesaid Elizabeth and George Cox till they attaine their Ages of one and Twenty years Item all the rest and residue of my goods chattells debts ready mony and personall Estate after my debts legacies and Funerall Expences are paid and discharged I give and bequeath unto my Master William Best of Seavenock aforesaid Inholder and I make and ordaine the said William Best sole Executor of this my last will and Testament desyering him to performe the same In witness whereof I the said Edward Thornton have to this my last will and Testament revoking all former wills by mee made written in two Sheets of paper to Each Sheet thereof sett to my hand and seale the Day and year First above written

the marke of Edward Thornton

Signed Sealed published and declared to be the last will and Testament of the said Edward Thornton in the presence of us the marke of Elizabeth Downes Tho. Streatfeild

John Harrison

134

PIERREPONT Elizabeth bur. 2 Nov. 1680
W. 9 Oct. 1680 prov. 19 Nov. 1680 Prob. 11. 364 f. 152
October 9th 1680

In the name of God I Elizabeth Pierrepont Doe make and Declare this to bee my Will I give my Mother Twenty pound I give to my brother Pieerepont his wife and Children Fifty pounds to buy Mourneing I give to my Ante Leghe Couzen Burton and Couzen Thomas Leghe Tenn pounds a peece for Mourneing and to my couzen John Leghe and his wife Tenn pounds a peece for Mourneing and Cusen Gacen [or Gacer] and his wife Tenn pounds a peece for Mourneing I give my Goddater my Couzen Terrss [?Teresa's] Dater Fifty pounds on her day of marriage I give to my Cusen Frankes Fifty pounds but her husband shall not know of it I give to Mrs Elizabeth Kooke Mr Samuels Dater hoe I call sister Fifty pounds I give my brother Humfry Twenty pounds I give my Cusen Anne Bull all my estate in Riverhead and Sinocke and I make my sister Bull my Executor and to bury me out of my estate in White Chappell this is my will Elizabeth Pierrepont And I give Betty my Mothers maid hare Mourneing witnessed by
Ralph Petley Vic Henry Mallory Samuell Seyliard

135

WOOD Richard Yeoman bur. 13 Mar. 1681
I. 24 Mar. 1681 prov. 16 Apr. 1681 PRS/I/23/86

A true and perfect Inventory of all and singular the goods and Chattells of Richard Wood Late of Seavenoake in the County of Kent, Yoman deceased taken valued and apprized the fower and Twentyeth day of March in the Three and Thirtyeth yeare of the Reigne of our soveraigne Lord Charles The second by the grace of god Kinge of England Scotland France and Ireland Defender of the Faith etc Annoque Domini 1680 as followeth (that is to say)

	£	s	d
Imprimis His Weareing apparrell	01	00	00
Item money in his purse	00	05	00
In the Hall			
Item A Table a settle with Fower joyned stooles and some other Lumber	00	10	00
In the milke house			
Item A Cupboard and a bakeing trough and Twelve Trayes or milk bowles and other Lumber	01	00	00
In the Celler			
Item nine Tubbs with other Lumber	02	00	00
In the Kitchen			

Item one forme Two brasse Kettles Three brasse skylletts a warmeing pan Two Iron potts one Iron Kettle fyer pan Tonges & pothangers and irons and Two spitts & pans with some other Lumber)	03	00	00
In the Hall Chamber			
Item A bedsted a bed and boulster Curtaines and vallence Rugg & blancketts)	05	00	00
Item Two joyned Chestes Two plaine Chestes one Trunke Two Cobirons fyeir pan and Tonges)	01	10	00
Item Twelve pair of sheets with some other Lynnen	07	00	00
In the Chamber over the milkehouse			
Item One old bedsted with some bedding a box and an old Truncke with some other Lumber)	01	10	00
In the Chamber over the Kitchen			
Item An old bed & bedsted with some bedding and other Lumber)	02	00	00
Item Five small dishes of pewter with some other pewter	01	00	00
Item For ploweing and seed to sowe Two and Twenty acres of Corne)	16	00	00
Item Two Courts and his plowes & Harrowes	07	10	00
Item for the poles uppon the hopground	06	00	00
Item Thirty sheepe	10	00	00
Item Seaventeene bullocks	40	0	0
Item Fower horses & Two Colts & Three old Harnesse)	16	00	00
Item Seaven Hoggs	3	10	00
Item Eight Loads of hay	8	00	00
	132	15	00

Apprized by us John Allen John Holte

136

PEAKE Richard — Yeoman — *bur. 20 Mar. 1682
W. 11 Apr. 1681 — prov. 12 Feb. 1684 — Prob. 11. 375 f. 21
*carried to Chevening

In the name of god Amen I Richard Peake of Riverhead in the parish of Seavenoke in the County of Kent Yeoman this Eleaventh day of April in the Three and Thirtieth yeare of the Raigne of our Soveraigne Lord Charles the Second by the grace of God King of England Scotland France and Ireland defender of the Faith etc. Anno Domini One Thousand Six Hundred Eighty One being sick and weake in body but of sound and disposeing mind and memory praised be God for the same doe make and ordaine this my last will and testament in manner following That is to say First I commend my soule into the hands of Allmighty God hopeing and assuredly beleeveing through the merritts death and passion of my blessed Saviour and redeemer Jesus Christ to receive a full and free pardon for all my sinns and a joyfull resurrection in the Kingdome of Heaven And my body I committ to the earth from whence it came to be decently buried at the discretion of my Executors hereafter named And as to what Worldly Estate it hath pleased God to bless me withall both reall and personall I dispose thereof as followeth Imprimis I give and bequeath unto the poore of the severall parishes of Seavenokes and Chevening in the County of Kent the summe of five pounds a peice of Lawfull mony of England to each parish to be paid and distributed unto them by my Executors hereafter named at their discretion two Moneths after my decease Item I give and bequeath unto my Master Ralph Petley Esqr the summe of Tenn pounds of Lawfull mony of England To his sonne Thomas the like summe of tenn pounds and to his son John and his daughter Jane the summe of five pounds a peice of like mony of England to be paid unto them by my Executors hereafter named within one year after my decease Item I give and bequeath unto Richard Fotherstone my Sister sonne the summe of one hundred and Three score pounds of lawfull mony of England to be paid unto him by my Executors hereafter named within one year after my Decease Item I give and bequeath unto my Kinswoman Anne Gooden Daughter of my Sister Ann Fotherstone deceased the summe of four score pounds of lawfull mony of England to be paid unto her by my Executors hereafter named within one year after my decease Item I give and bequeath unto the Five Children of my Kinswoman Susan Rogers deceased the summe of Five pounds a peice of lawfull mony of England to be paid unto them by my Executors hereafter named within one year after my decease Item I give and bequeath unto Robert Russell the elder and Ann his wife the sum of five pounds a peice To their sonne Robert Russell the younger my Godsonn the sum of Twenty pounds And to their daughter Ann Russell the summe of five pounds of lawfull mony of England to be paid unto them by my Executors hereafter named within one year after my decease Item I give and bequeath unto my Kinswoman Elizabeth Johnson of Crockenhill and her Three Children the summe of five pounds a peice of lawfull mony of England to be paid unto them by my Executors hereafter named within one year after my decease Item I give and bequeath unto my Kinswoman John Goodens Five Children the summe of five pounds a peice to be paid unto them by my Executors hereafter named within one year after my decease Item I give and bequeath unto the eldest sonne of the aforesaid Richard Fotherstone the summe of tenn pounds And to all the other children of the said Richard Fotherstone the summe of five pounds a peice of lawfull mony of England to be paid unto them by my Executors hereafter named within one year after my decease Item I give and bequeath unto Thomas Dasten of Seavenoke and to my Goddaughter Anne wife of Powsey of Shoreham And to Ellen Tye wife of Thomas Tye of Seavenoke the Two Daughters of the said Thomas Dasten the summe of five pounds a peice and to the Five other Daughters of the said Thomas Dasten the summe of three pounds a peice of lawfull mony of England to be paid unto them by my Executors hereafter named within one year after my decease Item I give and bequeath unto Marten Seamen unto Judeth Bunring Martha Roberts Rebecca Cakott four of the servants of my aforesaid Master Mr Petley the summe of forty shillings a peice and to George Finch the Fott boy the summe of twenty shillings of lawfull mony of England to be paid unto them by my Executors hereafter named within one year after my decease Item I give and bequeath unto Mrs Silence wife of Thomas Carnewel to my kinsman Richard Peake of Cuddham To my kinsman Peake of Idehill To the son of Alexander Garland of Riverhead to Edward Gilbert and Richard Hayman the summe of five pounds a peice of lawfull mony of England to be paid unto them by my Executors hereafter named within one year after my decease Item I give and bequeath unto the Two Daughters of the aforesaid Alexander Garland which he had by my Kinswoman and to my Goddaughter Elizabeth wife of Robert Gooden deceased the summe of three pounds a peice of lawfull mony of England to be paid unto them by my Executors hereafter named within one year after my decease Item I give and bequeath unto Mr. Thomas Streatfield of Seavenoke and Martha his wife the summe of Forty shillings a peice of lawfully mony of England to be paid unto them by my Executors hereafter named within one year after my decease Item I give and bequeath unto Mathew Hatridge and John Durlin the summe of twenty shillings a peice of lawfull mony of England to be paid unto them by my Executors hereafter named within one year after my decease Item I will and order that my Executors hereafter named shall expend and lay out on my funerall the summe of six and forty pounds of lawfull mony of England Item I give and bequeath unto Leonard Gale of Crawley in the County of Sussex Gent one of my Executors hereafter named the summe of One Hundred pounds of lawfull mony of England to be paid and received out of my personall Estate within one year after my decease Item I give and bequeath unto John Beardsworth of Seavenoke aforesaid my other Executor hereafter named the summe of thirty pounds of lawfull mony of England to be paid and received out of my personall Estate within one year after my decease Item all the rest and residue of my goods Chattells ready mony debts bonds bills mortgages and personall estate whatsoever I give and bequeath unto the aforesaid Leonard Gale and John Beardsworth whom I make and ordaine Sole Executors of this my last Will and Testament desireing them well and truely to performe the same And my will and meaning is and I doe hereby order and appoint that all my aforesaid Legatees to whom I have in this my will given Legacies that are not of the age of one and twenty years that my aforesaid Executors shall reteyne and keep in their hands their legacies given as aforesaid untill they shall attaine to their ages of one and twenty years and till they shall attaine to the said age of one and twenty years shall pay unto them or either of them after the rate of one shilling in the pound for the interest of the said legacies Item I give and bequeath unto the wife of Samuel Bird of Camberwell my Sisters Daughter All that my Messuage or tenement with the Barn Stable outhouses yards gardens orchards and two peices or parcells of Land and premises thereunto belonging lying in Whitley in the parish of Chevening in the County of Kent late in the occupation of Richard Ausby to have and to

hold to her the said wife of Samuel Bird his heires and Assignes for ever Item I give and bequeath unto Richard Goodden son of my Kinswoman Ann Goodden All that my Messuage or Tenement with the outhouse yard Garden Orchard and premises thereunto belonging lying in Riverhead in the aforesaid parish of Seavenoke in the occupation of John Hope or his Assignes to have and to hold to him the said Richard Goodden and to his heires and Assignes for ever Item I doe further give and forgive to the aforesaid Samuel Bird the summe of Tenn pounds which he oweth unto mee on bond In witness whereof I the said Richard Peake have to this my last Will and Testament Revokeing all former Wills by mee made written of four sheets of paper to every sheet thereof set to my hand and seale the day and year first above written
the marke of Richard Peake
Signed sealed delivered published and declared by the said Richard Peake to be his last will and testament in the presence of
Tho Streatfield John Harrison Martin Seaman

137

PEAKE Richard		bur. 20 Mar. 1682
I. 12 Mar. 1682	prov. 12 Feb. 1684	Prob. 4.10922

An Inventory of the Goods and chattells of Richard Peake of Seavenoke [yeoman] taken and apprized the Twelveth day of March 1682 and the Fowre and Thirtyeth year of the Raigne of our Soveraigne Lord King Charles the Second over England Scotland France and Ireland

Imprimis his purse ready mony and weareing apparrell	133	0	0
Item mony on bond and on Mortgage and other debts some good and some desperate	585	0	0
Item Three old Trunks Three Boxes and some other Lumber	2	0	0
Item things forgotten and not seene	0	5	0
	720	5	0

Apprized by us
William Allen Peter Trice

138

BLOME John	Gentleman	bur. 10 Oct. 1684
W. 30 Mar. 1682	prov. 21 Oct. 1684	Prob. 11. 377 f.122

In the name of God Amen the thirtyeth day of March in the foure and thirtyeth yeare of the reigne of our Sovereigne Lord Charles the Second of

England Scotland France and Ireland King Defendor of the Faith etc. Annoque Domini One Thousand Six Hundred Eightytwo I John Blome of Seavenoke in the County of Kent Gent being I praise God in good health perfect memory and understanding but observing the mortality of mankind and to the intent to make what provision I can for my Wife and Children wherewith it hath pleased God to bless me that all questions and controversyes concerning my Estate may as much as in me lyeth I doe by and with the consent of my loving wife Jane which is testifyed by her signing and sealing hereof declare this my last Will and Testament in manner following And first I commend my soule into the hands of my God and Saviour Jesus Christ not doubting through his merits and out of the experience that I have of his infinite mercys and preservacions of me to have a joyful resurrection with the Rightious and to be pertaker of his Heavenly Kingdome by him prepared for those that love and endeavour to obey him And for my body I leave the burying thereof to the discretion of my Executrix hereafter named only desiring that the same may be with as little charge and expence as may be reasonably contrived Item I give and bequeath to the Sixteen poore People in the Almshouse in Seavenoke aforesaid Five pounds which I desire the Warden and Assistants for the time being to imploy and lay out towards buying them Coates and Gownes And I alsoe give to every one of the said poore people six pence a peice which together with the said Five pounds I appoint to be paid at the end of twelve monethes after my decease Item I give to Forty the poorest people in the said parish of Seavenoke whether married or single four pence a peece and to Forty of the poorest children there two pence a piece to be paid unto the Churchwardens and Overseers of the same parish at the end of one month next after my decease Item I give and bequeath to every one of my Brothers in Law Mr Thomas Fisher his Children that shall be living at the time of my death Tenne shillings a peice to buy them Rings Item I give and bequeath unto my very loving Brothers Mr. Daniel Newman Mr Herbert Randolph and Mr Thomas Pettit and to their severall wives Tenn shillings a peice to buy them Rings Item I give and bequeath to every one of my servants that shall be living with me at the time of my death five shillings a peice over and above such wages as shall be then due unto them Item my will and meaning is that Jane my loving wife shall during the term of her naturall life hold and enjoy all those Messuages Lands and Tenements in the Isle of Oxney and alsoe all those lands in Higham and Cliff in the County of Kent which came unto me in her right And alsoe all that peice of Marsh land which I lately purchased in Oxney of John Hall And after her decease I give and bequeath unto my sonne John Blome all those lands in Higham and Cliff now in the occupacion of William Fletcher to hold to him my said sonne John his heires and Assignes forever Item I give and bequeath unto my sonne Charles Blome after my wifes decease all that my messuage or Tenement Farm and lands in Stone and Wittersham in the Isle of Oxney called the Hole Farm and all that Marsh lands lately by me purchased of John Hall called Craynes Marsh now in the occupacion of George Mount and all those woods and Woodlands lying within the said Hole Farm to hold to him the said Charles Blome his heires and Assignes for ever Item I give and bequeath unto my sonne Francis Blome after my wifes decease the moyety or one halfe of all that my farm called Stone Farm now in the occupacion of John Columben in Stone aforesaid together with a moiety of all those Woodlands lying within the same Farm to hold to him his heires and Assignes forever And the other moiety or halfe part of the said farm called Stone Farm and the Woods therein being after my wifes decease I give and bequeath unto my sonne Richard Blome and to his heires and Assignes forever And my will and meaning is that if any of my said four sonnes John Charles Frances and Richard shall happen to dye before their respective ages of two and twenty yeares that then the part or share of him or them soe dying shall goe to such of them as shall be then living and to their heires and Assignes forever Item I will and bequeath unto my sonne William Blome all that my part or share of the Mannor of Otford with its appurtenences to hold to him his heires and Assignes forever Alsoe I give and devise to him all that Lease of the School Lands in Seavenoke which is taken in the name of my Cozen William Wall in trust for me Also I appoint that the Lease which I have from William Spencer of the way neare my Tenement in Seavenoke now in the occupacion of Henry Swaysland shall allwayes during the continuance thereof waite upon and goe along to such person and persons as from time to time shall have the freehold and inheritance of the said Tenement And whereas I have now in my hands the summe of Fifty pounds which John Hodge gave unto my daughter Jane in full recompence and satisfaction for the same and of all such interest as shall be due from me for the same at the time of my death and for the maintenance and provision of my said daughter Jane I give and bequeath unto her the summe of eight hundred pounds to be paid unto her at her age of one and twenty yeares or day of marryage which shall first happen if she shall live to attaine either of them Item I give and bequeath unto my three Daughters Elizabeth Grace and Judith to each of them five hundred pounds to be paid at their respective ages of one and twenty yeares or dayes of marryage which shall first happen if they shall respectively live to attaine either of them And my will and meaning is that if any of my said foure Daughters shall happen to dye before they attaine their respective ages aforesaid or their dayes of marryage that then the porcions hereby by me bequeathed to her or them soe dying shall be equally divided amongst such of them as shall be then living share and share alike And my will and meaning is that the interest and benefitt of the said severall summes of money by me as aforesaid given to my said foure Daughters shall be by my wife received and imployed for and towards their education and maintenance untill they attaine their respective ages of one and twenty yeares or dayes of marryage as aforesaid And I do give and bequeath unto my said Wife her heires and Assignes for ever All those my two Messuages or Tenements with their appurtenences scituate at the Churchgate in Seavenoke now in the occupacion of William Richardson John Medhurst and James Walter to the intent and purpose the better to enable her to performe this my will and that she may together with the rest and residue of my personall Estate (which I hereby bequeath unto her) have wherewithall to support herselfe and to raise the said porcions hereby by me given and as occasion shall require to be helpful and assisting to my said Children and to be kind to those that shall be most dutifull to her and best deserve the same as she shall think fitt And whereas upon a Settlement by me made on the marryage of my sonne William Blome I have reserved the summe of five hundred pounds chargeable upon my dwelling House and other Messuages and Lands in Seavenoke aforesaid to such uses and purposes as I shall appoint Now my will and meaning is and I doe hereby direct and appoint that the same shall be paid to my Wife her Executors Administrators or Assignes to be imployed if occasion require for the better raising such Porcions in the first place as I have hereby given to my Daughters if the same happen to fall shorte but in case my other Estate will amount to pay what I have hereby given my four Daughters then my will and meaning is that the same shall be distributed to such of my Children as my said Wife shall under her hand and seale or by her last will and Testament think fitt and appoint and for want of such her appointment that then the same when it becomes due and payable shall be equally divided amongst each of my Children as shall be then living And of this my will I make my loving wife Jane Blome my sole Executrix and I request her on all occasions of controversy or difficulty that may happen or arise in the setling ordering or managing the Estate that will be left her to consult with and be advised by my constant and approved knowing Friend George Clifford Esq. of Pennis in Folkham whom I make overseer of this my Will whose continuall love to me encourages my requesting his best assistance to my said Wife and Children And I give unto him Twenty shillings to buy him a Ring or what else he pleaseth In Witnes wherof revokeing all former wills I have set my hand to the first of these two sheets wherein my will is written all with my owne hand and to the last sheet I have set my hand and seale the day and yeare first above written

John Blome Jane Blome

Signed sealed and published by the said John Blome to be his last Will and Testament and sealed and subscribed by the said Jane Blome his wife testifying her consent thereunto in the presence of us

Herbt Randolph Wm Allen Tho Sheppard Sym Baxter

139

RUSEL Robert	Yeoman	bur. 18 Jun. 1682
W. 18 Apr. 1682	prov. 12 Jul. 1682	PRS/W/14/88

In the name of God Amen Aprill the 18th 1682 I Robert Rusel of the Parish of Sevenoke in the County of Kent yeoman being Sick and weake in body yet perfect in mind and memory doe make and ordaine this my last will and testament:

Imprimis I bequeath my Soule to God that gave it my body to the earth to be decently buryed by mine executrix

Item I give and bequeath to my Son Robert Rusel this present Summers profitt of about three Acres of land lying about the house Called South field and I allow him twelve bushels of Oats for seed to sow the said field and what belongs to it and so to take the Cropp and to leave the land at Michaelmas

without any hurt wast spoile or dammage done to the hedges or fences And In Regard my Son Robert aforesaid hath already Received a large parte and portion of my goods and Chattles I doe hereby Will and declare that he shal have neither part or portion of any thing more then what he hath already received and what is above specified. Lastly I doe hereby Constitute and appoynt my Daughter Ann Rusell to be my Whole and Sole executrix of al my goods and Chattles and of all my debts dues and demaunds whatsoever that are or shalbe oweing or belonging to me at the time of my decease And hereby I doe Utterly disanull and make Voyd all other Wills and bequests heretofore Whatsoever:
Robert Rusel his mark
Signed Sealed and Delivered in the presence of
Richard Hilles
Richard Peake his mark} Wittnesses
Stephen Landen

140

BUTCHER Marthe	Spinster	bur. 1 Feb. 1684
W. 22 May 1682	prov. 12 Mar. 1684	Prob. 11. 375 f. 27

In the name of God Amen the two and Twentieth day of May in the thirty-fourth yeare of the reigne of our Sovereigne Lord Charles the Second King of England etc. I Marthe Butcher alias Piper of Sinock in the County of Kent Spinster being weak in body but of perfect memory Doe make and ordaine this my last will and testament in manner and form following Imprimis I bequeath my Soule into the hands of Almighty God and my body to the ground to be decently buried in the churchyard of Sinock Imp. I give to my Kinsman Thomas Hollingham the summe of one shilling Imp. I give to my Kinsman Thomas Norten the summe of five shillings Imp. I give to my sister Anne Norten the summe of Four Pounds Imp. I will and bequeath that after my debts and Legacies and funerall charges are paid all the remainder of my goods and Chattells I give to my loveing sister Dorothy Lander And I doe nominate and appoint my loveing sister Dorothy Lander to be sole Executrix of this my will and testament thus revokeing all former wills I declare this to be my last will and testament In witness hereof I have hereunto sett my hand and Seale
Marthe Bucher her marke
Edm. Negus Richard Averye his marke
Robert Goan his marke

141

BOSWELL Margaret	Widow	bur. 31 Aug. 1682
W. 7 Aug. 1682	prov. 24 Aug. 1682	Prob. 11.370 f. 94

In the name of God Amen the seaventh day of August in the Foure and Thirtieth yeare of the reigne of our Sovereigne Lord Charles the Second of England Scotland France and Ireland King Defendor of the Faith etc. Annoque Domini One Thousand Six Hundred Eighty and Two I Dame Margaret Boswell the widow and relict of Sir William Boswell late of Bradbourne in the parish of Seavenoke in the County of Kent Knight deceased being now of perfect mind and understanding and fixed on the extraordinary marcies of my Saviour Jesus Christ to mee in many and sundry deliverances both by Sea and by Land thinke it my Duty to bee warned and provided in all events hereafter that I may not be surprized in my soule body or estate and for that purpose hereby and by these presents Revokeing all former and other Wills Testaments Guifts and Bequests whatsoever by mee at any tyme or times heretofore made or published I doe make and ordeyne this my last Will and Testament in manner and forme following that is to say First and principally I doe Committ my Soule into the hands of Allmighty God that gave it and my body to bee decently buried in the parish church of Seavenoke aforesaid And as concerning that estate wherewith it hath pleased God to blesse mee I give and bequeath the same in manner and forme following (that is to say) I give and bequeath unto my Cozen Mr William Bosvile sonne of Mr Robert Bosvile deceased All such ready money Summe and Summes of money as I shall happen to have in my now dwelling house at Bradbourne aforesaid at the time of my death upon condition neverthelesse and to the intent and purpose that he the said William Bosvile shall out thereof and out of such Messuages Lands and Tenements and the rents and profitts thereof as I have heretofore settled upon him or that I have any power to make any appoyntment of pay and discharge all such debts as I shall owe at the time of my death and also beare pay and discharge all my funerall expences and charge of such mourning as he and my Executices hereafter named or the major part of them shall thinke fitt to give and likewise he shall pay and discharge the severall legacies herein after by mee given and bequeathed (that is to say) unto the poore people in the Almeshouses in the parish of Seavenoke aforesaid the summe of Five pounds And to such householdservants as I shall have dwelling with me over and above what wages shall bee due unto them the summe of Tenn pounds which Two Legacies I appoint shall be devided in such proporcions as the said William Bosvile and my Executrices hereafter named or the major part of them shall think fitt Also I give and bequeath unto Mrs Anne Cruttenden now dwelling with the Lady Seyliard the summe of Forty pounds of lawful money of England out of which I desire her to buy herselfe Mourning And I give and bequeath unto Mrs Margaret Chorley wife of Thomas Chorley of Seavenoke aforesaid Gentleman and to Margaret Chorley daughter of the said Thomas Chorley to each of them Five pounds. Item I give and bequeath unto Mr John Stone my Chaplyn the summe of Twenty pounds per annum to be yearly paid

unto him dureing the term of his naturall life Item I give and bequeath unto my Cosens Elizabeth Worsley and Anne Worsley (who have taken much paines and care of mee in my old age) the summe of Two Hundred pounds a peece Item I give and bequeath unto Anne Bosvile mother of the said William Bosvile Forty pounds per annum durine the term of her naturall life to bee paid yearly at the two most usual feasts in the yeare that is to say on the feast day of St Michael The Archangel and the Annunciacion of the Blessd Virgin Mary by even and equal porcions the first payment thereof to begin and to be made unto her at the first of the said feasts that shall first happen next after my decease (if she shall be then living) Item I give and bequeath unto Margaret and Isabella Bosvile the two sisters of the said William Bosvile the summe of one hundred pounds a peece to be paid them within six moneths after my decease All which said severall legacies yearely payments summe and summes of money aforesaid funerall Charges and Debts my will and meaning is shall be paid by and Chargeable upon the said William Bosvile and shall be by him paid out of the said ready money and Estates soe by me to him given and upon him settled as aforesaid All the rest and residue of my goods Cattel Chattells both real and personall householdstuffe moneys and securities for money and other personal estate whatsoever or in whose hands wheresoever (excepting only the said ready money which shall happen to be in my now dwelling house at the tyme of my death) I hereby freely give and bequeath unto my said loving Cosens Elizabeth and Anne Worsley whom together with the said William Bosvile I make the joint Executor and Executrices of this my last Will and Testament and to them my said Executor and Executrices (at the charge of the said William Bosvile) I commit the care of the printing my Bookes and Manuscripts which I desire may be speedily done after my death and the erecting in the parish church of Seavenoke aforesaid a Decent Monument of the value of at least one hundred pounds to be expended and laid out of the money and estate by mee given to the said William Bosvile with the advie and direction of the said Elizabeth and Anne Worsley And I committ the government care and management of my said Cosen William Bosvile and his estate unto the said Elizabeth and Anne Worsley until he shall attaine his age of one and twenty yeares And now having sett my house in order and haveing nothing to do but to dye O Lord I crave the mercy and pardon for all my sinns and for the merritts of thy dearly beloved sonnes sake receive my Soule and body into thy everlasting blisse and never so remember my wretched Sinns as thereby to forgett they owne name a Saviour wherein with thy glories joyned our Safety with his name can I end with a reverential and an Actuall Amen
Margaret Boswell

This was read to the aforesaid Dame Margaret Boswell and by her signed sealed and published to be her last Will and Testament in the presence of us

H. Powle Ralph Petley
Hugh Own Vic. Mathew Hartridge

142

MANTLE Trustraham	Carpenter	bur. 16 Mar. 1686
W. 17 Oct. 1682	prov 6 May 1686	PRS/W/11/124

In the name of God Amen I Trustraham Mantle of Sevenoke in the County of Kent Carpenter beinge weake and aged in Body but of sound and perfect mind and memory praysed by Almighty God therefore Revoakinge all former wills by me made doe this Seaventeenth Day of October in the Fower and Thirtieth year of the Raigne of our Soveraigne Lord Kinge Charles the second etc Annoque Domini 1682 make and ordaine this my last will and Testament in manner and forme followinge Inprimis I recommend my Soule into the hands of Almighty God who first gave it me hopeing through the only merritts of Jesus Christ my blessed Saviour and Redeemer to obtain Remission of all my Sinns and a joyfull Resurreccion to life everlastinge And my body I committ to the Earth to be decently buried att the Discretion of my Executor heerafter named And for my worldly goods I give and Dispose thereof as followeth vizt. Inprimis I give and bequeath unto my Daughter Morleyes Children soe many of them as shalbe liveinge att the time of my Decease Tenn shillings a peece to be paid them within one Moneth next after my Decease by my Executor heerafter named And for my Messuages and Tenements in Sevenoke aforesaid now in my occupacion and in the occupacion of James Beecher I give and Devise the same unto my sonn William Mantle his heires and assignes for ever And I doe make and ordaine my said sonn William Mantle Sole Executor of this my last will and Testament unto whom I give and bequeath my Debts and Legacyes aforesaid & funerall Charges beinge first paid and Descharged all the rest and residue of my estate both reall and personall whatsoever and wheresoever In witnes whereof I have heerunto sett my hand and seale the day and yeare first above written.
The marke of Trustraham Mantle
Signed Sealed published and Declared by the said Trustraham Mantle to be his last will and Testament in th presence of
Wm Richardson Edward Kirkin John Brattle

143

HAYNES John	Cordwainer	bur. 28 May 1683
W. 1 May 1683	prov. 12 Jul. 1683	PRS/W/8/172

In the name of God Amen I John Haynes of the parish of Sevenoks in the Countey of Kent Cordvayner this the First of May in the Five and Therteth year of the Rayne of our Soverent Lord King Charles the Secont Annoque Domini 1683 being seck and week in bodey but of perfect memorey prased bee God doe make and ordaine this my Last Will and Testament in manor following That is to say I Comend my Sowle in to the hands of Allmeitey God hoping therowh the merits of my Saver Jesus Christ to receave pardon for my sines and a joyfull resurection in the Kingdom of heven and my bodey I Comet to the Earth to be decentley bured bey the destreson of my execut erix her after menconed and asconcerning the esteat that it hath pleased God to bles me with all I despose ther of as Followeth Item I give to my sister Ann Hey Tenn shillings of Lawfull money to be paid hour bey my executerix with in on year and aday after my daes Item I give Ann Winget Tenn pounds of lawfull money the daster of Jmes Winget to be paid hour bey my executrix at the day or hour mareg or at the age of one and Twentey yers which shall hapen foust Item I give unto John Durtnall sun of Daved Durtnall Tenn shillings Item I give to John Brite sun of the widow Brite Tenn shillings Item I give unto John Greene sonn of Thomas Greene Tenn shillings To be paid bey mey executarex with in a yeare and aday after my deces Item I give unto Susand Denes Five shillings to paid to hour forth with after my deces bey mey executarex And I doe her bey make and ordaine my Loving Brother Thomas Haynes Full and Soll executarex of this my Last will and testement and doe freley give unto hem All my Land and esteat whatsoever he paying and discharging All the Lageses aforesaid In witnes to this my Last will and Testement I have her to set my hand and seall the day and year fust aboufe Ritten

John Haines

Signed sealled publeshed and delceared to be the last will and testement of the said John Hayns in the presents of

Daved Durtnall marke Thomas Waller Thomas Greene

144

WALL William bur. 6. Jul. 1683

W. 6 Jun. 1683 prov. 30 Aug. 1683 Prob. 11. 373 f. 99

In the name of God Amen I William Wall of the parish of Seavenoke in the County of Kent being of perfect memory (Praised be God) doe make this my last will and testament in manner and forme as followeth First I bequeath my soule into the hands of Jesus Christ my blessed Saviour and Redeemer And my body to the Earth from whence it came to be decently buried in the parish church of Seavenoke And as for the Temporall goods wherewith it hath pleased God to Blesse me I give and bequeath them as followeth First I give to the poore of Seavenokes five pounds to be disposed among them by my Executors within one month after my decease Also I give to my daughter Mary the wife of Thomas Taylor the sum of one hundred and fifty pounds to be paid her by my Executors at the end of one year after my decease if she shalbe then liveing But if she shall be then dead equally to be divided among such children of hers as shall survive her and to be paid to the said Thomas Taylor for their use to be imployed by him for their advantage Also I give to my daughter Dorothy the sum of three hundred pounds to be paid her by my Executors immediately after my decease And I give her more the sum of one hundred and fifty pounds to be paid her by my Executors at the end of one year after my decease Also I give to my youngest son Oliver all my cattle corn hay and implements of husbandry and all my stock upon the farm that is now in my occupation immediatly after my decease And I give to my said son Oliver all my plate pewter brass lynnen beds and all my householdstuffe whatsoever he allowing and paying to every one of my children William Geoffrey Mary Elizabeth and Dorothy so much of the said householdstuffe as shall be worth five pounds or else giving each of them fivepounds in money in liew thereof Also I give to my eldest son William the first and next avoidance of the Parsonage or Churches of Chelsfield and Farnborough in the County of Kent to him his Executors Administrators and Assignes with all the priviledges power right and title to the said avoidance and in and to the presentation to the said Parsonage that I have may can or ought to have Also I give to my youngest son Oliver all my part and share in the mannor of Otford and Forest of Whitcliffe to him and his heires for ever Also I give to my son Geoffrey all my land in the parish of Yalding in Kent now in the occupation of Henry Scot to my said son and his heires forever Also I give to my sons Geoffrey and Oliver my house and land called Bayliffs Hill and Willow Crofts lying in the parishes of Seavenokes and Chevening in the County of Kent in the occupation of William Morgan to them and their heires forever equally to be divided betwixt them Also I give my house and land at Newfound Street in the said parish of Seavenokes in the occupation of John Wood with the coppices or woods thereto belonging which are in my own occupation to my three sons William Geoffrey and Oliver to them and their heires forever equally to be divided betwixt them on condition that they make out of it these payments following First that (whereas I have formerly given to Edward Smith of the said parish of Seavenokes five pounds per annum during his life to be paid out of the said land) my said three sons do pay the same according to the rate and proportion following (vizt) Oliver three pounds per annum and William and Geoffrey each one pound per annum Also that my said sons doe pay out of the said land to my daughter Elizabeth wife of William Rolph the sum of six pounds per annum during her life Also that after her death they pay to the children of her body that shall survive her the sum of one hundred and fifty pounds equally to be divided betwixt them which payment shall be made to the sons when they arrive to the age of twenty one years and to the daughters when they arrive to the said age or on the day of their respective marriages if my said daughter be then dead if not then immediatly after her death But if my said daughter dye before her children do arrive to the said respective ages or marriage then the said six pounds per annum to be paid for the use of the said children until they shall respectively receive their several portions of the said sum of one hundred and fifty pounds My meaning being that when any of the said children shall have received their share of the said one hundred and fifty pounds that then a proportionable part of the said six pounds per annum according to such sum as shall be paid shall be abated and retained in the hands of them the said William Geoffrey and Oliver to their own use And no further payment shall be made of the said six pounds per annum or any part thereof to or for the use of such of the said children as shall have received their part of the said one hundred and fifty pounds Also I give to my son

William forty pounds Also I give to my Honored Friend Mr John Blome forty shillings for a ring desireing him to be an assister of my children after my decease All the rest of my lands money goods bonds bills dues and chattells whatsoever I give to my three sons William Geoffrey and Oliver equally to be divided betwixt them they paying my debts legacies and funerall charges which said sons William Geoffrey and Oliver I doe nominate and appoint joint Executors of this my will And I doe hereby renounce all former wills and declare this to be my last will and testament In witness whereof I have hereunto put my hand and seale the sixth day of June in the thirty fifth year of the reign of our Sovereign Lord King Charles the Second Annoque Domini 1683
William Wall
Signed sealed and declared by the said William Wall to be his last will and testament in the presence of Peter Everest
Edward Smith The marke of John Small

145

WALL William	Gentleman	bur. 6 Jul. 1683
I. 9 Jul. 1683	prov. 20 Aug. 1683	Prob. 4.6220

A True and perfect Inventory of all and singular the goods and Chattells of William Wall late of Seavenoke in the county of Kent gent deceased taken and appraysed the ninth day of July in the five and thirtyeth yeare of the Raigne of our Soveraigne Lord Charles the Second etc. Annoque Domini 1683 By David Dennch and Thomas Morley as followeth

	£	*s.*	*d.*
Inprimis Weareing apparrell and money in his purse	10	0	0
In the Kitchen			
Item one Table and frame one forme a Cupboard foure joyned Stooles three Chaires an Ironback and paire of cast Andirons fire shovell and Tongs Two paire of potthangers and Links an Iron to lay before the fire a Gridiron a Candle box a winding Jack Rope and Weight two Chaffing dishes three smoothing Irons a paire of Bellowes a Window Curtaine and Curtaine Rodd two Burding peeces and a Muskett	3	11	8
In the Brewhouse			
Item two Furnaces the brewing vessells of all sorts a bunting hutch and Sives and a cheese presse	5	0	0
In the Buttery			
Item Three Staulders thirteen drink vessells an Iron Pottage Pott a Brasse pott two frying panns and two leather bottles	2	10	0

In the Milke House			
Item five leads twelve Crocks a Charne two pow dering Tubbs and two Staulders and three pailes	2	4	0
In the Hall			
Item one Clock and Weights one paire of Andirons two beams scales and weights an Iron pitcher one Table and frame one forme a Settle six joyned stooles a Still one Cupboard a Glass cage and six Cushions and a Pike	5	3	0
In the Parlor			
Item two paire of Andirons fire shovel and Tongs one Cupboard one Sideboard Cupboard one Table and frame twelve joyned Stooles two formes six Turkey work Chaires and two Cushions and fowre leather Chaires	5	14	0
Item a Carpett and a Cupboard Cloath a Sconce and a paire of Snuffers	0	15	0
Item Brass and Pewter of all sorts	5	0	0
Item one joyned Chest a Table and frame a Chest of Drawers a Sideboard one feather bedd Blanketts Rugg boulster Steddle and all things thereto belonging	10	0	0
Item one feather boulster Pillowes Steddle curtaines curtaine Rodds valence matt and Cord blanketts and Rugg one joyned Chest one Trunke and a Chest of Drawers	5	0	0
Item severall peeces of Silver Plate	25	0	0
Item two feather bedds boulsters blanketts Coverletts Pillowes Steddles Curtaines Curtain Rodds Vallence Matts and Cords one joyned chest and two Trunks	8	0	0
Item one feather bedd feather boulster blankett Coverlett Steddle Matt and Cord one press Cupboard a Table three Chests	3	0	0
Item a paire of Scales and some small things in the Clossett of		5	0
Item fowre dozen Bottles		10	0
Item a Bedsteadle and the things in the Maids Chamber	3	0	0
Item a Scry a dozen of Sacks and twelve Bushells of Wheate	3	8	0
Item a Corne Tubb two Bushells one halfe Bushell one old Chest and two Sives a Shall and a Scuppett	0	12	0
Item a Bedd and furniture thereto belonging in the Mans Chamber	2	0	0
Item eighteene Milke Bowles		9	0
Item the Lynnen of all Sorts	32	3	0
Item Seaven Cowes and a Bull	20	0	0
Item two Steeres	6	0	0

Item three Calves	2	0	0
Item six Sheepe and two Lambs	2	13	4
Item two Mares and Colts and one Horse	14	0	0
Item three Sheetes and three Piggs	2	0	0
Item the Wheate and Oates on the Ground	18	0	0
Item a Stack of Hay	4	0	0
Item Clover and new Hay	4	4	0
Item old lumber and things forgotten and not seene	1	0	0
Item ready money and debts due and oweing to the Testator at the tyme of his decease	1125	13	8
Suma Totalis huius modi Inventarii	£mccccxxii	xv[s]	viii[d]

146

SPILSTEAD William — Weaver — bur. 8 Oct. 1684
W. 28 Jul. 1683 — prov. 8 Nov. 1684 — PRS/W/15/143

In the name of God Amen I William Spilstead of Seavenocke in the County of Kent Weaver this Eight and Twentyeth day of July in the Five and Thirtyeth yeare of the raigne of our Sovereigne Lord Charles the second by the Grace of God King of England Scotland France and Ireland Defender of the faith etc Annoq Domini 1683 Being sicke and weake in body but of sound and disposeing mind and memory praised bee god for the same Doe make and ordaine this my last will and Testament in manner followeing (that is to say) First I comend my soule into the hands of Allmighty God hopeing and Assuredly beleveing through the meritts Death and passion of my blessed saviour and redeemer Jesus Christ to receive a full and free pardon of all my sinns and a joyfull reserrection in the Kingdome of Heaven and my body I comitt to the Earth from whence it came to bee decently buryed at the Discression of my Executrix hereafter named And as for my personall Estate I give and dispose thereof as followeth, Imprimis I give and bequeath unto my brother John Spilstead and to my sister Dorothy Tayler the sume of Five shillings apeice of Lawfull money of England to bee paid unto them by my Executrix hereafter named within Three months after my Decease Item I give and bequeath unto John Saxten Henry Saxten Sarah Saxten and to Elizabeth the wife of Thomas Dunkin the sonns and Daughters of my sister Mary Saxten decd. the sume of Twenty pounds apeice of Lawfull money of England To bee paid unto them by the Executors or Administrators of my loveing wife and Executrix hereafter named within Two months after her decease Item I give and bequeath unto Robert Spilstead and Richard Spilstead the Two sonns of my brother Francis Spilstead Decd the like sume of Twenty pounds apeice of Lawfull money of England To bee paid unto them by the Executors or Administrators of my wife and Executrix hereafter named within Two months after her Decease Item I give and bequeath unto Thomas Fuller sonn of my Kindswoman Mary late wife of William Fuller and

to Thomas Margarett and John Saxten the Three Children of my aforesaid Kindsman John Saxten the sume of Five pounds apeice of Lawful money of England to bee paid unto them by the Executors or Administrators of my wife and Executrix hereafter named within Two Months after the Decease of my said wife Item all the rest and residue of my goods chattells debts ready mony and personall Estate I give and bequeath unto my loveing wife Mary And I make and ordaine the said Mary my wife sole Executrix of this my last will and testament Desireing her faithfully to performe the same In Wittnesse whereof I the said William Spilstead have to this my last will and Testament revoaking All other wills by mee made written in one sheete of paper sett to my hand and seale the Day and yeare first above written
the marke of William Spilstead
Signed sealed published and declared by the said William Spilstead to bee his last will and Testament in the presence of us
the marke of Elizabeth powell
the marke of James Clarke Tho. Streatfeild

147

SPILSTEAD William	Weaver	bur. 8 Oct. 1684
I. 17 Oct. 1684	prov. 15 Nov. 1684	PRS/I/19/107

A true and perfect Inventory of all & singuler the goods chattells debts Credits and personall estate of William Spilstead of Seavenocke in the County of Kent Weaver deceased taken & aprized the seaventeenth day of October in the Six and Thirtyeth Yeare of the Raigne of our Soveraign Lord Charles the second by the grace of God King of England Scotland France & Ireland Defender of the faith etc Annoque Domini 1684 By us whose names are hereunder written as followeth (vizt.)

in the hall	£.	s.	d.
Imprimis the deceaseds wareing apparrell of all sorts	5.	0.	0.
Item one Iron Backe one payer of Andirons fire shovell & tongues one payer of Pothangers Fower spitts Two Dripping panns one Tosting Iron & one smothing Iron	0.	18.	6.
Item one table one forme Seaven chaires one Little table one Stoole one Cupboard & one settle	1.	10.	0.
Item Two brass Kettles Two Brass Skilletts one Iron pott Two brass potts Fower brass Candlesticks Three other Candlesticks one Jacke Eight Cussions & one carpett	1.	12.	6.

Item one douzen and a halfe of peuter dishes one peuter quart pott Three porringers & other small peeces of pewter)	1.	13.	0.
In the Buttery			
Item one Little Brass Furnace Six small tubbs one bunting hutch one frying pann & one Stalder)	1.	5.	0.
In the Shopp			
Item Two Loomes & all tackling and ymployments belonging to the trade of a weaver)	5.	0.	0.
In the Hall Chamber			
Item one feather bed one feather boulster Two pillowes one blankett one coverlett one bedsteadle with curtaines vallance matt and cord one Trundle bedstedle one flock bed & one Coverlett)	6.	10.	0.
Item one Chest of Drawes Three other chests one Little Box one table one chayer one payer of andirons fyer pann and tongues & one warming pan)	2.	15.	6.
Item Nyne payer of Sheets Three payer of Pillow beeres Six table cloath Three Douzen of Napkins fower towells and other small Lynnen)	8.	0.	0.
In the Chamber over the Shopp			
Item one feather bedd one feather boulster one Counterpaine bedsteadle curtaines and vallance matt & cord Two blanketts & one Coverlett)	3.	5.	0.
Item Three greate chests one table & Three chaires	1.	15.	0.
Item one peece of new Lynnen cloath	0.	10.	0.
In the passage on the stayres			
Item fower Drinketubbs one chest one box and one chaire	0.	15.	4.
Item old Lumber thing seene unseene and forgotten	1.	0.	0.
Item the deceaseds ready mony in the house	5.	0.	0.
Item in good debts due to the testator	140.	0.	0.
Item Debts Desperate	10.	0.	0.
Total	196.	09.	10.

Thomas Greene)
John Beardsworth) Aprizers
Rob. Chapman

148

PERPOINT Mary Widow
W. 19 Sep. 1683 prov. 20 Nov. 1683 Prob. 11. 374 f.129

In the name of God Amen the Nineteenth of September in the yeare of our Lord one thousand six hundred eighty and three And in the reigne of our Sovereigne Lord King Charles the Second over England etc. And in the thirty fifth yeare of his reigne according to the computation of the Church of England I Mary Perpoint of Riverhead in the parish of Seavenokes in the County of Kent Widdow being of perfect memory and remembrance thanks be to God for it Doe make and ordaine this my last will and testament (hereby revokeing all other wills by me formerly made) in manner and form following vizt. First I bequeath my soule into the hands of Almighty God my maker hopeing that through the meritorious death and passion of Jesus Christ my only Saviour and Redeemer to receive free pardon and forgiveness of all my sins And as for my bodie to bee buried in decent Christian buriall at the discretion of my Executrix hereafter nominated Imprimis I give to my son Humphrey Smith twenty pounds which money is in the hands of Ann Russell to be paid to him after my decease as soon as it can be gathered in Item I give more to my son Humphrey Smith two feather beds the hangings in the hall chamber and the hangings in the next chamber to it and the hanging in his own chamber where [he] now lieth and the table in the Hall and the two tables in the two parlors and the tables and dressers in the Kitchen and the carpet in the Parlor two tableclothes two pair of sheets two pair of pillow coates six napkins four towells and I give him more all the Turkeyworke chaires and stooles which formerly did belong to the little parlor and the red leather chaires in the hall Now all these particulers or legacies I give to my son Humphrey Smith upon Condicion that hee doth not interrupt or cause to be interrupted by reason of selling or carrying away anything that shall belong to my Executrix that then all these legacies shall be forfeited Item I give to my grandchild Anne Bull my silver Tankard and my silver plate which belongeth to it Item more I give her one feather bed and bedstedle and curtaines belonging to it Item I give to Thomas and Elizabeth Perpoint my two grandchildren to either of them an old piece of gold after my decease Item all the rest of my goodes monies moveables rents due householdstuffe whatsoever within doores or without I give unto my daughter Mary Bull whom I make my sole Executrix of this my last will and testament to her and her (assignes) for ever upon condicion that my daughter Mary my Executrix doe discharge all my funerall expences and deliver up and pay all my debts and legacies And further my mind and will is that my son Humphrey Smith shall give my daughter Mary Bull my Executrix of this my last will and testament she her heires Executors administrators or assignes sufficient time with egresse and regresse to carry away or sell or any other ways convey away after my decease without any molestation or interruption of the said

Humphrey Smith or his heires or assignes Revokeing all other wills and testaments In witness whereof I have hereunto set my hand [and] seale the day and yeare first above written
Mary Perpoint her marke
Sealed and delivered in the presence of Henry Tickner
Dorothy Hinge   Wm Dannett Scri.

149

EARPE Robert
I. 15 Oct. 1683   prov. 11 Nov. 1683   PRS/I/20/1

An Inventory of all the goods and Chattels of Robert Earpe late of Seavenoke in the County of Kent deceased taken and appraised the fifteenth day of October in the three and thirtyeth yeare of the Raigne of our Soveraigne Lord King Charles the second Annoque Domini 1683 by us Thomas Greene and Walter Bassett as followes

Inprimis two milch Cowes	7.	10.	0.
Item two young Budds	1.	10.	0.
Item one old horse one old Mare and a Colt	4.	10.	0.
Item two sheetes two piggs and a Sow	1.	15.	0.
Item the Corne of three acres of Oates	3.	5.	0.
Item halfe an acre of Wheate and an acre of Pease	2.	2.	6.
Item the Barne and Lease held of Mr. Thomas Rootes	3.	10.	0.
Item one acre and a halfe of Barley	1.	15.	6.
Item one Load of Hay		18.	0.
	26.	16.	0

Robt Bargrave

150

BESWICK Charles   Gentleman   bur. 29 Jun. 1684
W. 23 Jun. 1684   prov. 10 Jun. 1685   PRS/W/2/67

In the Name of God Amen I Charles Beswick of Sevenoke in the County of Kent gent beinge aged in body but of sound and perfect mind and memory praysed be Almighty God therefore Revokeing all former wills by me made doe this Three and Twentieth Day of June in the Sixe and Thirtieth yeare of the Raigne of our Soveraigne Lord Kinge Charles the Second etc. Annoque Domini 1684 make and ordaine this my last will and Testament in manner and forme followinge Inprimis I Recommend my Soul into the hands of Almighty God who first gave it me hopeinge through the only merritts of

Jesus Christ my blessed Saviour and Redeemer to obtaine remission of all my Sinns and a Joyfull Resurreccion to life everlastinge and my body I committ to the Earth from whence it was taken to be decently buried att the Discretion of my Executrix hereafter named, and for my worldly goods I give and dispose thereof as followeth Item I give and bequeath unto my Daughter in Law Elizabeth Boreman the wife of Thomas Boreman of Sevenoke aforesaid victualler the summe of sixe pounds per Annum Dureinge her naturall life to be paid her quarterly out of the rents and proffitts of my Messuage now in Two Dwellings in the occupacion of John Phillipps and William Rascoe in Milford Lane neer St Clements Church without Temple Barr Item I give and bequeath unto Nicholetta Boreman the Daughter of the said Thomas and Elizabeth Boreman the summe of Forty shillings per annum Dureinge the like Terme of her naturall life to be likewise paid her out of the rents and proffitts of the said Messuage att the fower usuall quarter dayes in the yeare Item I give and bequeath the said Messuage and premisses with all and singuler Thappurenences unto Elizabeth Beswick the Daughter of my sonn Charles Beswick deceased her heires and assignes for evere chargable and charged with the said Annunities of sixe pounds per annum and Forty shillings per annum which said Annuities my will is shalbe paid by my Grandchild the said Elizabeth Beswick her heires and assignes and in case of non payment it shall and may be lawfull to and for the said Elizabeth Boreman and Nicholetta Boreman and their assignes to enter and distreyne in and uppon the said Messuage for the said severall Annuities and everye or any parte thereof Item I give and bequeath all my moveable goods my debts and funerall charges beinge first paid and discharged to the said Elizabeth Beswick and Nicholetta Boreman equally to be divided between them Item I give and bequeath to my sonn in Law the said Thomas Boreman one Gold seal ring Item I make and ordaine the said Elizaebeth Beswick my Grandchild sole Executrix of this my last will and Testament, and I doe desire and make John Brattle of Sevenoke aforesaid gent and the said Thomas Boreman to be Overseers of this my last will to see the same performed In witnes whereof I have hereunto sett my hand and seale the day and yeare first above written

The marke of the said Charles Beswick

Signed sealed published and declared to be the last will and Testament of the said Charles Beswick in the presence of us

James Beecher Thomas Barret Henry Casselton

151

EVEREST Elizabeth	Widow	bur. 27 Nov. 1684
W. 7 Oct. 1684	prov. 4 Jul. 1685	PRS/W/5/202

In the Name of God Amen I Elizabeth Everest of Seavenock in the County of Kent Widdow This Seaventh Day of October in the Six and Thirtyeth Yeare of the Raigne of our Soveraigne Lord Charles the second by the Grace of God King of England Scotland France and Ireland Defender of the Faith etc Annoque Domini 1684 being sick and weake in body but of sound and disposeing mind and memory praised bee God therefore doe make and ordaine this My last will and Testament in manner and forme followeing First I bequeath my soule into the hands of Allmighty God my Creator and his sonn Jesus Christ my redeemer In whome through his death I trust to bee saved and my body I comitt to the Earth whence it was taken to bee decently buried att the discretion of my Executor hereafter named And as to the estate God hath Lent mee hereon Earth I give and dispose thereof as followeth Item I give and bequeath unto my loveing brother in Law Peter Trice of Seavenocke aforesaid Blacksmith for the use and benefitt of My Daughter Margarett Everest All my goods chattells houshouldstuffe plate Ready mony and personall Estate whatsoever and I hereby nominate and appoint the said Peter Trice sole executor of this my last will and Testament uppon trust and confidence in him reposed that hee shall receive what monys is due to mee att the tyme of my decease and sell and dispose of sutch or soe many of my Goods houshouldstuffe and parsonnall Estate as hee shall thinke fitt to sell and dispose of and the rest to lay by and keepe for sutch use and uses as hereafter is mencioned and Expressed and to pay and dispose of what monyes my said Executor shall soe raise after my debts and funerall Expences and my Executors chardges and disbursements are paid and discharged as followeth (vizt) soe much thereof for and Towards my daughters mainteynance and Education as my said Executor shall thinke fitt and Convenient, and the Remainder of the monys goods and houshouldstuffe which shall remaine in my Executors hands hee shall pay and deliver unto my said daughter Margarett when shee shall attaine to her age of one and Twenty years or day of Marriage which shall first happen But if it shall fortune that my said Daughter Margarett shall departe this life before shee shall attaine to her said age of one and Twenty yeares or day of Marriage Then my will and meaning is and I hereby give and bequeath all sutch monyes goods & personall Estate as shall remaine in my Executors hands att the decease of my said Daughter unto my Three Sisters Mary wife of John Woodgate Dorothy wife of William Ducke and Margarett wife of the aforesaid Peter Trice Equally to bee devided betweene them In Wittnesse whereof I the said Elizabeth Everest have to this my Last will and Testament revoaking all former wills by mee made written in Two sheets of paper to each sheete thereof sett to my hand and seale the day and Yeare first above written.

the marke of Elizabeth Everest

Signed sealed published and declared by the said Elizabeth Everest to bee her Last will and Testament in the presence of us

Margaret Boss the marke of

Elizabeth platt   Tho. Streatfeild

152

EVEREST Elizabeth	Widow	bur. 27 Nov. 1684
I. 2 Jul. 1685	prov. 4 Jul. 1685	PRS/I/5/29

A True and perfect Inventory Indented of all & singuler the goods chattells household stuffe & personall estate of Elizabeth Everest late of Seavenoake in the County of Kent widdow deceased taken and Aprized the second Day of July Annoq Domini 1685 By us whose names are hereunder written as followeth vizt

	£.	s.	d.
Imprimis the deceaseds wareing Aparell of all sorts and ready mony in his [sic] purs	6.	2.	6
Item one old joyned beddstedle curtaines vallance Matt and cord one Flock bedd one Feather boulster one Flock boulster 3 Blanketts and one Coverlett	1.	15.	0
Item one little beddstedle one little Feather bedd one Feather boulster and one blankett	1.	X.	0
Item one greate table 2 little tables 3 low leather chayers one Wicker chayer one cuppboard one chest of drawers & one chest	2.	6.	0
Item one little hand Jacke one Warmeing pan one payer of Andirons tongs Fyerpann Gridd Iron tosting Iron Frying pan one Iron Pott & one Iron Kettle	0.	15.	6
Item 4 silver spoones one Silver Cupp 7 Gold Rings and 4 Silver Bodkins	3.	0.	0
Item 5 pewter dishes one Bason one pewter pott & 2 porrengers	1.	0.	0
Item eight payer of sheetes 2 payer of pillowbeers 2 douzen & a halfe of napkins 2 tablecloaths 6 towell and other old lynnen	5.	17.	6
Item one brewing tubb 4 drinke tubbs 3 chests 2 Joyned stools one little Iron pott and one brass Skillett	1.	14.	0

Item old lumber thinges seene unseene and forgotten	0.	6.	8
Summ Totallis	24.	7.	2

William Heath)
Robert Hockham) Apprizers
Fran: Nixon

153

SMITH Thomas Husbandman
NW. 20 Oct. 1684 prov. 7 Nov. 1684 Prob. 11. 378 f.154

Memorandum the Twentieth day of October in the six and thirtieth year of the reign of our Sovereign Lord King Charles the Second over England etc. Thomas Smith of Seavenoke in the County of Kent husbandman then lodging at the house of William Bowls of Chatham in the said County of Kent Carpenter being sick and weak in body but of sound and disposing mind and memory did then in the presence of us John Rosewell William Hills and Sarah stevens make and declare his last Will Nuncupative in these words following (or words to the like effect) I give to my daughter in law Sarah Martin my flockbed with the furniture thereto belonging to the value of about five pounds and to my friend there pointing to Mary Foreman (being Mary Foreman of Chatham aforesaid Spinster) all other my estate personal which (naming) Mary Foreman I do appoint to be the full and sole Executrix of this my last Will and Testament
Witness our hands this three and twentieth day of October abovesaid Anno Domini one thousand six hundred eighty four
John Rosewell William Hills
the marke of the abovesaid Sarah Stevens

APPENDIX A

HEARTH TAX RETURN 1664

SEAVENOCKES TOWNE

Chargeable		*Chargeable*	
Earle of Dorsett	lxxxv	Thomas Lambard Esq	xiiii
Francis Farnaby Gent	xviii	Mr John Cooper	xii
Mr Olliver Theobald	vi	Mr Walter Smyth	viii
Mrs Elizabeth Hooper	ii	Mr John Bloome	x
John Cronke	iii	Mr William Allen	iiii
Richard Aslett	ii	William Cockett	vi
George Johnson	iii	Phillip Ridgis	ii
Richard Rogers	ii	John Groombridge	iiii
Richard Cockett	iiii	Timothy Stone	iii
Henry Murgin	ii	Joane Bostone	iiii
Jane Baker	ii	William Everist	ii
Richard Salmon	ii	Edward Baker	x
Robert Bourman	ii	Thomas Wood	ii
William Richardson	ii	Widdow Murgin	iii
Edward Stringer	ii	John Allen	i
Jo: Gaces	ii	Edward Ridgis	v
Elizabeth Butterfield	ii	James Porter	i
Mr Turner	xi	Mrs Francis Best	viii
Mr Thomas Wesson	vii	Thomas Allen	iiii
George Wood	ii	John Beardsworth	iii
John Thornton	viii	John Staple	ii
Robert Skinner	ii	John Jenkins	i
Robert Tarpe	ii	Mrs Dorothy Chapman	ii
Richard Bantken	iii	Thomas Beetchar	ii
William Spilsted	ii	Samuell Wellar	ii
Mr Richard Boss	v	Gilbert Kipps	iii
Richard Cronke	iiii	George Novis	ii
Jo: Allen	ii	Percevall Smyth	ii
Thomas Wheeler	ii	Moss Ffrancis	ii
Mr Edmund Wesson	ii	Widdow Cooke	vi
John Wilson	ii	Mrs. Wesson	vi
George Crafts	vi	Alexander Fowle	ii
Widdow Beetchar	ii	Widdow Burges	vii
John Walter	ii	David Durtnall	ii
Henry Bostock	iiii	Henry Swaesland	ii
William Lawrence	i	Robert George	xi
Truss. Mantle	iii	John Flood	ii

Mr Thomas Charley	viii
Mrs. Groome	ii
William Mantle	ii
Francis Baker	ii
Nicholas Masters	ii
Bartholomew Wood	vi
David Woodriffe	ii
Edward Sone	i
John Kelsey	ii
Henry Sisley	ii
Richard Randall	iii
Nicholas Trice	iii
Edward Wood	iiii
John Martin	ii
Nicholas Martin	v
Jane Lane	ii
Nicholas Kelsey	i

Not Chargeable

Thomas Lawrence	ii
Richard Alchin	ii
William Scot	i
Henry Thorpe	i
Widdow Fant	ii
William Akers	ii
John Clarke	ii
James Browne	ii
Edmund Pattenden	i
Thomas Marten	i
Ad. Small	i
Goodman Ring	i
Widdow Collyer	i
John Fletcher	ii
William Walters	ii
James Hampton & Samuel Kester	iiii
Widdow Chakelin	i
John Henderson	ii
William Giles	i
Widdow Merrum	i
Reignald Medherst	i
Robert Cole	iii
Ralph Bayman	ii
Goodw: Hollaway	i
Thomas Sone	ii
John Downes	i
Trustram Strayner	ii

Widdow Lovelace	ii
Giles Lawe	ii
Walter Browne	ii
William Flote	i
Mr. Robert Newman	ix
Widdow Beardsworth	iiii
Widow Sone	ii
Widow Cole	iiii
Nicholas Whale	ii
Mr. Edward Courthopp	iiii
William Spenser	ii
Thomas Wiggenden	ii
William Upstone	iii
Nathaniell Owin	iii
Thomas Green	iii
Richard Spilsted	ii

Not Chargeable

Goodman Ridge	i
Thomas Dalchin	iii
Luke Hammerson	i
Widdow Bassett	i
Robert Tye	ii
James Munnion	i
Goodwife Bellchamber	i
Widow Bates	i
John Medhurst	i
Widdow West	i
John Crafts	ii
Robert Phipp	iii
John French	ii
Goodman Still	ii
John Johnson	i
Robert Martin	i
Widdow Sinklis	i
John Gates	ii
John Pattenden	i
William Smaile	i
Richard Atkins	ii
Thomas Hinge	ii
William Belchar	ii
Widdow Muddey	i
James Walter	i
Thomas Thorneton	ii
Thomas Lander	i
James Beecher	i

John Merrum	ii	William Baker	ii
Goodman Olliver	ii	Thomas Crafts	i
Widdow Crafts	ii	Goodman Downe	i
James Browne	i	Widow Tanton	ii
Peter Durance	ii	Harry Colegate	i
Widdow Francis	ii	John Hilles	i
Benjamin Whiffin	i	William Turner	i
Widdow Tye	i	Sid. Francis	i
Widdow Durance	i	Clim: Cockett	i
Edward Maidhouse	i	James Smyth	ii
Goodwife Edwards	i	Goodman Stevens	i
Goodman Munchin	i	Robert George Borsholder	i

SEAVENOCKES WEILD

Chargeable		*Chargeable*	
Mr. Olliver	vi	James Hunt	vi
Thomas Hilles	iiii	Thomas Moreland	iiii
John Everest	ii	Mr William Wall	vi
Thomas Rigsby	iiii	Thomas Carryer	ii
Thomas Skinner	ii	John Baker	iii
Francis Spilsted	ii	Edward Smyth	i
Richard Everist	i	Widow Nicholls	iii
Edward Fletcher	ii	Robert Everest	v
Stephen Hall	ii	John Hall	ii
William Turner	iii	Thomas Rogers	vii
Edward Stimson	ii	Thomas Vines	ii
William Fremlyn	v	Augustine Webb	i
Thomas Tayler	iii	Thomas Waller	ii
Richard Uridge	iiii	Richard Morgan	iiii
Widdow Hawse	i	Phillip Dennis	i
William Murgin	iii	John Hawse	ii
Thomas White	ii	William Kenwood	ii
John Cogger	iii	John Beadle	ii
George Wood	iii	Richard Purvey	ii
Daniell Everist	ii	Lyonell Sutton	i
Edward Lampard	iiii	William Thisleton	iii
Thomas Hibben	ii	Richard Childrens	i
Not Chargeable		*Not Chargeable*	
Widdow Greenehill	i	John West	ii
Thomas Holloway	ii	Richard Masters	ii
Edmund Head	ii	Robert Pickett	ii
Widdow Sutton	ii	John Goodshew	i
Andrew Waters	i	Joane Randall	i
Sampson Allen	i	James Skinner	ii

John Clements	i
Widdow Fant	i
Humphrey Taylor	ii
Nicholas Taylor	i
Thomas Hawse	i
Widdow Garrett	i
William Humphrey	ii
Robert Clifford	i
Arthur Clifford	i
Thomas Humphrey	ii
Widdow Crowhurst	i
Cris Welles	i
Widdow Wakefield	i
John Driver	i
Thomas Brigtridge	ii
John Taylor	ii
Richard Marten	i
John Milles	i
Robert Clifford	i
Richard Woodgate	ii
Thomas Giles	ii
Widdow Muglett	i
John Clifford	ii
William Plastoe	ii
Thomas Wells	i
Richard Grove	i
Anthony Thatcher	ii
John Wells	i
Widdow Marten	i
Richard Morgan Borsholder	

LIBERTY OF RIVERHEAD

Chargeable

The Lady Bosville	xviii
Richard Rigsby	iiii
Mr Jeston	iiii
Mrs Peirepoint	x
John Copland	ii
Richard Everest	ii
Edmund Chapman	iii
David Jeffery	ii
Henry Hall	iiii
Henry Wakerell	ii
Alexander Garland	i
William Charlewood	ii
Widdow Jeffrey	iii
John Middleton	i
Richard Hills	iii
John Haynes	iii
Robert Betts	ii
William Fuller	ii
Richard Evridge	v
Mr Hacksupp	v
John Stileman in an empty house	ii

Chargeable

Mrs Culpepper	x
Mr Rerisford	vi
Mr. Clarke	vii
Symon Payne	ii
Thomas Ward	i
Robert Turke	i
Thomas Stileman	vii
William Round	ii
John Banester	i
Edward Hampton	ii
John Hawes	ii
Thomas Masters	ii
Robert Russell	ii
Margaret Tomlyn	i
James Lawrence	ii
Widdow Hunt	ii
Edward Porter	iii
Widdow Soane	i
Mr Winn	v
Widdow Hope	iiii
Widdow Hewson	ii
Richard Smyth	ii

Not Chargeable

John Swatford	ii
William Clifford	ii
Widdow Cuss	iii

Not Chargeable

George Canfield	ii
Richard Waghorne	ii
William Nitingale	i

Thomas Brad	ii	Allen Cryer	ii
Robert Charlwood	ii	Thomas Turke	ii
Widdow Nitingale	ii	Brian Oliver	ii
Widdow Partridge	ii	Simon Payne Borsholder	

KAO., QR. Th.

APPENDIX B

A Rental of all the particuler rents belonging to the Mannor of Seavenoke made the seaven and twentieth day of October *Anno Domini* 1665

A	Josua Allen a tenement	0. 0. 6	where he lives in the shamble rowe
	Sampson Allen a tenement and backside	0. 0. 2	he is lately dead and his death presented this house is where he dwelt in the weild now belongs to John and Tho Brasier infants and heirs of Elizabeth sole daughter of Sampson Allen
	William Allen a shamble shopp	0. 0. 4	the tenant of this is one Tharpe a Chandler and it was lately bought of Tharpe of Westerham the Clothier
	more lands which he lately purchased of John Beckett called South Deanes lyeing nere Rethered	0. 1. 0	these are Foxglove fields and the woodlands in his owne occupation
	more for Clodhamer mead lyeing at the brooke in the way from 7oke to Rethered which he late purchased of John Becher	0. 1. 0	now in Edmund Chapmans occupacion
	for the yoke of Clodhamer	0. 0. 4	

	for a tenement and Lands now in his owne occupacion against the markett crose in 7oke	0. 3. 5	this he purchased this last yeare of my brother Fisher and is entered tenant
B			
	Lady Margarett Boswell lands in Bradbourne	0. 3. 0	
	more for Capons and Cradles	0. 1. 2	this land lyes at Baylies Hill and is in Rich Evredge his occupacion
	more for Harts lands	0. 2. 0	this lyes nere the footeway from 7oke to Seale and is in John Thorntons occupacion
	more for Barnefields and Little Redinge	0. 3. 4	
	more lands once Tanners	0. 2. 6	
	more for lands once Childrens	0. 3. 0	
	more a Croft behind the howse	0. 0. 3½	
	for Rose Croft	0. 0. 6	
	for lands once Chapmans	0. 0. 10	
	for the yoke Newmans	0. 0. 4	
	Richard Besbeech his heirs a tenement and lands	0. 4. 0	this joynes to Thisletons land at Newfound Streete towards the North & West tenant
		1. 7. 8½	John Cogger
	Edward Besbeech his heires	0. 2. 6	Riverhill lands tenant James Hunt occupacion now belonging to young Arthur Childrens James Herrod tenant

Thomas Burges his heires	0. 2. 0	a howse where they dwell and land called Longe Strack Margery Burges her death presented 1672 and Edmund Burges admitted 167?
more for the Pydbull and a tenement in the shambles	0. 1. 7	the Pydbull in John Thornetons and the other tenement in Widow Frauncis occupacion
John Beckett his heires lands nere Brittaines called Goddards	0. 1. 8	these are in myne and Edward Chapmans occupacion now Mr Farnabys
more for lands there called South Deanes	0. 2. 8	these lands are some in myne and some in William Allens occupacion ?presentlie now Mr Farnabyes
Jesupp Beckett a tenement & lands	0. 3. 2	these are at Seavenoke towne end in the widow Bakers and Bostockes occupacion he was entered tenant 24 Oct. 1665 tenant now John Thorneton
Barnard Beckett a tenement in the Towne	0. 0. 6	where Giles Law now dwells this is sold to Percivall Smith presented 1671
Richard Bankin a tenement in the towne	0. 0. 3	in his owne occupacion
more for a Butchers shopp	0. 0. 6	the upper new built shopp
Thomas Beecher a tenement	0. 0. 4	the howse in which he now dwells
Mary Beardswarth widow a tenement	0. 0.10	the Bell where she dwells now Beardsworth and he entered tenant

James Beecher for Retherden	0. 1. 0	he lives at Eatonbridge and the tenants name is William Turnor the land lies in the weild
Nicholas Bratle his heires for Hobbins mead	0. 0. 6	tenant Christopher Thomas this lyes between Dibden Hill and Salters heath at the
more for lands called Bendix and Coldings ashe	0. 1. 7½	now called the George lands nere to Kippington
Richard Browne lands called Ketles	0. 1. 0	a little beyound Shangden pond towards Riverhill
John Blome certaine tenements nere the markett crosse	0. 1. 3	tenants Isaac Day Kippes & Ridges
more the howse where he dwells called walnutree feild	0. 0. 2	
more lands therewith used called the Deanes	0. 3. 6	
more a tenement nere the Crowne	0. 0. 2½	tenant Nicholas Masters
more two tenements and a backside nere the Church	0. 0. 3	
William Beecher a Butchers shopp	0. 0. 4	this sold to Anthony Symons and 1672
Richard Croncke a tenement against the markett crosse late purchased of one Bray	0. 0. 2	where he dwells
	1. 6. 0	

	Edward Cosier a tenement & lands	0. 1. 8	now in the occupacion of the Widow Weston now Mr Blomes
	more a Butchers shopp	0. 0. 4	now in Nicholas Masters his occupacion
Admitted 1669	John Coggar two tenements at Dibden	0. 0. 5	where he dwells young Coggar admitted
	more a tenement and lands called Little Kippington	0. 2. 6½	in the widow Butterfields occupacion admitted
	more a tenement and lands at the foote of Dibden Hill	0. 0. 8	these were late purchased of William Blome young Coggar admitted
	John Culpeper gent his heires lands in Rethered	0. 4. 10	
	for Parnell More & Brested feild	0. 2. 6	
	more lands once Crouchleyes	0. 0. 2	
	for Jone lands	0 . 3. 4	
Admitted 1669	John Cowlard a tenement & backside	0. 1. 1	the Kingehead where William Caccott dwells
	Thomas Chorley gent a howse & lands	0. 1. 3	this is the howse and lands in his occupacion
	lands once Moses	0. 0. 3½	
	for the yoke Andrewes	0. 0. 4	
	Churchwardens of St Buttolphs	0. 3. 8	nere the Vine Richard Caccott tenant
Entered 1669	Martin Caccott his heires a tenement	0. 1. 6	nere the Towne well William Baker tenant his two daughters are Eliz King & Ann Beecher now entered

William Cooks his heires a tenement	0. 0. 2	where the widow Cooke now dwells
for his yoke Carfers	0. 0. 4	
Thomas Chowneing his heires a tenement and croft	0. 2. 10	called the blackboy Peter Cothopps occupacion
Mathew Couchmans his heires for Bablands	0. 1. 6	on the Vine below old Skynners now in Nicholas Martins occupacion his death presented 1674
Richard Croncke of the Weild more parte of Wickhurst farme which is parte of the yoke	0. 1. 5	now tenant one Russell the same tenant 1679
Pickman	0. 0. 9	
more for lands late purchased of John Rich	0. 0. 11	this in the occupacion of Richard Everest and is a tenement orchard & garden
Richard Croncke of Tandridge	0. 1. 4	nere the Herst in the weild a tenement in the occupacion of Edward Smith
Richard Croncke of Trosley	0. 1. 0	tenant Edmund Smith lands called brookecroft this is now sold to John Everest Junr presented 1671 & admitted
more a tenement and parte of Whites	0. 0. 8½	tenant Daniell Everest now The Hills now Edward Alderidge
more a meadow and other lands called Jenkins	0. 1. 8½	Skynners of Panthurst were tenants now John Goodhugh now John and Daniel Sutton
a Butchers shopp	0. 0. 4	Spilsted was tenant now sold to Nicholas Beardsworth presented 1671

for Cobham feild and Dewland mead	0. 0. 8	this land is in the Weild and Lyes nere Little Westwood Thomas Rogers is tenant now Stephen Hall
Edward Colvin lands lately purchased of Thomas French called Bigfield	0. 0. 8	this where Thomas French late dwelt and now one of old Robert Skynners sonnes at Under River now in Popes occupacion
	1. 17. 0	
Richard Duke for Arkesden	0. 5. 0	this lyes about Shorham and is now sold to one Nathaniel Tench Esq. presented 1671
Richard Everest a tenament and lands	0. 0. 5½	all called Wakelyns now old William Walls the Smith forge presented
more a parcell of land called Wakelyns plaine		
William Everest a tenement & backside	0. 0. 5	hs death presented 1671
Francis Farnaby gent for his howse and garden	0. 1. 4	
lands late in the occupacion of Keble	0. 7. 0	
lands called Cantsedge	0. 5. 0	this lyes beyond Thomas Woods new built howse and was lately woodlands
lands in Thomas Wickendens occupacion	0. 1. 4	
lands in widow Wells her occupacion	0. 6. 1	
lands in John Coggars occupacion	0. 1. 0	

	lands late in John Hase his occupacion	0. 1. 3	
	the lands late in Russells now in Butterfields occupacion	0. 3. 6 1. 6. 6.	
	Francis French his heires lands called Wilds & Swans croft	0. 2. 8	it lyes westwood and conteynes about 20 acres joyned to the lands of William Fremlyn North and it joynes to the lands goeing to Hale
	John Floate a tenement etc.	0. 0. 1	
Admitted 1669	Edward Falter his heires	0. 13. 9	this is for part of Wickhurst Richard Morgan is tenant
	for the yoke Pickman	0. 0. 4	now Francis French hath it (?) Rathsens death presented 1672
	William Francklyn his heires for a tenement and land called Birchfield	0. 0. 10	this is in Thisletons occupacion beyond Shangden sold to Francis and Thomas Rogers presented 1671 Thomas Rogers admitted to all 21 Oct 1675
	William Garland	0. 0. 6½	in Whitley Augustines Garland hath only a howse and 3 acres of land tenant William Hawes
	Robert Goodhew his heires for Levett lands	0. 2. 4	lyeing on the further side of Hobland Richard Goodhew admitted 1671
	Thomas Grene lands at Boswell late purchased of Thomas White	0. 0. 2	this is sold by him to Robert Bowman and by him to one Thomas Walls presented 1671

	a tenement and lands in Whitley called Clenches late purchased of John Cronck	0. 1. 6	
	William Hinton a tenement in Rethered	0. 0. 4	
	Nicholas Hamon his heires for Redlands	0. 1. 0	Mr. Wynn tenant
		2. 16. 5	
	more for a peece of land	0. 0. 2	
	called Nisells		Mr Wynn tenant
	for two yokes called Carfers and Beechers	0. 2. 4	
	Francis Hills his heires a tenement	0. 0. 2	the hand and Pen George Croft tenant now myne
	Nicholas Hacksup a tenement	0. 0. 10	Goodman Charlewood tenant midway to Rethered
	another tenement in Rethered	0. 0. 2	Edmund Chapman tenant being the Porcupine
Admitted 1669	Stephen Hall lands in the Weild called Swithin	0. 1. 1	nere Westwood East to a lane* leading from Hale to 7oke North and West and to a lane leading to Westwood towards the South conteynes 10 acres
	John Hollamby his heires lands in the Wield	0. 0. 6	at the foote of Baylis Hill one Purvey tenant
	Elizabeth Jordan a Butchers shop	0. 0. 4	this shop is now downe it stood at the North end of Widow Frances on the backside of the bull Mr

			Burges hath now bought the ground of Isaac Day who bought it of Elizabeth Jordon presented 1671
	John Kelsey a tenement in his owne occupacion	0. 0. 2	against the Towne well
	John Lucke a tenement in 7oke	0. 0. 3½	in Henry Colgates occupacion sold to Edward Soand new built Anno 1670
	Thomas Lambard Esqr for Juds in Edward Ridges his occupacion	0. 0. 4	
	for 7oke Parke & Julyan Hills	0. 11. 11	

* Later corrected to read 'Rounding to Westwood West to a Lane . . . .'

	for Christmas croft and well mead in Richard Rundalls occupacion	0. 0. 4	
	three acres in his occupacion adjoining to the Parke	0. 1. 4	
	for parte of the Mannor of Rumshott in James Hunts occupacion	0. 10. 10	
	for the yoke Aylands	0. 0. 4	
	for the yoke Russells	0. 0. 4	
Admitted 1669	Edward Lampard 5½d & woodlands 4d	0. 0. 9½	late purchased of Mr Walter lyeing on Seavenoke Common Lampards death presented 1673
Admitted 1669	George Morgan his heires a tenement and lands where they dwell	0. 1. 0	

	more a croft of lands late Robert Wimbles	0. 0. 6	adjoining to theire howse
	more a Butchers shop purchased of John Thorneton	0. 0. 6	where they stand
	more a long shopp where Hills & Payne did stand	0. 0. 8	
	one little stable used by George Johnson	0. 0. 2	quare if this be not Josua Allens and but mortgaged to them
		1. 14. 9	
	Edward Mitchell his heires lands once Tottehursts	0. 11. 10	
	for the yoke called Pound	0. 0. 4	
	John Martin entered his 3 tenements and admitted 1671	0. 0. 3	
	Rogers Nicholas his heires for Pettfeild	0. 0. 2	beyound the Hurst tenants William and Robert Sutton Ann 1679
	Robert Oliver gent for lands called Smiths farthing	0. 2. 8	(?) mort nere Blackehall gate in Robert French his occ.
	for that yoke	0. 0. 4	
	Nathaniel Owen a tenement in Seavenoke	0. 0. 9	where he and Mr Cesar dwell against the crosse late purchased of Floate
Quare	Symon Payne a butchers shopp	0. 0. 4	
	Ralph Petley a tenement in Rethered	0. 1. 0	where Ralph Clarke late dwelt

Quare	Penngate a shopp	0. 0. 4	now George Morgans purchased of O Wall this a Tanners shopp
Admitted 1669	Ann Page a tenement in 7oke	0. 0. 6	late purchased of John Thorneton tenants John Staple Samuel Weller
	Mr Thomas Polhill lands called Godlake	0. 1. 8	this land was late in Spilsteds and now in John Bakers occupacion and lyes below Grations land ne(re) Whitly forrest
	Edward Porter a tenement & lands	0. 3. 0	where he dwells at Skenehill nere Knowle Parke parte of these lands which went at 1s.8d. per Acre were purchased of Robert Oliver they are now descended to Allen Pope and James Walker and to William Porter and the rent devided Anno 1670
	Peter Prince lands late Cleds in the occupacion of Aslett in 7oke	0. 4. 3	
Sold to R.Croncke	John Rich lands late Thomas Rich Entered to Richard Croncke	0. 0. 11	this is in the occupacion of Richard Everest in the Weild and is a tenement orchard and meadow
Sold to R.Rich	more for lands parte of Wickhurst heritable	0. 1. 9	in Richard Everest his occupacion
	Richard Rich gent a parcel of land given his father Admitted by Thomas Rich his will of Seale	0. 5. 0	parte of Wickhurst heritable and in the occupacion of Thomas Tailor
	more for Longefield & Clay hill	0. 1. 8	quare these lye at Kettles hill

	Richard Rundall a tenement & lands	0. 1. 8	where he dwells
	Richard Rogers Glasier	0. 0. 1	where he dwells sold to N Kelsey he admitted
	Richard Rogers his sonne	0. 0.1½	next tenement above sold to Kelsey admitted
	Alexander Rottenbridge a shopp	0. 0. 8	sold to William Locke presented 1671
		1. 19. 0½	
	Percival Smith a tenement & lands	0. 3. 3	in his owne occupacion
	more a tenement against the well in 7oke	0. 0. 4	where Thomas Craft widow Downes etc dwell
Weston admitted 1669	William Spilsted a tenement	0. 0. 6	where he dwells late purchased of Thomas Beecher halfe of this sold to Edmund Weston and by him resold to Weston 1673 and Spilsted then admitted
	William Spencer a tenement late purchased of John Chowning of 7oke	0. 0. 2	tenant John Wilson
	Walter Smith gent lands late purchased of Mr Cooper		up Blands Lane
	Stephen Stretfeild for lands once Symondes	0. 0. 8	at Bowsell
	Richard Stevens lands once Mr Lones	0. 2. 0	nere Whitley young Ridges tenant now it belongs to widow Stephens who dwells at Borehill nere Hidhill purchased by Edward Ridges

	Edward Soane his heires a tenement and lands vizt Braingly croft 1s.3d and lands once Edward Sones 8d	0. 1. 11	where they dwell at the Tubbs parte of this is sold to John Cowlard for which he is to pay 8d per Annum and then Soane is to pay 1s.3d presented 1672 and Cowlard admitted 1673 Anno 1673 Thomas Soane sells to John Jeffery 2 messuages a garden acre of hopground 2 acres of lands per 8d and Soane to pay 8d more
	John Stileman lands in Rethered	0. 0. 5	
	more for two tenements one orchard and the west end of a Barne once Henry Stilemans	0. 0. 4½	
	more for two tenements once George Whites	0. 0. 4	
	more a tenement in 7oke against the well	0. 0. 2	
Staple admitted 1669	Thomas Stileman his heires a tenement called new howse another called the old Kitchin and two orchards	0. 0. 4½	Robert Staple
	for lands once Lockes and before Vanes	0. 0. 6	Robert Staple
	more for lands once Vanes	0. 0. 8	Robert Staple
Rich admitted	for Barnefield and little meadow	0. 1. 2	Mr Rich hath purchased this
	for a tenement once Bodylies	0. 0. 4	Norton tenant it belongs to Staple

	Thomas Tailor a tenement and lands once Symondses	0. 0. 8	mort. where Thomas Tailor dwells in the Weild
	John Twisleton gent a tenement & lands	0. 7. 0	tenant William Wall in the Weild
	Edmund Thomas his heires for Culverden	0. 0. 7	in Whitley betweene Sir N Strod and Mr Owtrems woods
	more for Retherden and another croft there	0. 1. 4	
	for Grittneys Mill	0. 0. 8	
	Christopher Thomas scholes Mew	0. 1. 4	
		1. 6. 7	
	Nicholas Trice a tenement once Floates	0. 1. 0	where he dwells
Admitted 1669	more lands at Shangden late purchased of Mr Lambard	0. 0. 8	
Thomas	John Thisleton his heires a tenement and lands late purchased of Frankwell	0. 0. 4	beyound Little Kippington called Butlers
Admitted 1669 to a moyety			
John jun. admitted 1669	John Thorneton certaine tenements once Hutchins	0. 0. 4	to Ratchell Craft for life and then John Thornton next below the Catts above that bought by Mrs Wilkes
	for scoolelands	0. 2. 3	12 Oct 1669
	a leather shopp	0. 0. 2	Robert Thorneton
	Webbs shop	0. 0. 4	John Thornton

	Rounds shop	0. 0. 6	John Thornetons
Quare	James shop	0. 0. 6	Pounder purchased it from George Francis and he bought it of John Thornton senior
Now Will Everest	John Francis his shop	0. 1. 0	Johns he now stands there now Mr stands there its sold to Everest William 1673 and he admitted
	Wests shop	0. 0. 4	John Nicholas Masters hires it
	Tailors shop	0. 0. 4	Johns tenant William Watts
Kingsland	a tenement late Burkhams	0. 0. 4	the upper howse in middle row now Henry Thorntons who married to ? James Kingsland and then sold it to Nicholas Kelsey presented 1671
	parte of Grigles	0. 0. 3	Johns
O. 7. 8	a tenement late Bostons	0. 1. 4	Johns
	Thomas and William Vines for parte of Wickhurst heritable	0. 0. 11½	
	Robert Wimble one tenement and croft	0. 0. 4	against slutts well quare
	Thomas Wood lands called Barbor	0. 1. 0	where he lives sold to Richard Hawkes and he admitted 1671
	more a tenement	0. 0. 4	tenant Martin

	Thomas White a tenement	0. 0. 8	tenant Edward Stringer sold to John Beardsworth
	Robert Watts a tenement	0. 0. 6	at the markett crosse tenant William Spencer now it belongs to Thomas Wise and he presented 1671 and he then admitted
	John Walter of Swanscombe for greate Whites	0. 6. 0	tenant Thomas Rigesby it lyes at the foote of the Hurst betweene the Hurst and Westwood
	more a tenement and lands called Wakelyns Plaine	0. 0. 4	
		0. 19. 9½	
	John Walter of Westwood lands called Coppinge		at Westwood
	more for a grove once Staples	0. 0. 4	
	Oliver Wall his heires for lands called Falters late William Walters of Trench	0. 2. 0	tenant Thomas Morley
	William Wall for a tenement & lands at new found street	0. 4. 9	tenant George Wood
Quare	the tenement where Fletcher late dwelt	0. 0. 4	
	Thomas Weller gent a shop	0. 0. 4	
	George Wood three parts of five parts of a	0. 0. 2	in Whitley his death presented there is two

tenement purchased of the heires of William Garland		tenements and parcels of land being six acres George junior admitted 1671
	0. 10. 0½	
Some totall is	13. 17. 4	and Martins 3 tenements since entered at 3d per Annum

KAO., U269, M156

APPENDIX C

The condition of this Recognizance is such that whereas the above bownden Francis Best is admitted and allowed to keep a common Alehouse & victualling house (by the said Justices) until the 29th of January next ensewinge the date hereof, & no longer in the house wherein he now dwelleth Commonly called the Sygne of the Crowne in Sennocke in the said County of Kent & not ellswhere, If therefore the said Francis Best shall not during the time aforesaid permitt or suffer, or have any playing at Dice, Cards, Tables, Quoits, Loggets, Bowles, or any other unlawfull Game or Games, in his house, yard, Garden or backside nor shall suffer to bee, or remain in his house any person or persons (not being his ordinary household servant), uppon any sabbath day, or holy day, duringe the time of Divine service or sermon; Nor shall suffer any person to Lodge, or stay in his house above one day & one nighte, but such whose true name, & sirname he shall deliver to some one of the Constables, or in his absence to some of the officers of the same parish the next day followinge, unlesse they shall be such person or persons as he or shee verry well knoweth, & will answer, for his or theire forthcoming: Nor suffer any person to remain in his house Tipplinge or Drinkinge contrary to the Lawe; Nor yet to be there tipplinge after Nine of the Clocke in the night time; Nor buy or take any pawne or stolen goods: Nor willing harbour in his said house, or in his Barnes, stables, or otherwhere any Rogues, vagabonds, sturdy beggers, Masterless men or other notorious offendors whatsoever Nor suffer any person or persons to sell or alter any Beere or Ale or other victuall by deputation or by Color of his License; and also if he shall keepe the true Assise & measure in his potts, bread & otherwise in his altering of his Ale Beare or bread & the same Beere & Ale to sell by sealed measure & according to the Assise & not otherwise not alter any stronge Beere, or strong Ale above a penny the quart & soe after the same rates That then this recognizance to be void and of none effecte, or ells to remaine in full force & vertue.

KAO., Q/RLVI/8

APPENDIX D

Table 1 Prices of livestock in Sevenoaks inventories 1665–1683

	1665	1666	1667	1668	1669	1672	1674	1677	1678	1679	1680	1683
Buds*											15*s*.	
Bulls									£2 10*s*.			
Bullocks	£1 10*s*.										£2 7*s*.	
Colts						£1 10*s*.						
						£2						
Cows	£2	£2 10*s*.	£4			£2 10*s*.	£3		£3 5*s*.	£2 15*s*.		£3 15*s*.
						£3			£3 7*s*.			
						£3 5*s*.						
Hogs	£1 10*s*.	14*s*. 6*d*.	15*s*.			10*s*.	12*s*.		18*s*.		10*s*.	
			8*s*.						10*s*.			
Horses						£3				£3		
Lambs			3*s*.			4*s*.						
Mares			£3			£2 10*s*.			£3			
Oxen		£4 12*s*.				£4 15*s*.			£4 15*s*.			
Pigs						8*s*.						
Sheets**						8*s*. 6*d*.			10*s*.			
Steers						£3 5*s*.						
Steers, fatling				£6 6*s*. 8*d*.								

*Buds = weaned calf not being a heifer
**Sheets = young hog of first year

Table 2 Crop prices in Sevenoaks inventories 1665–1680

	1665	1666	1668	1672	1674	1677	1678	1679	1680
Barley sown per acre				£1					
Barley per cop*	3*s*. 6*d*.								
Hay per load		£1		£1	15s			£1	£1
Hops per cwt						£2			
Hops per bag							£2 10*s*.		
Oats sown per acre			£1	14*s*. 6*d* £1					
Oats per cop	3*s*.			3*s*.	2*s*. 6*d*.				
Peas per load		£1							
Wheat sown per acre			14*s*. 6*d*	£1 3*s*. £1 13*s*. 4*d*.					
Wheat per cop	5*s*.			2*s*. 9*d*.					

* Cop = a heap of an unbound grain crop

GENERAL INDEX

Common items which occur in every inventory are omitted from the index.

PLATE I

Lidded flagon, inscribed Bredhurst Church, pewter, 1600–1610, and pewter charger.

PLATE II

Wine bottle and 'Bellarmine' stoneware jug.

PLATE III

Two earthenware pipkins and ointment pot.

PLATE IV

Bronze mortar and bell metal skillet.

PLATE V

Oak chair with arms.

PLATE VI

Chair, walnut, Charles II.

PLATE VII

Oak court cupboard.

PLATE VIII

Cupboard with drawers, oak frame.